THE
FOREX
EDGE

UNCOVER THE SECRET SCAMS AND TRICKS
TO PROFIT IN THE WORLD'S LARGEST FINANCIAL MARKET

JAMES DICKS

New York   Chicago   San Francisco   Lisbon
London   Madrid   Mexico City   Milan   New Delhi
San Juan   Seoul   Singapore   Sydney   Toronto

1 2 3 4 5 6 7 8 9 10   QFR/QFR   1 6 5 4 3 2 1

ISBN 978-0-07-178118-3
MHID 0-07-178118-8

e-ISBN 978-0-07-178119-0
e-MHID 0-07-178119-6

This publication is designed to provide accurate and authoritative information in regard to the subject matter covered. It is sold with the understanding that neither the author nor the publisher is engaged in rendering legal, accounting, securities trading, or other professional services. If legal advice or other expert assistance is required, the services of a competent professional person should be sought.

—From a Declaration of Principles Jointly Adopted by a Committee of the American Bar Association and a Committee of Publishers and Associations

Entries in the glossary have been taken from Investopedia (www.investopedia .com), the Forex Glossary (www.forexglossary.com), and OptionTradingpedia (www.optiontradingpedia.com).

McGraw-Hill products are available at special quantity discounts to use as premiums and sales promotions or for use in corporate training programs. To contact a representative, please e-mail us at bulksales@mcgraw-hill.com.

This book is printed on acid-free paper.

The tough economic times have hurt all of us in many different ways. I too have been affected over the years. You know the saying "It's not about how many times you get knocked down but how many times you get back up." Keep that in mind. Just because things get tough doesn't mean you have to give up. Keep working hard, and things will always get better.

I would like to dedicate this book to those who have worked hard and never given up. To those who see this as their next step to getting back up I say work hard. I would also like to especially thank my team, or shall I say my family, that has stuck by me for many, many years. Thanks RJ, Rob, Robert, Michael T., Adam (RIP), Michael N., Terrance, and Rocky. You guys are the best!

CONTENTS

PREFACE

It is amazing for me to actually be sitting here and writing this book. It seems like only yesterday I started down this road of trading in the forex market. It has been a fun and fast-paced adventure in my quest for the ultimate in portfolio diversification. The first book I wrote was specifically to introduce people to the world of trading in the over-the-counter spot forex market. The book was only an introduction; one that would share what I believed to be the next great frontier in trading. That book, *Forex Made Easy*, is still in print and continues selling well. It has served its purpose, and I have seen the forex market go from a virtually unknown investment opportunity in the United States to a common and familiar marketplace.

I started the hard way, by trial and error. I entered the forex and started trading using a practice account and then opened one of my many live accounts. It took me a number of years to feel confident trading in the forex market. I made many mistakes, but I learned from all of them. Not to say I didn't make the same mistake twice, because unfortunately I did. But I don't make a habit of doing the same thing over and over again unless it is successful.

This brings me to the point of this book. Over the past 11 years of trading the forex, I have started to see some patterns develop, patterns that have caused me much concern and that forced me to spend a tremendous amount of time investigating the very forex brokers I personally traded with. I have seen some suspect trade fills and order rejections, raising my suspicions about these brokers being able to do various deceitful things in order to hinder me from becoming a successful trader, and I have heard similar allegations from others. But I have never really had any concrete proof they were doing it until recently.

During my investigations, I discovered that my broker actually had someone on the inside watching accounts to try to detect how a trader was trading. If the broker could, in fact, determine what trading style or strategy a customer was using, the broker would start to trade against the customer. If that didn't work, the broker would deploy various devious tactics to beat the customer out of his or her money. I am going to share these findings with you throughout this book.

But not to worry—you can still trade the forex market; you just need to arm yourself with the right tools, knowledge, and training. I am going to share with you some strategies that you can use to beat the brokers at their own game. Don't be discouraged about the fraudulent actions of a few brokers. Keep in mind that the equities markets, sadly, do have unscrupulous practices and brokers. But you can still make money by trading equities; again you need to know and understand your environment.

I have made some drastic changes in my trading strategies as well as where I trade; I will share that with you in the pages to follow. I have already started on my next book in the forex series and have several others ready to follow. One of the topics that we will explore in this book will be forex options. I believe this will be the next big opportunity in the forex marketplace and is already used widely by major corporations, hedge funds, and banks. Forex options will allow traders to use some of the same strategies that equities traders use with their options.

Whatever you do, don't put this book down; make sure you read through it before you place another trade.

ACKNOWLEDGMENTS

It would not be fair if I didn't quickly say thanks to a few people for helping to put this book together, for helping me bring my personal investigations in the retail forex marketplace to view. As always, I want to say thanks to the best publisher and my only publisher, McGraw-Hill, to Jennifer, Peter, and their McGraw-Hill team. Caroline, I have to say thanks to you for your years of assistance on our forex book projects—again, thanks for being part of the team. My right-hand man, Jack, thanks for always reviewing my writing for grammar and spelling mistakes; we all appreciate it. Michael T., as always, thanks for your assistance in helping to get this book out in a timely manner; this was a big project, and I could not have completed it without your help. Last and most important, to my family, for their patience during this project and their understanding about the long nights and weekends I had to put in getting this book to completion, thank you. I would like to add a special acknowledgment to a good friend, Adam, who was in the trenches with me trading for years and who was tragically killed in a motorcycle accident at a young age just prior to the book being released. Thanks, Adam, for all your help.

DISCLAIMER

The information in this book is for educational purposes only. I am not giving advice or specific financial recommendations. You must seek guidance from your personal advisors before acting on this information. Trading can result in losses. I accept no responsibility for any losses you may incur. **Do not invest more than you can afford to lose.**

NFA AND CFTC REQUIRED DISCLAIMERS

Trading in the forex market is a challenging opportunity where above-average returns are available for educated and experienced investors who are willing to take above-average risk. However, before deciding to participate in forex trading, you should carefully consider your investment objectives, level of experience, and risk appetite. Do not invest money you cannot afford to lose.

Forex trading, futures trading, and options trading all have large potential rewards, but also large potential risk. You must be aware of the risks and be willing to accept them in order to invest in the forex, futures, and options markets. Don't trade with money you can't afford to lose.

This book is neither a solicitation nor an offer to buy or sell forex futures or options. No representation is being made that any account will or is likely to achieve profits or losses similar to those discussed in this book. The past performance of any trading system or methodology is not necessarily indicative of future results.

There is considerable exposure to risk in any forex transaction. Any transaction involving currencies involves risks including, but not limited to, the potential for changing political or economic conditions that may substantially affect the price or liquidity of a currency.

Moreover, the leveraged nature of forex trading means that any market movement will have an equally proportional effect on your deposited funds. This may work against you as well as for you. The possibility exists that you could sustain a total loss of initial margin funds and be required to deposit additional funds to maintain your position. If you fail to meet any margin call within the time prescribed, your position will be liquidated, and you will be responsible for any resulting losses. Investors may lower their exposure to risk by employing risk-reducing strategies such as stop-loss or limit orders.

CFTC RULE 4.41

Hypothetical or simulated performance results have certain limitations. Unlike an actual performance record, simulated results do not represent actual trading. Also, since the trades have not been executed, the results may have undercompensated or overcompensated for the impact, if any, of certain market factors, such as lack of liquidity. Simulated trading programs in general are also subject to the fact that they are designed with the benefit of hindsight. No representation is being made that any account will or is likely to achieve profits or losses similar to those shown.

INTRODUCTION

It has been nearly 10 years since I wrote my first book on forex. I, like many of you, have worked my way through many trials and tribulations of trading. This book is yet another installment of what I have learned, or shall I say, what I have exposed in recent years.

Before we get into what I believe will be one of the most important books you will have on your shelf concerning forex and your trading, I want to reiterate how exciting this marketplace is. The forex is still the largest financial market in the world, and although there is still no centralized location to trade, the forex market is becoming more accessible to individual traders. I believe over the next three to five years you will see some exciting improvements that will ultimately benefit the small retail trader.

When I first started talking about the forex market back in 2000, it was truly the "Wild West" of investing. There were very few regulations and certainly limited oversight. That has changed over the last 11 years, and just the last 2 years have brought the most changes affecting oversight, which added many new regulatory changes.

As I share with you my insight, what I have discovered and what I have investigated over the last few years, you will see an alarming pattern that I only wish I knew about earlier and could have shared with you prior to this book. But unfortunately, like you, I learned most of this through my own trading while watching anomalies that probably were not quite so random. I am going to stay away from finger-pointing and outright naming some brokers who I feel are unscrupulous and whom I have even referred people to in the past, not knowing their tactics. I see no reason to do that at this point. I will make sure that you have all the information at hand to be able to choose your broker wisely.

To keep my loyal followers up to speed and those who are new to the marketplace in the know, I will continue to keep my www.jdfn.com Web site up to date with pertinent information to help you make your decisions about trading. Keep in mind that the site is free and that it is designed for traders, by traders. These traders are proving a tremendous support network for you by posting unique insights into the forex market, as well as their opinions on various brokers and trading opportunities. I encourage you to log on and give back. Share your experiences and your trading insight. The more that you participate, the more beneficial the information becomes.

As I began my forex trading, like many of you, I started with a practice account, or demo account. Unfortunately I thought, as many of you do, that demo accounts were exactly the same as the real thing, using the same price and executions. I thought what better way to learn the market than to perfect your trading using virtual money. Why not make bad trades on purpose and learn from your mistakes. When you are confident that you can consistently make money, then, and only then, you go live. So I thought.

Well, the unfortunate realization is that the live accounts don't trade like a demo account. The brokers don't care how you trade your demo account, but if you start trading a live account with real money and start winning on a constant basis, you will draw the ire of the brokers, and they will basically seek you out and destroy you. That's strong language, but in my experience it is the truth.

I now know that, in certain instances, if a customer is consistently successful, he or she can actually be blacklisted. I am serious! You can actually be put on a blacklist. In my investigations, I have seen the actual blacklist accounts at certain brokerage houses. Should you get on that list, you will no longer be successful on a consistent basis no matter how good you are at trading. You might as well throw in the towel because you are done there.

In my own experience, I was running my very first managed account in the forex market using spot forex. I had nine straight month-over-month successes with no drawdowns, meaning I never lost any money by month's end. Of course, I would have some losses, or intermonth drawdowns, but never a losing month in nine straight months.

Then I received an e-mail from the broker one day, saying that I was going to be moved to a new server to better execute my trades

The e-mail said, "Please make the appropriate changes so that your trading platform will work correctly." Sure enough, come Monday, I was on a new server. You can only imagine what happened from then on. This is as real as it gets. I never had another winning month again, and I ultimately had to close the account.

You cannot imagine my frustration; I traded for nearly a year with precisionlike accuracy, slaying pips on a daily basis while watching my accounts soar to new highs month after month only to wind up, no matter what I did, in a losing trade. It was so frustrating. Over the course of four months, I witnessed all the games brokers play, but I didn't exactly know they were games at the time. My intense investigation has led me to the games that were being initiated against me, and I want to share them with you in the coming chapters of this book.

The unfortunate reality is that I am and have already begun to be blacklisted within the industry, and frankly I don't care. I am going to expose the forex industry and the brokers that prey on unsuspecting traders like you and me.

Keep in mind that this is not a book on the negative aspects of trading. This is a book that will expose what brokers are doing, and I will show you how you can use that information against them. You can still make money trading this market, and you can make lots of money. But as so many have realized, you can lose lots of money too. As with any investing, I think the biggest thing to note is that all investing should be deeply considered and that your risk tolerance must be taken into account before making any investment. The forex marketplace is no different. It is a great way to diversify your portfolio, but you should still use risk capital that you are willing to lose. Keep in mind that you can reduce some of this risk by using less margin.

While reading this book, you will see that I have taken many steps to help ensure I have more control of my trading. You will see and learn how I stay ahead of the brokers. I will disclose up front that I simply cannot openly discuss all those strategies, or I will be giving the very brokers I am trying to expose more information on how to beat today's traders. This is not a book for brokers to use against us, but for traders to use against brokers. In the end, I will do my best to make my personal trading strategies available to you either through personal appearances or through www.jdfn.com. Together we can beat these brokers and help create a fair and orderly marketplace and a level playing field.

I have suffered from the tough economic times, as many of you have. With all the regulatory oversight and changes in the forex market, my business has had to readjust and change no less than four times. This time I am fighting back. I am creating the necessary infrastructure to compete in this highly regulated industry, and I am driven to shift the focus on individual customer success. I believe that the success of your business depends on the longevity of your customer. In the past, I have relied on other brokers to ensure success for me, my companies, and my customers, but not anymore. I am going to weed out the bad ones, and I am going to personally take an active role in where my readers and customers are trading. I want to see my customers using a straight-through process, avoiding all the games that the current brokers are playing. If your brokerage firm says it is a market maker or it creates a market ... run! The broker is a game master, for sure.

I am creating a trading environment that is exactly what I want, and I figure if it is good enough for my accounts and me, it will be good enough for you. How I do this is just some of what I am going to share with you in this book. First we have to learn what is going on in the marketplace, how to recognize the games, and how to avoid them. Then we must learn where we can apply what we have learned so that we can be successful and begin achieving our personal financial goals.

I want to challenge you to spend the necessary time to understand the concepts I will explain. I want to challenge you to forget all the garbage you are reading on the various message boards. I have personally read inside information from brokers discussing how they create false accounts on the many message boards and chat rooms; the biggest ones out there are disseminating false and misleading information to traders like you and me. Don't be surprised; it happens; I have seen it firsthand. I know of brokers asking employees, using false names and accounts, to post information in chat rooms about other brokers' customers so that unsuspecting new traders see how bad other brokers are or how they nickel-and-dime their customers. I have read inside memorandums on how the brokers are bashing other brokers or posting misleading facts about themselves. This practice is rampant. Right now you are probably as flabbergasted as I was when I first started learning about this kind of activity.

Before we all start playing the blame game, keep in mind that my trading knowledge of the forex and my forex career have evolved like many of yours, and I have always shared what I knew to be correct with others. So if you read anything that may contradict something I have said in the past, then so be it. I have learned more through my in-depth investigations of the industry, and that is what I am sharing with you now.

I know that you are saying to yourself, if this is so bad, how can James be trading it? Well, that is what you are going to learn, and that is what I am going to share. While you are reading through the pages to come, I challenge you to go out and do some research yourself to see firsthand some of the games these brokers are playing. Go to the chat rooms and forums and notice which brokers are sponsoring and advertising on them. Read the comments and rebuttals that are clearly made by insiders or employees. It is almost comical when you are made aware of this kind of activity. I know that one broker almost solely sponsors one of the biggest forex forums on the Web today, and that broker controls all the content on the site. If you see a broker advertised on a forum or message board, run, or at the very least be suspicious.

That leads me to my own books. If you ever come across reviews that may not be so positive, keep in mind that I know for a fact other competitors have sought to discredit my books. Why? Simple. I have always shared strategies to help others trade the markets more successfully. I have lots of readers and prospective trading customers wanting to know where they should trade, and if I did not recommend a particular broker, then you can only imagine what the brokers thought of me and what I was saying. This book will be no different; in fact, if anything, it will be far worse for the brokers and competitors. At the time of this writing, some pretty strong allegations are flying around federal court about certain brokers. I know these actions will come and go, but I am sure that you and I will benefit, since the brokers will have no choice but to clean up their acts.

I also know that many of the brokers out there, primarily because of new regulations, have started changing their practices, but not all. Some of the so-called bucket shops will probably never change. I believe that regardless of whether the brokers have changed or not, they should not be let off the hook so easily. If you used to steal cars but no longer do, that doesn't make you innocent. Unfortunately, I have to say that I no longer recommend the brokers I used to recommend. But I haven't stopped trading; I just took the information that I am sharing with you and armed myself; I moved on to greener pastures.

I hope you can take what I have brought to these pages and modify your existing trading plan. If you are new to the marketplace, this information should help you design your own successful trading plan.

I look forward to reading your many successful stories in the years to come; you will always be able to post those at www.jdfn.com.

As I always say, Happy Investing!

THE FOREX MARKET AND ALTERNATIVES

1

THE FOREX MARKET
AND FRAUD

HOW THE FOREX STARTED

In theory, foreign exchange (forex) trading dates back to ancient times when traders first began exchanging coins from different countries and groups. In 1944, the postwar forex system was established as a result of a multination conference held at Bretton Woods, New Hampshire, and remained intact until the early 1970s.

At this conference, representatives from 45 nations met to discuss the forex system. The conference resulted in the formation of the International Monetary Fund. It also produced an agreement that fixed currencies in an exchange rate system that tolerated 1 percent currency fluctuations to gold values, or to the dollar, that was previously established as the gold standard. The system of connecting the currency's value to gold or the U.S. dollar was called *pegging*.

In 1971, the Bretton Woods Accord was first tested because of dramatic, uncontrollable currency rate fluctuations. This started a chain reaction, and by 1973, the gold standard was abandoned by President Richard M. Nixon. The fixed-rate system collapsed under heavy market pressures, and currencies were finally allowed to float freely. Thereafter, the forex quickly established itself as *the* financial market—the world's largest financial market.

WHERE THE FOREX MARKET IS

Forex trading is not bound to any one trading floor and is not a market in the traditional sense because there is no central exchange. Instead the entire market is run electronically among a network of banks, continuously over a 24-hour period. This market is considered an over-the-counter market, providing off-exchange spot foreign currency transactions.

Banks have a natural flow of forex business from their customers, who buy and sell currency according to individual needs. The banks must manage their currency deposits in the changing light of their customers' transactions.

Investment managers deal globally and must take positions in the currencies, as well as in more traditional instruments such as bonds and equities. For example, if a fund is invested in U.S. bonds, the manager must decide if the fund should be invested in U.S. dollars or a different currency. Again, it is a question of hedging, another layer of risk to manage.

WHERE THE FOREX MARKET IS GOING

According to the Bank for International Settlements, as of April 2010, the average daily turnover in global forex markets is estimated at $3.98 trillion, a growth of approximately 20 percent over the $3.21 trillion daily volume as of April 2007. Some firms specializing on the forex market have put the average daily turnover in excess of $4 trillion.

The $3.98 trillion breakdown is as follows:

- $1.490 trillion in spot transactions
- $475 billion in outright forwards
- $1.765 trillion in forex swaps
- $43 billion currency swaps
- $207 billion in options and other products

In addition to the above-listed growth, retail transactions on the forex will continue to grow. The United States will remain comparatively small in the overall growth of forex transactions, with overseas, China, and surrounding areas being the driving force behind the huge growth.

With all the new regulatory oversight of the forex industry, I have noticed that the forex brokers are starting to look at different business models. They will continue to offer retail off-exchange forex, but the forex brokers in the United States are going to be looking into offering swaps, forwards, and other regulated investment vehicles.

The word I am hearing on the street is that if the forex brokers are going to be so highly regulated in the United States, then they might as well get in all the way. What I mean by this is that the forex brokers are going to be offering commodities and equities in the near future.

In addition to commodities and equities, you are going to see forex options become much more mainstream for the average retail forex customer. I already know of two brokers that have not traditionally carried a forex options product but will be offering such products by the time this book has been printed.

While the big equities brokers are out there struggling to get new customers, the forex brokers are not having that problem since, by continuing to add new trading services that include equities and commodities, they are the ones getting all the leads. As a result of the changes in forex services, the big equities brokers will start looking at the big forex brokers as targets for acquisitions, thus increasing the customer acquisitions of the big equity brokers. So look for industrywide consolidation coming soon.

WHO ARE THE VICTIMS?

These days, and particularly in the United States, there is a huge investment-oriented culture. The list of financial investing instruments freely available to the retail individuals is expanding day by day. We can choose among forex currency trading, options, futures, stocks, bonds, real estate, franchises, and other business ventures that contribute to reinforce the economy of the country while securing good profits and making the markets move.

This variety and freedom has allowed some unscrupulous individuals and companies to simulate legal investment schemes and abuse the investors through the promotion of unrealistic returns and well-elaborated but deceitful programs, only seeking to make money for themselves.

Anyone can be the prey of these fraudsters, and especially those of you who think you will never fall for such a scheme. Financial swindlers are quite clever and know very well how to manipulate and target all kinds of potential investors, from the wealthiest ones down to precisely those who might be struggling with financial difficulties or have little or no capital.

The less wealthy will be more sensitive to the offers that promise large returns overnight. One of the most employed sales pitches is that only the "guru" is able to show you how to become rich and teach you the precise and "proven" investment strategies that all the wealthy people or the "big boys in-the-know" usually employ.

Don't get me wrong; I personally follow many so-called gurus, though I always take everything they say with a grain of salt; but you cannot go around with blinders on and be so negative that you can't see the forest for the trees. I have gotten little golden nuggets from many people out there who may not be the best traders or have the best intentions, but they certainly gave me some great ideas that I was able to research and develop into some really good trading strategies.

The victims of investment scams come from very diverse backgrounds. Among them, we can find successful professionals and political figures, as well as thousands of hardworking people. However, all of them share two important characteristics: unlimited *greed* and a desperate need to believe whatever feeds or promises to feed that greed.

INVESTMENT FRAUDSTERS: WHO ARE THEY?

Many of these swindlers and scammers are very successful, and the total amount of stolen funds has been estimated at billions of dollars a year. They will convince you of their legality and use every ingenious trick they can think of to assure you that they are the real thing so that they can gain your trust and cooperation. They will offer you such an exclusive and time-limited opportunity to make lots of money easily and quickly, moving you around and pushing your "greed and need" buttons so cleverly that you will believe what they say if you are not prepared and do not know about their usual modus operandi.

If you find yourself on the spot in a pressure situation, the best advice is to take a step back and go out and do some homework. You can rest assured that in most cases, or at least in the legitimate cases, you will be able to still take advantage of any special deals, and there will be some to hold on to and some to stay away from.

The reason it is so difficult to identify financial scammers is that they do not exhibit a definite profile. Therefore, you will need to get rid of any stereotype you might have about the looks or attitudes of a potential fraudster as a first step in protecting yourself. It could be anyone around you, previously known or unknown. The only common trait among all of them is that they possess a tremendous and compelling power to convince other people to believe in them.

Some of these fraudsters may not have always been so. There are instances where highly trusted and esteemed individuals in the accounting or legal business, financial brokers, and even medical doctors have succumbed to temptation and renounced their ethics to make quick money through an investment scam, and, of course, to benefit from their formerly accepted and transparent social position.

In other instances, some of the legitimate investment programs failed because of bad management or unpredictable events, and the directors ended up mishandling or losing their investors' funds. Whether planned or not, the results of an investment scam are the same; you, as the client, will lose your hard-earned money.

HOW THE FRAUDS WORK

Fraudsters will try to imitate the marketing pitch of perfectly legal investment companies. Therefore, the method they might use to contact their potential victims is not always an indication of a scam. Getting in touch with customers directly by phone and mailing lists or indirectly through advertising and the Internet are some of the methods employed by many legitimate businesses to identify and select people who may be potential investors and might be interested in their financial products and services. Investigate carefully and independently their approach and understand how these swindlers might benefit from either of the above marketing schemes.

Direct Personal Contact through Telephone and Mailing Lists

Swindlers will usually contact hundreds of potential investors, either by telephone or by mail, after getting specifically targeted mailing lists from other sources, such as subscriptions to investment-related publications and financial forums. The swindlers will say enough to catch your interest so you will write or call for more information, but little enough so they can remain under the radar of the authorities.

Indirect Contact through Advertising and the Internet

Regulatory agencies usually monitor all advertising in major publications. However, this does not stop swindlers from using this type of media to set up their bait-and-switch system, offering amazingly attractive profits aiming to catch investors unaware in a short-term move. Some others will choose smaller publications where there is less risk of being caught by a regulator.

One aspect of this is the forex broker demo bait and switch, which I describe in more detail in Chapter 16.

As a result of its increased expansion and potential, the Internet has attracted those fraudsters too, and they use it to implement the same old scams, formerly conducted through normal mail or phone, but now through e-mail, subscriptions lists, and flashy Web sites that are advertised in strategic places such as social media, forums, and investment-related sites.

Using Your Own Professional, Social, or Even Familiar Circles

One of the easiest and most effectively used methods is the referral scheme, where the first investors receive large profits on time and so will be eager to recommend the forex program to their family members, friends, and colleagues. Most often those profits are paid from the investors' own funds (as there is no forex trading backing up the investment) or from the investments of other victims.

The power of referral from one investor to another is so strong that the fraudsters will not need to find any new victims. The investors will come to them, and what is even better, they will already be convinced of the authenticity, profitability, and trustworthiness of the fake forex investment program. This method is really more related to pyramid schemes. Most of us are familiar with the biggest of them all, the one that originated in New York in the 1990s (or possibly earlier). Ultimately, the man behind that one ended up in prison for the rest of his life. Bernie Madoff prided himself on his social ties and built his business on referrals. In the end, the business came crashing down, and everyone lost money.

I am not saying don't invest; you really don't have a choice. Well, I guess you have two choices: sit on the sidelines and let inflation wipe out any real value of your savings; or get off the sidelines, use good money management and diversification, and take the appropriate risk to reward. You will lose money, and you will make money, but obviously your goal is to make more than you lose. To do that, you will have to take some calculated risks. Most of the time, referrals are a good way to find investment opportunities so long as you do some due diligence.

The "Facade": Looking Good Enough to Build a Reputation

Some fraudsters will try to look really professional and reputable by renting luxurious offices in the high-class financial areas of the city. Some will go so far as to have enough personnel to give the impression of being an important and busy company. They will even require you to ask for an appointment and keep you waiting for a while, building up your interest with an apparent nonchalance in getting your account under their belt.

Those scammers might also participate in several public associations and give the image of the perfect citizen; meanwhile the only purpose for all the scenery is to get a solid grasp on your account.

Buttons They Push and Weaknesses They Exploit

As stated earlier, greed is the main element that will attract plenty of potential victims to the fraudster's evil plan. Fraudsters can promise you anything as big as it can be, but in the end they do not have the intention to fulfill those promises. All they want is your hard-earned money, and they want it as soon as possible.

Here is a list of the key elements that are signs of a potential investment scam:

- *Creating expectations for huge profits.* This really is not so difficult. Remember, past performance is not an indication of future performance. Contemplate your potential investment with the dollars that you are willing to lose and that you can afford to lose. You never know what will happen in the markets, especially the forex market. The forex market can be drastically affected by any major news event from around the globe.

  Some money management firms will offer profits big enough so they can catch your interest, but not so excessive that you might become suspicious. These unscrupulous people may suggest that the investment has a greater potential and will gauge your reactions to follow on with the scamming scheme. Bear in mind that if the returns on a given investment seem too good to be true, you might be the prey of one of these swindlers.

- *Omitting the mention of the risks involved.* The last thing a scammer wants you to think about is that you might eventually lose your money. The emphasis will always be set on "low risk" and "guaranteed" returns so that you might believe there is no risk at all. If you insist and ask about the potential risks, fraudsters could eventually admit there are some but assure you that they are very small and that the profits will be much higher. In general, fraudsters will try to change the subject quickly or even show impatience and try to turn you down so you won't insist on the issue.

- *Creating a sense of urgency and exclusivity.* Limited offers, limited time—fraudsters are always in a rush and will urge you to invest "right now" because you might miss the opportunity. You may be told about a very special offer, only for the select few. The real reason behind this is that the fraudsters do not want you to think about their offers in depth, as you might become suspicious and decide to check further or turn the offer down. They are also in a rush because they might already be planning to leave the place very soon.

- *Building trust.* Scammers will center their efforts on conveying total confidence about the returns of the investment they want you to get in, the solidity of the proposal, and the almost no-risk situation so that you trust them enough to lend them your funds easily and quickly. The message they intend to pass is that the opportunity they are offering you is practically a favor; they might even suggest that if you are not interested, they will bring the offer to someone else, trying to appear detached from the fact that it is *your* money they want to pocket. Of course, this attitude is aimed at getting the potential investor to react by expressing his or her interest, and voilá—the mystification is almost done! Swindlers are real masters at manipulating and controlling the conversation, and so there is little chance for the investor to ask them embarrassing questions.

Another typical example is how they can build confidence by word of mouth of initial investors who are paid large profits and become inadvertently "recruited" to spread the word to their friends or relatives. This is mostly seen in the high-yield investment program–type schemes. After a period during which consistent profits are paid out on time (from the new deposits of the most recent victims), older investors become bold and start investing larger sums of money, and new investors are attracted to the scheme because of the excellent reputation the swindler has built by recycling new payments into fake profits. In the end, after pocketing enough of the monies, the swindler will leave the scene.

Another scheme swindlers can employ to gain trust in their supposed forex trading abilities is the "slow approach," where they offer forecasts free of charge and never ask for the potential investor's money up front. Half the investors are given one forecast, and the rest are given the opposite forecast. After several cycles, the remaining few who have had all the "good" forecasts want desperately to invest with the swindler, because they believe undoubtedly in the swindler's accuracy at predicting market prices. The swindler might even protest a little and play hard to get in order to increase the anxiety of potential investors.

Remember, there is no definite profile for an investment scammer. It could be anyone from the anonymous caller on the phone to a well-dressed executive in an expensive office to a supposedly informative and educational forex Web site to friends of friends, with or without a series of impressive titles and awards.

First and External Signs of Potential Internet-Based Scams

You have to take a close look at the overall Web site content. Are there strange and nonprofessional names; noncredible claims and excessive guarantees; serial, cut-and-paste FAQs and templates with the same exact content for different forex investment Web sites; lack of corporate identity in logos and images? These are all signs of potential scams.

The most blatant sign is the investment plan itself and the lack of detail about how the exceptionally high returns are really obtained. Never invest if the company or its representatives are unable to provide complete disclosure about their financial activities and overall business management.

Preventive Actions

1. How to Find Out

As a fundamental rule, you should never participate in any investment activity that you do not fully understand, and you should never believe any performance claims that you would not be able to replicate by using the same methods. Fraudsters who try to promote alleged forex investments will usually make claims of possessing special and secret techniques that allow them to obtain extremely high profits with consistency, but seldom will they go into detail, because most of the time those are fake claims—the only secret activity those fraudsters engage in is to wipe your account clean.

If "profits" are there, they will most often be a recycling of your own deposited funds. Do not risk your savings on what is being advertised, especially if the returns that are "guaranteed" seem too good to be true, unless you know exactly what you are doing and there is transparency in regard to the methods that are employed.

Here is a list of some questions you can ask that will undoubtedly make fraudsters feel uncomfortable and probably also will lead them to back off and turn to a less- informed new prey.

- *Personal data.* If you have been contacted by a total stranger through a phone call or e-mail, ask the originator where he or she obtained your personal data.
- *Risks.* Ask the promoter about the risks of the investment being proposed. Each and every investment involves some risks—especially those that theoretically offer excessively high returns.
- *Documentation.* Fraudsters will be quite reluctant to give you access to written documents and risk disclosures, as those could be used against them in case of a fraud trial. Ask for additional information and a detailed explanation of the whole investment that is being proposed, as well as a complete risk disclosure statement. This will usually make the scammers run away.
- *Management and performance.* Ask for the names of the company's management staff. Some people who operate dishonest forex investment businesses might give you false names, but the fact that you are checking into details can alarm them.

    Investigate the past of the company itself: Ask how many years it has been in business. Ask to see its track record and trading performance, which should be proportionate to that time. Some start-up businesses can be totally reputable; however, it is important to dig a little into the past activities of the people you are talking to. Of course, a scammer won't be at all eager to talk about this.

Asking for written performance reports is a must, and it's even better to have them certified by an accountant or equivalent. It is true that the past performance is in no way a guarantee that the future performance will be similar; however, a well-established company with several years of activity should be able to produce those reports easily and in a verifiable form.

Ask for a personal meeting and visit the firm's office. If it is a scam, the fraudsters surely don't want you to see where they operate from or risk being recognized.

- *Third parties.* Is the company capable of providing verifiable and trustworthy references that you can contact? Would the representatives agree to further explain the forex investment proposal and submit it for analysis to more prepared third parties, such as your accountant, banker, attorney, or investment advisor? Hesitation and excuses on this are clear indications that you should absolutely not invest with such an individual or company.

- *Regulations and legal conditions.* Inquire about which regulatory agencies supervise the investments you are being offered and ask if they are traded on a regulated exchange. Regulations imply a structure of protection and strict rule enforcement through sanctions to those individuals or companies that do not observe them. A fraudulent investment will never be under regulation. Tell the person who is proposing the deal to you that you want to check the company's status before deciding.

If it is a scam, prepare to hear some evasive responses. Finally, ask about the legal frame that the company uses to solve any dispute or controversy that might arise. If there is any sign of discomfort or impatience from the vendor at this point, do not go further.

There are some Web sites where people can post and vent their frustrations and experiences. Most of these sites have hidden agendas. If you dig around the sites that seem to only have negative information, it is more than likely you will find that the negative comments are the work of a competing company. It is okay to read the postings—just take what you read with a grain of salt.

- *Accounting.* Ask how your money will be managed and in what type of account, as well as which kind of accounting statements you can expect to receive and how often; also ask if there is a regular auditing of the company's records.

  You also need to know the detailed costs of the fund's management—for example, what are the performance fees, commissions, and overall management fees—and you want to obtain all this information in written form.

  Finally, and most important, ask how you will be able to liquidate the contract and recover your money if you decide to terminate the investment agreement, including any type of specific costs and delays.

You should obtain straight, detailed, and transparent answers to these questions.

2. How to Protect Yourself

Investigate before you invest. The previous list of questions will not guarantee you honest and straightforward feedback from the individual who is promoting the investment scheme; however, the questions will help you in the detection of dubious situations. The last thing a con artist wants is to be checked up on, and fraudsters are highly experienced in evading any questions that could expose their true colors. Bear in mind that they will try to emphasize the "huge profits to be made" and minimize or simply ignore some of your queries, which is precisely what will expose their agenda.

Most fraudsters will try to operate under the radar by:

- Choosing either types of investments or locations that have little or no regulatory requirements
- Adopting different names
- Changing their promotion techniques
- Insisting on the exclusive urgency of the investment, thus not allowing you the time to investigate
- And, in general, targeting ill-informed potential victims that have no idea how to verify their claims or check the company's activities

This is why there are so many forex scams. Until recently, the forex market had been unregulated. Many of the commodities professionals who were not so professional and who had disciplinary actions against them moved to the forex marketplace. This allowed these people to continue trading without violating the disciplinary orders handed down by the U.S. Commodity Futures Trading Commission (CFTC). The good news is that with all the new regulatory reform, the forex market is well on its way to becoming a great market.

One thing is certain: there are no guarantees that any investment, even a legitimate one, will make money, but you can be absolutely sure that your money is already lost the moment you lend it to a fraudster.

You can go a long way to protecting yourself by doing research:

- *Contact local institutions and the media.* Look for complaints filed against the individual or the company at the local police department, Better Business Bureau, consumer protection organizations, and local newspapers; also look on the Internet. You might start by contacting the National Fraud Information Center (NFIC) at www.fraud.org or call the NFIC hotline at 1–800–876–7060; this is a public service of the National Consumers League, and the staff can direct you to other agencies for information.
- *Contact the regulatory offices.* Individuals and companies that offer investments and other financial instruments are, at least in the United States, subject to one or more types of regulations. It might be more difficult to research operations in other countries, but here is a short list of institutions that can be of help in verifying what the specific legal requirements are for a particular investment and in checking the background of the firms that are soliciting your funds or with which you intend to invest:
  - United States:
    CFTC,www.cftc.gov
    National Futures Association (NFA), www.nfa.futures
    .org/basicnet
  - United Kingdom: Financial Services Authority, www.fsa.gov.uk

- ○ Cyprus: Cyprus Securities and Exchange Commission, www.cysec.gov.cy/licence_members_1_en.aspx
- ○ Ireland: MiFID, www.mifid.ie/index.html
- ○ Germany: BaFin, www.bafin.de

Futures contracts and options on futures are regulated by the CFTC, which is a federal agency, as well as the NFA, which is a self-regulatory organization authorized by Congress. The NFA maintains a database of futures-related disciplinary information that investors can access by calling the Disciplinary Information Access Line at 800–621–3570 or 800–676–4NFA.

Conducting a thorough investigation before risking your hard-earned money in a dubious investment proposal will take time and effort on your part. This is a must and is totally worth the time and trouble. When you contact the regulators, you will be able to find out if the individual or business is duly registered and has the appropriate rights to work in the forex investment business. Additionally, you will find out if the business has been the object of public claims or disciplinary actions in the past.

Other institutions that you can contact in the United States include these:

- The office of the local public prosecutor
- The state attorney general
- The state securities administrator
- Federal postal inspectors if the promotion of the scheme is being sent through the mail
- The Federal Bureau of Investigation

3. Keep Close Track of Your Money

After having completed all the above steps, even if the forex investment you are being offered seems completely legitimate and you decide to invest, you still need to continue monitoring and be alert for any signs of things that might go wrong: a sudden lack of communication with the individual or company that sold you the investment, failure to receive accounting statements or important documents that were promised, lack of further information or discrepancies between what was stated in the beginning and actual data, and, especially, failure of scheduled payments.

If at a certain point you become suspicious and cannot obtain the proper answers or resolve the previously described situations, you should immediately try to get out of that investment and ask for a liquidation of your monies—and if needed, threaten to contact the authorities. If there is fraud going on, the company might prefer to send your money back rather than risking its scheme being discovered.

Be prepared to hear new excuses, explanations, and reasons why you should keep your investment with the company. Insist on a refund no matter what the people there tell you and do not accept any excuses or further attempts to convince you to the contrary.

If you get your funds back, consider yourself lucky. Most of the time you will not, and in that case you should immediately report the situation to the authorities. In fact, even if you get your investment back, you should contact the authorities if you still suspect fraud was involved.

2

YOU VERSUS THEM

To be successful trading in the spot forex marketplace, you will need to arm yourself with all the knowledge and tools you can find. The brokers are out to get you, at least most of them. With ever-changing regulatory oversight, the industry is on its way to being the greatest financial marketplace in the world. It will take regulatory oversight to get rid of the bad practices that some of the brokers out there are still using to separate you from your money.

To beat the brokers at their own game you will need to know a few things. We will cover many of those throughout this book, and in most cases you will ultimately feel that it is you versus them. That's okay so as long as you know what to look for and how to protect yourself while trading this exciting marketplace.

HOW FOREX BROKERS MAKE MONEY

A forex brokerage firm is a business just like any other, and as such, it must generate a profit in order to ensure the firm's permanence and functionalities. Brokers provide a service to both individual and corporate traders, acting as intermediaries between the interbank and its clients. Among the brokers, we can find different levels of ethics and trustworthiness, ranging from the mere "bucket shops" with little or no care at all for the client's needs and the mindset of a casino owner to bigger companies where all the ethical criteria are met and total transparency and efficient customer service are their guidelines.

Brokers are an integral part of the market's hierarchical structure, which begins with first-tier financial institutions and goes on down; depending on their company size, capital, structure, and volume of operations, brokers can be placed in the second or third tier.

OVERVIEW OF THE MARKET STRUCTURE

Top Tier = Central Banks, Largest Investment Banks

At this level, all transactions are totally transparent, and every participant can see all the rates offered from one another through the Electronic Broking Services Spot Dealing System, which accounts for the currency pairs involving the euro, U.S. dollar, yen, and Swiss franc. All other currency pairs are handled through Reuters Dealing 3000 Spot Matching.

This tier is composed by the largest central banks of the world, which are free to trade all currencies at any rates they decide to agree upon.

Second Tier = Smaller Banks, Multinational Bank Branches and Financial Institutions, Large Funds, and Wealthy Private Investors

Large multinational corporations and banks, including their subordinate branches, represent the second tier of the forex market. The commercial requirements of currency exchange are offered rates that usually differ from the interbank exchange rates, and quotes can also be significantly different from bank to bank. Huge capital funds and wealthy private individuals can have access to a variable array of liquidity providers for their transactions, and therefore they can be considered as belonging to this level.

A few retail brokers, especially electronic communication networks (ECNs), can also be classified as second-tier institutions.

Third Tier = Market Makers and Smaller Investors

The great majority of retail forex brokers fall in this category, and most of them only interact with a single liquidity provider from the second tier. Only ECNs and a few high-level brokerages, although also being classified as "retail," can offer direct access to a variety of liquidity providers and thus have to be placed under the second-tier label, as they send the trading orders from the clients directly to the interbank.

TYPES OF RETAIL FOREX SERVICE PROVIDERS

There are basically two types of brokers that provide access to the retail forex market: ECNs and market makers (see Table 2.1). Their presence allows small investors (who wouldn't be able to participate directly at the top-tier levels) to speculate and trade currencies alongside big financial institutions and private wealthy individuals, without the need to deposit large sums of money to be able to enter the markets.

ECNs usually require larger deposits but provide a more direct relationship with the interbank. Many of them can be considered to be at the second-tier level. Market makers seldom allow their clients to interact directly at those levels and belong to the third tier.

Finally, all the much smaller traders with smaller amounts to invest make up the lowest tier.

Market makers employ various ways to route their clients' orders: some are offset in a sort of inside market between different clients' opposite trades; in others the market makers take the other side of the trade; one more way is to hedge the position through liquidity providers or higher-tier institutions.

The most common tools that the forex brokers employ to make money for their business are listed below and then commented on in detail.

- Spreads and differences among liquidity providers
- The use of leverage
- Commissions and rollover or swap fees
- Hedging
- Interest collection
- In-house trading
- Recruitment of introducing brokers (IBs) and affiliates

Table 2.1   Some differences between ECNs and market makers

ECN	Market Maker
Higher starting capital is needed	You can open an account with very small amounts
Trades are directly conveyed to the interbank	Trades are kept in-house or hedged on the interbank; only really big trades might be conveyed directly
There are smaller spreads at some times but greater spread volatility	The spreads are fixed and often even guaranteed, with little volatility
Commission fees are earned on every trade	No commissions are earned (except on Sharia-compliant Islamic accounts)
Trades are characterized by transparency and impartiality	There can be conflicts of interest since the broker often acts as counterparty of the client's trades
Money is earned from commissions and spreads	Money is earned from spreads, and money is also earned if the client loses money when acting as a counterparty

The list contains mostly ethical options that brokers employ to receive a payment for their services. There are also less ethical and blatantly unethical procedures, such as the following:

- Countertrading, or trading against the traders
- Controlling the trading platform through plug-ins
- Manipulating prices directly
- Penalizing profitability

HOW ETHICAL DEALERS EARN THEIR MONEY

Spreads and Differences in Liquidity Providers

The primary source of income is the spread, or price difference between the bid and ask rates offered by the broker. These differ from rates the broker receives through the liquidity providers, which can offer the broker a very small spread or even no spread, thus earning the difference in the broker's favor. Also, in the case of in-house trades, the rate differential remains in its totality in the hands of the broker, as there are no external interventions.

The *ask* price is the price that the trader pays when opening a long position (buying the currency pair), and the *bid* price is the amount at which the trader will be able to sell back that same position to the market. Inversely, short-selling a currency pair is done at *bid* prices and closed at *ask* prices. This difference is expressed in *pips*, which is the standard, smallest unit of measure and is usually between 2 and 5 pips for most brokers. This is what the broker earns on all your transactions, no matter if the final outcome is positive or negative for your account.

The rates that the broker receives from the liquidity providers are also often different from the rates offered on the trading platform, with a smaller gap between bid and ask; or if the broker has access to a diversity of choices, as is the case for ECNs, the broker can pick the best rate on both sides of the transaction, giving an additional boost to the broker's benefit. Although 1 pip can seem a tiny sum (0.0001 of the value of the currency pair or 0.01 on yen-based pairs), trades are counted by standard lots of US$100,000 (where 1 pip on most majors equals $10). Additionally, high leverages and the overall amount of transactions in a market that moves trillions of dollars every day (nearly $4 trillion in April 2010, according to the Bank for International Settlements) account for a quite handsome profit for the brokers.

Normal market fluctuations creating preferred or void price zones account for the differences in bid/ask spreads, and the same goes for slippage (when there are no buyers or sellers at a given price, the execution of an order has to be done at the next available price). This is also why brokers that offer fixed spreads or guaranteed fills (or both) have to employ other strategies to limit their risk exposure, and most probably will give you a delayed execution or "server disconnections," especially at news times, when this kind of volatility is more likely to occur. When there is no counterparty to take the opposite side of a trade, the risks are on their side to assume the guarantee, and so they use delays and requotes whenever they need to protect themselves from such a risk.

Leverage

High leverage is an additional source of multiplied income, as the spreads are automatically leveraged and therefore the broker's gains are proportionally increased. For example, on a 1:50 leverage, brokers would earn 50 times more on the spreads than they would be able to do with no leverage or 1:1. Recent regulations have limited the maximum leverage to 1:50 on major currency pairs and 1:20 on exotics; however, there are plenty of offshore brokers who still offer as high as 1:400 and 1:500 leverages.

Commissions and Swap

One of the advantages of forex trading is the commission-free operation. Only Sharia-compliant accounts are charged a commission in place of the swaps on most market makers' trading platforms. ECNs do charge a commission on every trade independently from the outcome, plus the spread, which is usually very small except on very volatile sessions and particularly during news releases.

The swap or overnight rollover fee is a requirement from the liquidity providers, which is passed on to the clients (with the possibility of slightly different rates from those of the banks; in fact, almost every retail broker differs from every other on this particular). Swaps are calculated in regard to the interest rates of both currencies involved in a pair (the difference between paid and borrowed currency), and the broker will pay the swap to the trader when the ratio is positive on the open positions and will collect the overnight fee if the difference is negative. As these calculations also take into account the bid and ask prices, the paid swap ratio is always smaller than the collected swap; therefore the broker always ends at an advantage.

Make sure that you check out your broker of choice carefully. Some brokers will try to get out of paying the swap fee when you are long the high-yielding currency pair. For instance, I know some brokers that won't pay out any swaps if you are in a mini account. I know some brokers that won't pay out swaps on some pairs regardless. I have also had brokers that only paid after I questioned why I wasn't getting paid.

Finally, some brokers also charge payment processing fees at the moment of depositing or withdrawing from your account.

These fees are usually very small; they are meant to compensate even if partially some of the broker's expenses. You will find these sorts of fees specifically relating to wire transactions of payments in and out of your account. This used to be a rampant practice, and brokers would literally gouge their clients. Many brokers today are so competitive for an account that they will either waive this fee or not charge it at all.

Hedging

Hedging is performed through offsetting the broker's exposure in one market direction by establishing an equivalent position in another market to reduce the risks. This can be done through option trading, insurance policies, and other investment vehicles.

When hedging, you will more than likely have to go offshore, as recent U.S. regulations have disallowed this sort of trading. You can always use a correlated hedge. This is when you find another currency pair that will mimic or mirror what you are currently trading. The more correlated it is, the more risk you can reduce between your trades.

There can be some inherent problems with hedging in the same currency pair. I had a trade that was perfectly hedged, and still the account was liquidated. By design, you would think that by being long the EUR and short the EUR, you would have a perfect hedge. Well, think again. First you would not use a stop, since you have a perfect hedge. So here is the problem. I am hedged both sides, and the market moves big on news.

The bank (liquidity provider) decides to go after my account. I had the account up about 25 percent in a month, and obviously the bank didn't like it. So when the market moved big, the bank held up one side of the bid and ask. That way the spread was widened, in this case, about 150 pips. Seriously, in the worst trade gone bad I have ever experienced, the account was seen as overleveraged at that time, since I was technically open on both sides of the trade. So when the spread opened, the account dropped and hit its margin call, the bank closed the trade and liquidated the account, and then the bank just covered the trade and reverted to a normal spread.

By the way, I was on the phone the entire time this happened trying to get out of the trade, and the bank wouldn't let me out.

Ultimately the bank told me, "That's trading the spot in the over-the-counter market; you get what you get." I am still trying to get credit back for that garbage.

Interest Collected on Exchange Operations
Earned interest on deposited funds and on the conversion and holding of different currencies is another alternative that adds to the broker's profits. Some brokers pay back a part of this interest to the client, but most of them do not.

In-House Trading
Small retail operations, below one standard lot, are usually kept "in-house," where brokers offset opposite positions whenever possible among their own client pool. Trades can't be conveyed to the interbank because of their insufficient size, and very few market makers manage to group some of them when the entries are equivalent. (See Chapter 17, where I discuss B-books.)

IBs = Affiliates
Brokerage houses make money each time a trade is opened by any of their clients. The same holds true for the IBs, or affiliates.

Although this can be considered as an indirect way of earning, brokers increase their profit potential by recruiting IBs for their firm or signing up affiliates and offering them a share of the spread incentives. These individuals most often are given a branded personal Web site to channel new clients to the brokerage house; and given that their earnings basically depend on the amount of lots traded, either winning or losing, it can be very rewarding to both parties, unfortunately quite often to the detriment of the customer.

Keep in mind that the IB is really an intermediary. In most cases the broker just pays the IB part of the spread, and that doesn't necessarily mean that the spread is any higher for you, the trader, whether you are trading directly through the broker or through your IB. In some cases the broker will increase the spread to cover the added expense of the IB to the broker.

WHAT DO SHADY BROKERS DO TO EARN YOUR MONEY?

Countertrading

Trading against clients creates a conflict of interest and is a highly unethical practice. But it is very profitable for the broker. When all the conditions offered seem too good to be true—low spreads, high leverage, no trading or payment processing fees, and high paid rollover interests—you can suspect that the broker is trading against you to "earn" *your* money.

Brokers usually make the majority of their income on your losing trades rather than from the spreads or any earned interest on the capital that you have deposited in the account.

Plug-Ins

One of the most popular forex platforms comes along with an interesting virtual plug-in. This plug-in allows the brokers to manipulate prices and set a series of parameters that allows them to exert total control of client accounts. All actions are automated, including triggering stops at particular levels, moving stops and limits, setting a fixed slippage, overriding client parameters, performing selective and fixed execution delays, disabling pending orders at specific times (usually on news releases), programming platform freezes, selectively processing or rejecting trading requests, etc.

There are many other platforms that brokers are using with back-office software to manipulate the market and ultimately take your money. As a result, we will be talking about specific strategies to make the trading environment a much more level field.

Direct Price Manipulation

Prices can be manipulated through sudden spikes and widening of spreads that do not correspond to the real market activity. They also can be manipulated through hunting stops and by overly delaying orders, causing excessive slippage. In the equities market, these manipulative practices are sometimes called flash trades. All these will be discussed in depth in later chapters.

Profitability Blacklisted

Banning profitable traders is a sure sign of a scam broker. As soon
as these brokers see that you are making profits steadily, they will
close your account, usually invoking some obscure reason. I have
personally seen broker account listings labeled "Blacklisted." The
broker will literally seek out these profitable accounts and then do
everything possible to destroy the accounts' value.

I know that brokers use traders as well; their job is to review
profitable accounts. Then the broker's trader is instructed to look
for trading patterns of the profitable trading customer. So if you are
using, say, a 50-day moving average and the broker's trader figures
it out, the broker can then start trading against you. The broker now
knows when you get in and what you are looking at. The job of the
broker's trader is to beat you at your own trades.

These brokers also classify their clients into two groups: those
who lose money (which is around 95 to 98 percent of all traders, especially newcomers) and those who win and make money. At the beginning of the broker-client relationship, the assumption is that your
account belongs to the losing group. After a while, if you have been
making consistent profits, you will be reassigned to the winning
group, and trading conditions will start to become tighter: more
requotes and delays in execution, sudden server disconnections,
selective use of the above-mentioned virtual plug-ins, etc.

I have been there and done that, seen all the games, and they
will find you. Again, we have to deploy some tactics of our own to
beat the brokers at their own game. I know you are probably saying
that if the brokers are so unscrupulous, why keep trading? Great
question! The answer is because we can still make money, so there
is no reason to stop trading the world's largest financial market just
because of a few bad brokers or banks.

Also, your trades will be grouped with all those of the winning
group and hedged against on the interbank to offset any profits
made on those positions. Those brokers are mostly interested in getting "losing" accounts, given the fact that the trades never leave the
house; when a client takes a loss, all the money goes in the broker's
pocket.

An overseas broker told me that the rule of thumb was that brokers make about 120 to 125 percent of the clients' deposited funds.

CAN YOU TRADE THE FOREX?

I know what you are saying. After reading this far, you are asking yourself, "Can I trade the forex?" The answer is yes, you can trade the forex. When you get done reading this book, you will be better armed with the right tools and knowledge to go out and start trading the forex with a renewed sense of confidence.

I still trade the forex market and love it. Just like you, I don't enjoy butting heads with an unscrupulous broker that is out to steal my money. I am on a constant lookout for tricks or things in my trading account that don't add up, and I am always looking for good brokers. By the way, just because some brokers used to use some of the unscrupulous tactics outlined in this book does not mean that they can't change their stripes, so to speak.

There is always management turnover, and with new regulatory oversight, the bigger brokers are trying very hard to stay on the right side of the industry. Don't be afraid to test other brokers or go back to ones you may not have liked in the past. Just make sure you are testing them with money you can afford to lose. You never know.

WHY 98 PERCENT OF TRADERS LOSE MONEY

Access to the forex markets is a relatively recent possibility for individual traders, thanks to the development of communication technologies. This easy access has also contributed to all the hype and inaccurate comparisons to "get-rich-quick" schemes, which abound on the Internet. The promotional materials of some brokerages (although they always include the legal disclaimers in small letters) are almost always slanted to appeal to people's needs or greed. The words *easy* and *rich* are used so often that people end up thinking that's the natural outcome of forex trading and, what is worse, that forex trading is nothing more than a mere gambling activity.

Nothing is further from reality; the trading of forex is not a game or a gamble; instead, it's a tough and potentially very rewarding business if would-be traders are willing to dedicate their time and efforts to learn, understand, and thoroughly develop all the skills and abilities that are needed in this profession.

Just as a medical student wouldn't think of performing surgery on a patient without having mastered all the surgical skills and knowledge available and practicing for many years to become a flawless physician, the same mindset must be ingrained in every forex student if he or she really wants to achieve consistent and durable results.

The fundamental reason why 98 percent of traders lose money and are forced to quit the forex arena in their first year is due to a total lack of education on the subject. But there are also other obvious reasons, which I am going to categorize and describe below.

In my years of experience both trading and dealing with brokers, I have come to realize that undercapitalized accounts are doomed to fail. You simply have to have the appropriate amount of account size, depending on your type of trading. A broker once told me that his firm holds all accounts under $5,000 because it knows that 98 percent of them will lose their money.

The broker doesn't have to trade against you per se, just hold the other side of your trade. The broker knows you will make enough mistakes to wipe out your account, and who do you think profits from your losses? That's right—the broker.

In my opinion, there are three basic areas that can explain a trader's failure to meet his or her goals through forex: technical, emotional, and external. Technical reasons are mostly related to proper education, abilities, and skills. Emotional reasons involve the trader's own personality traits and reactions, as well as common beliefs that may be useful in life but are counterproductive in this particular industry. External reasons, although still somewhat the trader's responsibility, are trickier to handle and depend on the behavior of third parties. Let's examine each area in more detail.

TECHNICAL REASONS WHY TRADERS LOSE

1. Not Having Enough Education

This is the basic cause of all trading failures. New traders do not bother taking the time to learn what moves the different currencies or to get a grip on fundamentals or technical analysis; they just jump into the markets blindly, hoping the trades will take care of themselves.

2. Not Practicing Enough

Although lack of proper practice is cause for failure, this is a double-edged sword. Too much trading on a demo account can be harmful later on, because when trading on the demo, the trader tends to become careless about the outcome, since he or she isn't incurring any risk. The need for practicing is paramount. Demo accounts are good for learning the platform's operation, but the conditions are usually quite different from those of actual live accounts, because there are many brokers that allow trading accounts to be opened with a very small amount of capital.

Traders should start trading small until they obtain acceptable results and a proper grasp of the market behavior before trading more. By practicing beforehand, the trader acquires greater experience in the markets.

3. Trading with "Scared Money"

Disclaimers always enforce this rule, but in practice it is seldom respected. You should *never* trade with funds that you cannot afford to lose. The reason is pretty obvious; even the most cool-headed individuals will crash psychologically in front of a loss, and the added stress will lead to poor decision making and further losses in a dwindling spiral.

4. Having No Money Management Rules

The first and foremost rule to be established in a trading plan should specify how risk will be managed. Failing to do this could lead to committing too high a percentage of the capital and increasing the possibilities of getting a margin call or even blowing the account in its entirety. This goes hand in hand with the next reason—employing an excess of true leverage.

5. Overleveraging

True leverage differs from the broker's allowed leverage. You are trading at 1:1 true leverage if your total equity is $10,000 and your position size is one mini-lot ($10,000 exposure). Using your broker's maximum leverage capabilities is a recipe for disaster, increasing the potential losses in the same proportion as eventual profits. Betting the farm on a single trade is not a good policy.

Brokers offer higher leverages so that you might open larger positions, therefore increasing the income they obtain through the spreads; for a higher pip value, they get a higher total spread value.

6. Trading without a Complete Trading Plan

The trading plan is a forex trader's business plan. If you don't have a plan, you won't have an edge to turn the market in your favor. You need to build and write down a complete trading plan, which should include a series of specific rules according to the particular strategy you will apply: entry rules, exit rules, money management and risk-to-reward trade evaluation, time frames that will be used for entries, types of signals, and indicators. All of this is needed and then some to help you set a realistic and achievable goal.

If you don't have a plan, your trading will have no focus or direction. The trading plan should also include personal and psychological aspects that will have to be in place before you click on that BUY or SELL button. Finally, you must set a daily trade limit (you especially need to stick to a daily trade limit to avoid potential losing streaks) so that you don't fall into the next category: overtrading.

7. Overtrading

Getting enthusiastic after a few winning trades and taking revenge trades after a few losses both lead to the same mistake. Although scalpers might disagree, taking too many trades, locking your profits too early, and using stops that are too tight for the time frame employed will certainly make your broker very happy to collect all those spreads. But in the end, this is a losing strategy for you, as your profits end up being smaller than the spreads you've paid.

8. Choosing Bad Times to Trade

The best time for trading is when there is plenty of liquidity, that is, when at least two of the biggest markets are open. In times of low volume, volatility becomes erratic, and traders get mixed signals. Bank traders dominate the market in quieter times with their customer order flow. It is better to stay out of between-session hours. Also, the most significant moves occur shortly after news releases. There is high volume, and liquidity and changes in price reflect a real and important currency flow.

9. Taking into Account Only Half of the Elements of a Currency Pair

Both the base and quote currency strength must be assessed before making a trading decision. When acting upon the behavior of a single currency, you are missing half of the trade reality of that particular currency pair.

10. Implementing Insufficiently Tested Strategies—Dilettantism

Many traders are eager to jump in and out of strategies, without dedicating enough time to back and forward testing to see if a particular strategy really can be profitable. Instead, they discard it at the first sign of a loss, thus not allowing the method to show its real results and scope.

11. Trading Too Many Pairs

Currency pairs exhibit a different behavior from one another. If your attention is spread over too many of them, you won't be able to understand each one in detail. Focus is needed here, mastering one pair at a time.

12. Choosing the Wrong Time Frame

Some traders attempt to trade longer term while applying stops and profit-taking rules that belong to smaller time frames. If your trades are too short term, you will be wasting your efforts in spreads paid to the broker; if you try to forecast what will happen next month and base your trading decisions on distant overviews, you will not pay attention to what is happening at the moment. Trade in the *now*.

13. Trading against the Trend

Identify the main trend and do not try to pick tops or bottoms. Trade in the direction the price is moving.

14. Using Too Many Indicators

Throwing a bunch of indicators on a chart will create confusion and lead to analysis-paralysis, especially when the signals you get are in conflict with one another. Try cleaning up your charts and do not employ more than two indicators, or better, learn to identify price action by itself.

Most, if not all, indicators are lagging and only show what has already happened.

15. Making Careless Exits

Exiting a trade has to be planned as carefully as or even more carefully than the entries. Stop losses are emergency exit levels, but if you see that a trade is not working the way you expected, no need to wait until the stops are hit; try to minimize the losses. On the other hand, when you are into a winning trade, don't cut out profits too soon even if the tension builds up while monitoring the position. Wait patiently until the price reaches your expected target profit, and observe carefully any signs of reversal. Don't jump out because you were following a whim or because it is too boring to wait it out. Trading is boring and stressful, but it's rewarding if you follow the rules.

16. Watching One Pair and Trading Another

It is useful to observe the correlations between currency pairs, but you shouldn't assume that the pair you want to trade will be moving in the same direction or with the same impulse of the pair you just noticed moving. Each pair has its own reasons that determine its behavior. Trade the pair that moved.

17. Not Assessing Properly the Market's Technical Condition

It is important to observe when a market is overextended in any direction, as this is a condition where price action in reversal could be particularly sudden and strong. This could result in blowing out stop losses. Always check the overall situation before entering a trade.

EMOTIONAL AND PERSONALITY REASONS WHY TRADERS LOSE

Contrary to what you may think, emotional risks are subordinate to technical reasons in a great number of occasions. The lack of proper education leads a trader to fail by taking out-of-proportion risks, trading too many lots in regard to their actual equity, and opening random positions without a specific plan, thus missing an edge on the markets. The emotional frustration you will experience thereafter is a consequence of not possessing enough knowledge of forex and therefore being at the mercy of continuous ups and downs and stress accumulation because of the losses incurred.

Emotional self-control is an important asset, but by itself it will do nothing for your trading results if it is not paired with a thorough education and sufficient practice to develop appropriate trading skills.

1. Acting from Basic Emotions Related to Money

Fear and *greed* are the most basic emotions that lead traders to lose control of their performance. Fear of losing money that you can't afford to lose (see technical reason 3 above, "Trading with 'Scared Money'") can cause you to close positions too early and thus cut your profits too soon. Even worse, fear of losing money can cause you to leave losing positions open up to the point of no return in the hope that the market will come back instead of cutting your losses as soon as possible. Greed causes problems when you are in the middle of a winning streak and want more and more, leading to overtrading and giving back to the market all that was previously earned.

In addition to the emotions of fear and greed, I would add *need*: the need to produce more money and make a tiny account grow enough to make a living out of it by projecting unrealistic goals and false expectancies along with the wrong idea that forex trading will make you rich in no time.

2. Being Afraid to Take a Loss

One of the most deeply ingrained beliefs is that taking a loss implies a personal failure. This is something we all would like to avoid. No one wants to be labeled a loser. We have been taught to strive for success, and failure is frowned upon in our normal professional life. However, losses are part of the whole scene of forex trading, and you have to carefully plan so you do not compromise the overall performance in the long haul.

There is nothing wrong in taking a loss. It doesn't diminish your value as a trader—on the contrary. You can't control the market reactions, but you must be the master of your own reactions to the market, and this includes accepting the fact that you will sometimes be wrong about the movement of a trade.

3. Trading on a Hunch
Using feelings and emotions to enter a trade instead of using a carefully thought-out plan is a menu for disaster. Revenge trading also falls under this category. You see a surge in prices and you buy, or you see a sudden spike down and you sell, without taking into account the whole picture or the characteristics of the time frame you are watching. You get a series of losses, fear rears its ugly head, and you feel the need and greed, which pushes you to open trade after trade, hoping to make back all the money you lost.

4. Feeling a Lack of Confidence
The only way to build up true confidence in your trading is to get positive results, and those will only come after you learn this business thoroughly. A few lucky trades aren't enough, as they might propel you into the opposite emotional flaw—overconfidence.

5. Feeling Overconfident
One of the worst things that could happen to a new trader is to start by experiencing a series of winning trades by chance, without having a real grasp of the market's behavior mechanics. You suddenly feel all-powerful and take success for granted, losing perspective and thinking forex is easy. You will be more likely to trade carelessly and without a plan, and you will be totally unprepared when the first big loss comes around.

6. Doing Too Much Analysis
Trying to look beyond what is obvious and elaborating complicated theories about the markets will hinder your ability to see and trade what is really happening in plain sight. Keep it simple.

7. Trading 24 Hours a Day
Staying too long in front of the screen without proper rest reduces your ability to focus and builds up stress and fatigue in your brain and whole body. You need to be totally focused when taking on a

trade, and this is only possible for a limited amount of time. Do not trade when you are tired or when your attention is driven away by other daily preoccupations. Spend less time in front of the charts, but when you do spend time with them, be completely aware and awake.

8. Lacking the Will to Follow Your Own Rules

A trading plan is only as good as your ability to stick to its rules. Traders that always find excuses to bend the rules based on emotional reactions are only justifying their lack of discipline and will have poor results in the long run.

9. Being Fearful of "Pulling the Trigger"

Even with a well-thought-out plan, some traders freeze when their strategy triggers a trade, and so they consistently miss good entries. It is true that not trading won't bring losses, but it won't bring profits either. Trust your plan and have the courage to put it into practice when the time is right.

10. Moving Stops

This is another version of "letting losses run" and is the result of a "hope-and-pray" state of mind. You should never move a stop to a wider distance. If your preplanned stop is hit, either you were trading in the wrong direction, so moving the stops would only add to the impending disaster, or it was too tight and you'll need to reassess your risk management in regard to the time frame you are trading to avoid such a situation in the future.

11. Giving Up Because of Disappointment

Trading should be treated as a business at all times, and this includes setting a specific time to work on your trades, independently of their individual outcomes. If you start the day on the wrong foot, just take the loss and continue with your daily plan.

12. Counting Your Chickens before They Hatch

Setting realistic goals is good, but daydreaming about profits to be made or worrying about potential losses is of no use. Focus on your plan, wait for the trigger, and then just concentrate on your trade until it comes to completion.

13. Feeding on Adrenaline

Many people get into forex trading because of the emotional rush it gives them, just like gamblers get. This attitude is far from positive and can have disastrous effects on decision making. The ideal situation is to be as relaxed about your trades as you can—you should be alert and interested, but not excited. You need a tranquil mind to be able to exert total focus.

14. Feeling the Need to Be "In the Market" at All Times

Taking trades without a real trigger just because you want to be "in the market," or because you feel bored waiting for the appropriate setup, is the same as entering trades randomly. When there are no reasons to trade, just stay out.

EXTERNAL REASONS WHY TRADERS LOSE

1. Choosing the Wrong Broker

This should be the first lesson to learn before entering the forex arena. Gather as much information as possible about the potential broker so you can choose a good one, and avoid being ruined by a scam or just plain unethical bucket shops.

2. Setting Your Stops in the Open

Even with a decent retail broker, stops will occasionally be sought. Using stops that are set at obvious levels or that are set too tightly for the time frame chosen will invariably turn the odds against you. Be sure to allow your trades enough space to breathe and evolve.

3. Following Other Traders' Decisions

Sharing thoughts and analyses with fellow traders is a double-edged sword, especially for newcomers who have little understanding of the markets and seem desperately in need of a guide or mentor. Not all the traders that publicly post the positions they are about to enter are profitable; in fact, truly successful traders seldom participate in such social media; they are too busy trading and perfecting their strategies. You need to make your own decisions and develop your method(s), even if only adapted from a proven system.

4. Adopting an Automated Strategy
Based on Hypothetical Results

There are several "black-box" systems for sale out there, with amazing performance records, that have never really been tested on a live account. Hypothetical performance is equivalent to no performance at all, given that demo conditions are totally different from those of real trading. Keep in mind that the only true motivation behind those systems is for the seller to make money out of inexperienced traders.

5. Being Influenced by Rumors

A rumor or forecast circulating before news releases can be employed to take a closer look at the situation but should never be jumped upon blindly without a careful examination of both the currency pair's actual price action and the timing of the rumor itself. The source of the rumor is also a clue to its real motives, as often the purpose is to create exactly the opposite reaction to whichever direction the market is about to take and then to profit from the confusion.

6. Having a Poor Understanding of Fundamentals

News reports on economic releases are to be carefully examined, as they are often biased or offer just one side of the picture without taking into account all the elements involved. Whenever possible, read news releases at the source and learn to interpret and understand them correctly.

To conclude, being successful at forex trading is the result of a dedicated and consistent effort to learn the necessary skills and perfect them through continuous practice and preparation. Being able to identify the trading style that best suits your talent and personality, as well as your capital needs and time availability, will ultimately allow you to be successful in achieving your forex trading goals.

Finally, never stop reviewing your performance to spot any weak points you may need to correct, as well as to recognize your positive trades. This will allow you to increase your confidence and maintain focus on the strategy you have developed.

CHAPTER 3

FOREX OPTIONS

WHAT ARE FOREX OPTIONS

Forex, or currency, options are financial derivatives where the underlying instrument is a currency pair. The buyer of such an option acquires the right to buy (call) or sell (put) a currency pair at a given price and specific expiration date, but does not have the obligation to do so. Inversely, the seller of a currency option will have the obligation to buy or sell the instrument when it is exercised.

Originally this type of trading was performed in over-the-counter (OTC) markets and reserved to institutional traders as well as large corporations, which used the options to reduce the risks by hedging the exposure they might have in a particular foreign currency. Today, thanks to electronic trading and wider market access at the retail level, trading forex options is becoming more and more popular as an alternative or even a complement to the positions opened at direct spot forex rates.

There are several online forex brokers that include the availability of trading options on currency pairs among the financial instruments they handle. I will keep an updated list of these brokers at www.jdfn.com. A few futures and stock options platforms do offer currency options and spot forex trading, and most of them will allow you to trade options on single-currency futures (Globex). Although there might be some differences in volatility, trading futures options on the base currency of a particular currency pair can be an alternative, but direct correlation with the spot currency market might be lost if the aim is to use them for hedging.

Some brokers will offer both long and short call and put options (vanilla options), while others will only offer the long types. There are many binary option-specific intermediaries; a few include touch and boundary alternatives. Most often, forex options belong to the European style (discussed later in this chapter).

FOREX OPTIONS VERSUS STOCK OPTIONS

In essence, both currency and stock options follow the same principles; however, they do have significant differences, starting from the fact that a forex option implies a double contract. For example, when buying a long call on EUR/USD, you are simultaneously acquiring a call on the euro and a put on the U.S. dollar. This particularity makes market forecasting more difficult, as both currencies have to be assessed and will not always move in perfect correlation.

Another important issue is volatility: currency markets tend to move much faster and exhibit more directional swings than the great majority of stocks, and they also react swiftly in front of major economic news releases and general international events. Forex currency pairs have a higher level of leverage compared with that of stocks, thus increasing the profit potential but also the risks. Forex options are more sensitive to political and economic factors, whereas stocks will take into account the economic variables that affect the specific company.

Another risk worth mentioning is the counterparty risk, which is more often present in currency options than stock options because the currency options are mostly OTC instruments. If the broker or firm that holds the other side of the transaction goes into bankruptcy, any options contracts you are holding as a client might become worthless and will not carry the financial obligation to deliver the foreign currency. This occurs because there is no protection through a central clearinghouse when the dealers cannot meet the exercise obligations.

Finally, currency options can be traded continuously throughout the year, as the forex market is always open, while options on stocks can only be traded when the stock markets are functioning during normal business hours.

HOW TO FIND A FOREX OPTIONS BROKER

Many different options trading alternatives are available, and each one exhibits distinct risk levels and overall characteristics. Plain vanilla forex options are standard options contracts that are traded through either an exchange or an OTC dealing desk, where you can buy or sell standard calls or puts. There is good liquidity, and you can usually get real-time streaming quotes and enter or exit the market at any time during the trading week. Then there are the exotic options, which are a derivative of the standard vanilla kind, including binary options and other styles.

The online broker will provide electronic access to currency exchange liquidity pools; however, many of them consider options as OTC transactions, and the trades will be directly performed with the broker as the counterpart, instead of matching the orders with other traders. With many firms that offer forex options along with spot forex trading, you will find a considerable array of strike and expiration prices for you to choose from. Some firms might also let you decide on the expiry style.

Finding the appropriate broker to trade forex options can take some time, because there are not as many as plain-currency trading brokerages, and not all of them offer all the various styles or possible combinations. The best approach is to first learn about all the variants that are available and make a preliminary choice of the style you would prefer to employ; then open a demo account on different platforms and see which one suits you best. You need to make sure that everything you will require for trading is available.

Some of the option strategies are more complicated to understand than others, and you will have different levels of documentation on the specific options. Some brokers offer the potential for you to trade directly a particular strategy with a single click, and some don't. Also, there are different ways of handling the expiry and option exercising. And although some brokers do not offer an online platform, they will allow you to trade options through their dealing desk via telephone. Some will have both capabilities. The minimum deposits required will also vary from broker to broker. Finally, most retail forex brokers will require high levels of protective capital to allow the selling of options contracts, as writing options carries high risks of loss.

Do a thorough online search, one that includes checking for other traders' comments and evaluations in forums or reviews, just as you would do when looking for a forex trading platform; or you can visit www.jdfn.com. Then, when you think you have found what you are looking for and have thoroughly tested the platform, be sure to ask all the pertinent questions with the customer support desk before committing real money. You will need to know the trading account minimums and margin requirements, and you will also need to know if the options contracts can be opened and closed at any time or if you will be locked out until expiration; in addition (especially if it is not clearly signaled on the platform), you will need to find out about the procedures that are used to allow you to exercise the options on expiry.

ADVANTAGES AND DISADVANTAGES

Trading forex by using options, by either combining them with spot forex or using them on their own, keeps most of the advantages of traditional forex trading while eliminating many of its setbacks. For example:

- There is no leverage for the purchase of forex options. For the same reason, you don't have to pay interest on leveraged positions.
- The risk is limited to the amount paid at the moment of acquiring the option (the premium), and you get an unlimited profit potential.
- You can choose the strike price and expiration date for your transaction.

- The positions do not need to be monitored as often as with forex trading: options are less stressful and can save you time.
- There is no need for margin (except on short options). Therefore, you need less money to guarantee the transaction than for cash forex positions.
- You can use forex options along with normal forex trades to limit the risks and lock in profits through hedging.
- There is no need to risk huge amounts of capital when trying to predict the market moves in trading fundamental economic events; there are options strategies that allow you to profit in such situations independently of the outcome with a very limited risk.
- Besides standard call and put options, you have a vast array of choices in binary and single-payment options trading (SPOT) options.

Of course, there are also downsides to forex options:

- They can be more difficult to use.
- They are limited in time (the expiration date).
- You need the price of the underlying currency pair to move enough so that it covers the premium paid to just get to break even (this would be equivalent to getting back the spread points in forex trading, but premiums can be much wider).
- The premium is variable in regard to the strike prices and expiration dates. Thus the risk-to-reward ratio of the transaction will also be variable and less easy to calculate.
- Some types of options are a one-time choice and cannot be traded back into the market, for example, SPOT options.
- The fixed-date expiration and strike can become a hindrance, as it is difficult to predict the exact date and price levels at which the market will be moving.

However, despite those inconveniences, forex options can still be a very valuable instrument to add to your trading toolbox either to earn profits or to reduce the risks on traditional forex positions. They can be particularly good when there is higher market volatility, for example, during economic reports or special events.

OPTIONS ON CURRENCY FUTURES

Currency futures options offer another alternative for traders and have a greater availability than forex options on general online options-trading brokerages. The underlying asset here is a single-currency future. The advantage of trading options on currency futures is that while forex options are mostly traded in the OTC market, they can be traded directly on centralized exchanges like the Chicago Mercantile Exchange (CME), which has the world's widest array of currency futures and options.

OPTIONS TYPES

There are two basic types of options, calls and puts (equivalent to buy and sell, respectively), which can be either bought or sold depending on the combination you choose of both market direction and market volatility. Transactions made with options include the payment of a premium, calculated according to a specific formula that I will describe in more detail in the options pricing section of this chapter.

In the forex options market, just as in the spot forex scene, every transaction is dual. When you buy a call, you are automatically buying a put at the same time. There is usually a wide selection of alternatives to the price of the underlying expected volatility (delta) and date at which the option will be exercised. Traders get a quote that states the premium of the option, that is, the amount either that the trader has to pay for the transaction (long options) or that the trader will receive (short options). If the actual exchange rate of the underlying instrument places the options out-of-the-money (OTM), they will expire worthless.

Long (Buying) Calls or Puts

When buying calls or puts, the trader pays the premium and has the *right* to exercise the option at the strike price, either buying the underlying asset in the case of a long call or selling it if the option is a long put.

If the market price of the underlying at the moment of the expiry makes the option profitable, the trader will exercise the option and will gain the net difference between the profits made minus the premium already paid. If the option is not profitable, the trader lets it expire worthless, and his or her net losses will be limited to the amount of the premium.

The profit potential is unlimited if the market rallies (long calls) or sells off (long puts). In both cases, the risk is limited to the loss of the net premium that has been paid for the option.

Short (Selling) Calls or Puts

Here the seller receives the amount of the premium up front and acquires the *obligation* to exercise the option at the strike price, either selling the underlying asset in the case of a short call or buying it in the case of a short put. If the market has fallen, you would have to sell the call at a lesser price and lose the difference minus the premium you have already received; in the same way, if the market has rallied, you have to buy the put and will lose the difference to its strike price minus the amount of the premium.

The profit is limited to the net premium that has been received at the moment the option was written (sold). The risks are unlimited either when markets rally (short calls) or when markets fall (short puts).

Use of Different Options Types with Trading Scenarios

Long Call

These options are to be used when you expect the underlying market prices to rise (bullish direction) and are also bullish on the potential volatility. We can use Figure 3.1 as an example.

On February 20, 2011, I was expecting the euro to strengthen against the yen and the EUR/JPY to perform a significant rise above the current market price in the next few weeks. I decided to buy a EUR/JPY call option. Among the alternatives offered, I chose an OTM strike price at 115.04 and an expiration date set at April 4.

The premium paid for this option was 120 pips.

On April 4, 2011, the option expired in-the-money (ITM), which was 470 pips above the strike price, as the EURJPY spot rate increased to 119.74. I then exercised the right to buy the underlying currency pair at the 115.04 strike price. To lock in the profits, I immediately sold it back to close the position.

Figure 3.1　Long call EUR/JPY

The profits realized on this transaction are calculated as follows:

Spot price at position close − strike price = profit in pips
119.74 − 115.04 = 470 pips

Profit in pips − the premium paid = net profit
470 − 120 = 350 pips net profit

Should the spot forex rate have been quoted below the strike price of 115.04, the option would have still been OTM at expiry. As no profits could be realized in such a situation, I would have allowed the option to expire worthless, and my loss would have been limited to the 120 pips paid as premium with no further risks.

It is important to note that to calculate the breakeven point for this transaction, I need to add the premium paid to the strike price; this means that to be at least at that level (zero profit–zero loss) I would need the price of the EUR/JPY to have reached 115.04 + 1.20 = 116.24.

Buying a long call option is the easiest way to profit in a bullish market. You can reap significant and potentially unlimited benefits if the currency pair rallies; and should you be wrongly positioned or if the market decides to suddenly pull back, your risks and losses will be limited to the amount of money you have already paid with the premium.

Long Put

I will use a long put option if I am bearish in regard to the market direction and bullish on its volatility.

This time let's look at a failed option trade, depicted in Figure 3.2. I had thought the AUD/USD would bounce from a resistance and fall for the next few weeks. Therefore on April 10, 2011, I bought a long put option that would expire one month later, setting the strike price also OTM at 1.0514. The cost of the premium for this option was 98 pips, giving me a breakeven price level at 1.04160. If the price had fallen below this level, I would have had a profit.

Figure 3.2   Long put AUD/USD

However, the price rallied 321 pips above the strike price at the moment of expiration, so I didn't exercise my right to the option, letting it expire worthless instead. I only lost the amount already paid for the premium, 98 pips, which is only about 30 percent of the loss I would have had to assume on a normal spot forex trade.

Like a long call, a long put is a very good and easy way to limit the risks to a fixed minimum while offering the opportunity of making unlimited profits if the market direction chosen is correct. On this modality, you will be expecting the currency pair rate to decrease.

Short Call

Shorting, or writing a call option, can be used when you are bearish on both market direction and market volatility. A short call option is also referred to as a naked call. It's a position that carries a lot of risk, as its loss potential is unlimited should the market go against the direction chosen.

Figure 3.3 shows a short call option on the GBP/USD. With this option, I was expecting the price to keep falling below the strike price, also OTM at the moment for which the option was sold. This time the breakeven level was placed above the strike price, as I received the amount of the premium set for this option at 150 pips; thus price could go against my direction until 1.5630. My aim was to take possession of a GBP/USD short position at the moment of expiry, with the open price at 1.5480.

However, here again the market decided to rally further and ended at 1.6192, leaving me with a GBP/USD position 712 pips into the negative against the locked-open price (1.5480), which turns out to be a 562-pip loss after deducting the premium of 150 pips I had already gained with the transaction. You can easily see how the risk potential becomes nearly unlimited with this type of option, and it should only be taken (with much caution though) when the direction is clearly confirmed, or it should be employed along with other instruments in a specific strategy, as I will discuss later on in Chapter 24 on forex options strategies.

Figure 3.3   Short call GBP/USD

Short Put

When we expect the market to be bullish but its volatility to decrease, a short put option could be attempted. Similar to a short call option, this type of option is also referred to as a naked put.

Figure 3.4 offers an example of a short put. As you can see from the figure, the breakeven price level is below the strike price, as the risks are to the downside. With a 115-pip premium received, this is the amount you will have to deduct from the strike price to calculate the level.

When the option expired, it was automatically exercised, and I got a long position on EUR/USD from the strike price at 1.4104, which was 413 pips positive, plus I got to keep the 115-pip premium. Although the only profit made on the option was the premium, I was now well positioned on the market and could sell the EUR/USD position back to bank the 413 pips profited, as the option expired ITM.

Selling puts also carries an unlimited loss potential; however, it allows you to buy the underlying at a cheaper price.

Finally, Table 3.1 provides a short summary for a quick visual reference.

Figure 3.4   Short put EUR/USD

Table 3.1

Types of	Choices				
Options	Direction	Volatility	Profits	Losses	At Expiry
Long call	Bullish	Bullish		Limited to	Right to buy
Long put	Bearish	Bullish	Unlimited	premium paid	Right to sell
Short call	Bearish	Bearish	Limited to		Obligation to sell
Short put	Bullish	Bearish	premium received	Unlimited	Obligation to buy

OPTIONS STYLES

The most commonly traded forex options belong to either of the following basic styles for plain vanilla options: European style or American style.

European-style options cannot be exercised before their expiry date; however, you can sell them back in the options market at any time in between.

American-style options differ from European in that it is possible for the buyer to take possession of the underlying asset prior to the expiration date. They also can be negotiated back in the market.

In any of the above, the buyer acquires either a right to buy or sell a specific number of contracts on the underlying asset at a given price and date (long call or put) or the obligation to sell or buy the underlying at its strike price at a future date (short call or put).

A third style is exotics, which include SPOT and binary options as well as other less common substyles. An exotic option is any type of option that differs from the standard calls and puts that can be found on major exchanges.

Vanilla forex options have a very specific structure of their expiration and payouts. Exotic forex options contracts can be much more flexible than vanillas and have variable outcomes.

Traditional options (American options) have an advantage in that their premiums are usually lower than those of SPOTs and they grant you greater flexibility, as they can be negotiated back before their expiration date. SPOT options are easier to set up and execute.

SPOT, BINARY, AND DIGITAL OPTIONS

The same as for other options transactions, you will have to pay a quoted sum, the premium, which, in return, gives you an optional right. If you win the option, you will receive the premium paid plus a given percentage of this amount, called the *return* or *payout*, which has been stated up front at the moment of buying the option. On some binary options, if you lose, you will receive a small percentage of the premium as a consolation payout. There are no additional commissions or fees.

Unlike vanilla calls and puts, the amount of the payout does not increase with a rise in the underlying asset or a fall below the strike price; instead it is a fixed sum that will be earned at a given point.

These styles offer the traders an easier way of trading. You choose a particular scenario for a currency pair and do not need to monitor anything else until it plays out. If you are right, you receive the payout. If you are wrong, you only lose the premium paid.

Some of the alternatives to choose include:

- *One-touch SPOT.* You receive a payout if the price touches a certain level.
- *No-touch SPOT.* You receive a payout if the price doesn't touch a certain level.
- *Digital SPOT.* You receive a payout if the price is above or below a certain level.
- *Double one-touch SPOT.* You receive a payout if the price touches one of two set levels.
- *Double no-touch SPOT.* You receive a payout if the price doesn't touch any of the two set levels.

For example, you are bullish on the EUR/USD and think the pair will break 1.4200 in 10 days. If on that date the price of the EUR/USD is trading at or above 1.4200, you will collect the payout in cash in your account. But if the price is still below that level, you get nothing.

What are some disadvantages of these options? For one, the cost of the premium is usually higher than on standard vanilla options. Also you cannot change your mind and sell back the option before its expiry date. Another issue is the risk-to-reward ratio, which can't be calculated as it would be on a normal forex trade, because on this kind of option the reward will always be inferior to the risk. Thus you need to be right much more often to end up with a net profitable scene, as losing trades will cost you more than you can make on winning trades.

OPTION VALUE AND PRICING

The value of an option is established by means of mathematical models, which have been developed by quantitative analysts. The objective of these formulas is to predict the changes in an option value in regard to the changes in the conditions and elements that form it.

The variables that will be present in a forex option value calculation are:

- The price of the underlying asset (the spot forex rate of the currency pair)
- The local currency interest rate
- The foreign currency interest rate, or dividend yield
- The strike price (which is the rate at which the currency will be exchanged at the expiry)
- The expiration date of the option
- The volatility expected for the currency pair rate throughout the active life of the option

The most common mathematical model used in forex options, and especially for the European style, is the Black-Scholes-Merton model. This model uses five basic variables bearing names mostly from the Greek alphabet (frequently, as a group the variables are also referred to as "the Greeks"):

- *Delta*. Measures the changes of the option value in regard to the underlying asset
- *Gamma*. Is a derivative of delta
- *Theta*. Shows how fast the option loses value in regard to time
- *Vega* (not a Greek letter even though it may sound like one). Measures the effects of changes in the volatility of the underlying and the way they affect the option value
- *Rho*. Measures the changes and effects that stem from variations in the interest rates

Thanks to these calculations, we can gauge how the value of an option will change as time gets closer to the expiration date, or we can study the possible impact of a volatility increase of the currency pair rates. This helps in evaluating and quantifying all the risks implied in the ownership of an option, thus allowing more precise risk management.

Therefore, we have a series of factors that together determine the price or premium of a forex option.

Intrinsic Value

This is the exercise value of the option at that moment. There are three possible descriptions for this value: ITM, OTM, and ATM (at-the-money).

- *ITM*. The strike price is lower than the current market price of the underlying asset for call options or higher in the case of put options.
- *OTM*. The strike price is higher than the current market price of the currency pair for call options or lower in the case of put options.
- *ATM*. The strike price is exactly at the current market price.

The changes that occur in the underlying asset price (in the case of forex options, the currency pair on which the option is taken) will increase or decrease the value of the option. Their effects will be opposite on calls and puts. If the rate of the currency pair rises, call options will have a greater value while puts will diminish in value. When the rate of the underlying is falling, call options will reduce their value and puts will increase.

Time Value

This value represents the uncertainty of the price over time. The longer the time to expiry, the higher this value will be, thus increasing the cost of the premium. It can also be considered as the price that an investor is willing to pay above the intrinsic value of an option, in the expectation that its value will increase at a certain point before its expiration due to positive changes in the rate of the currency pair or underlying asset. The more time available for the market conditions to evolve in the benefit and direction taken by the investor, the higher the time value will be.

The time left until expiration will affect the time-value element of the premium. As we come closer to the expiration dates, both calls and puts will see their value decrease proportionally, even if being ITM.

Differential in Interest Rates

Changes in the currency's interest rates will modify the relationship between the actual market rate of a currency pair and the strike price of the option. The effects of the changes on the option premium are small and secondary, but they can be measured and will reflect the costs or dividends from rollover.

Volatility

Volatility is quite subjective and thus difficult to quantify; however, it bears a very significant impact on the time value of the option premium. A greater volatility will increase the possibility of reaching the strike price in less time, thus increasing the value of the option premium.

Volatility measures the potential variability of the price of the underlying asset. If greater fluctuations of prices are expected, the premium values for both calls and puts will increase.

Both interest rate differentials and volatility are factored into the time value.

OPTIONS VOLATILITY

Volatility is one of the elements taken into account in the time value of a forex option. The impact of the changes that occur in this factor can be good or bad depending on the strategies that you plan to implement. Both the general market direction and the volatility—bullishness or bearishness—are to be considered in most of the basic vanilla options strategies, which are described in detail in Chapter 24.

In addition to the implied volatility (IV), which is equivalent to vega, the historical or statistical volatility of an underlying asset has to be taken into account if we want to determine if the price of the option's premium is above or below its fair value. This can be very useful in deciding if the best strategy is to buy a particular option or sell it.

A lower volatility implies lower premiums, but also lower margins are required on written options. When you decide to short an option, your broker will allocate a portion of your account as the initial margin to guarantee against a move of the market in the opposite direction. Margins will also vary according to the levels of IV of the currency pair as the option underlying.

It can help to predict the prices either when they reach too far, looking then for a turn back to the mean, or when they exhibit extreme values without any event to back up these values. Most of the time, this can happen when future events are already priced into the volatility values, and so it can be a signal to expect significant moves to occur.

OPTIONS GREEKS

The Greeks are a series of calculations used to measure risks and serve as guidelines for the evaluation of profit and loss potential in diverse options strategies. Knowing how to interpret those values is crucial in order to have the most accurate idea possible about the profitability of a particular system and its underlying instrument.

Three basic elements must be to taken into account to interpret those risk and reward capabilities: price action, volatility fluctuations, and the correlation of value and time, which will tend to decline.

The most used Greeks in forex options are delta, gamma, theta, and vega.

Delta

This is a Greek value that is derived from an options pricing model, and it represents the equivalence of the underlying asset (in this case with forex options, the currency pair); its value can be different for the bid and ask prices even in an option with the same strike price and expiry date. Delta is represented with a positive percentage on calls (ranging from a value of zero when an option is totally OTM to a value of 100 when it is fully ITM) and with a negative percentage on puts (ranging from value 0 for OTM options to value –100).

A call forex option will be ITM when its strike price is lower than the current price of the underlying currency pair plus the premium paid. A put forex option will require the current price to be trading below the strike price and minus the premium paid.

A long call option on EUR/USD with a strike price at 1.3900 and a premium of 100 points will start being ITM when the market rate for the EUR/USD surpasses 1.4000.

A long put option on AUD/USD with strike price at 1.0900 and a premium of 140 points will start being ITM when the market rate for the currency pair falls below 1.0760.

Gamma

This Greek value is also represented as a percentage, and it is also derived from an options pricing model. It is used to calculate how many delta points the option will increase or decrease for each pip gained or lost on the rate of the currency pair. It measures the rate of change of delta in respect to the value of the underlying asset. When the options are deeply ITM or OTM, its value will be small. Its greater value shows when an option is near-the-money or ATM.

Theta

This value is expressed in points per day, and its calculation depends on the time left until the expiry date. The closer an option is to its expiration (where all options lose the whole of their premium value), the faster this value will increase. It shows how much of the option value will be lost after one day's time.

Vega

Another of the Greek values, vega indicates the expected amount an option can gain or lose in value, depending on a 1-point increase of the IV.

It is better to buy options when the IV is low because you will be paying a smaller time premium; and when there is a rise in the volatility later on, the price of the option will increase. For the same reasons, selling or writing options should be performed when the IV is high, as you will be receiving a bigger premium; and a decrease in volatility thereafter will reduce the price of the option.

Embedded in the structure of any options trading strategy are delta-, vega-, and theta-associated positions, as well as those of other minor Greeks. In either standard or combined options transactions, the net value of the positions can be calculated, which, in turn, will give us an evaluation of the amount of potential risks and rewards of that particular strategy.

For example, if you buy a forex option (long call or put), the risks you incur will depend on the price moving in the wrong direction, a decrease in the IV, and a time-based reduction of the intrinsic value of the option. Should you be a seller (short call or put), you will be incurring risk if the price moves in the opposite direction or the implied volatility increases, but the time-value decrease will not be a determinant.

FOREX OPTIONS QUOTE SCREEN

A typical forex options quote screen (see Figure 3.5) will show an array of available call and put options with different bid and ask strike prices and expiration dates, as well as the underlying current rates. It should include, at the least, some extra information, such as volatility and delta, to allow you to choose the best alternative for your strategy.

In Figure 3.5, we also can see what the breakeven rate is for any given option. This will greatly differ from broker to broker. In the case of currency futures options, you should find additional useful information including volume, open interest, and other Greeks such as gamma, vega, and theta values; there should also be alternatives to customize your data display, as well as a series of different exchanges from which you can choose to trade the option.

Here is a short summary of the main elements that can be present on your forex options screen:

- *Symbol.* The underlying currency pair or futures symbol (for example, EUR/USD for the spot forex EUR/USD currency pair or 6E plus the option-specific letters for EuroFx futures). The screen should also show the actual market rate and can include such details as the high, low, open, and close rates; percentage of change; average price; time and feed provider; etc.
- *Bid and ask prices.* The latest prices offered to buy or sell the option with a market order. Both will constantly vary along with the underlying rates and their own proximity to the expiry dates. It is very important to consider the width of the spread between the bid and ask prices to evaluate the risks, especially if you will be trading short term. Usually the most active options exhibit a tighter spread. These are also called intrinsic bid and ask prices.
- *Extrinsic bid and ask in points.* The time premium built into the option price at the moment of the transaction, which decreases in time until there is none left at expiration.

Cross Rate	Bid	Ask	Chg	%Chg	High	Low	Range	Open	Last	Party	Time	Pip	Pip($)	H-L Mid
GBP/USD	1.62118	1.62327	-.00133	-0.08 %	1.63036	1.61658	.01378	1.62251	1.62118	FXDesk Stream2	9:00 PM	10.00	10.00	1.62347

⦿ Calls   ○ Puts

Strike	Jun 16, 2011 Bid	Jun 16, 2011 Ask	Jul 21, 2011 Bid	Jul 21, 2011 Ask	Aug 18, 2011 Bid	Aug 18, 2011 Ask	Sep 15, 2011 Bid	Sep 15, 2011 Ask	Oct 20, 2011 Bid	Oct 20, 2011 Ask	Nov 17, 2011 Bid	Nov 17, 2011 Ask	Dec 15, 2011 Bid	Dec 15, 2011 Ask	Jan 19, 20.. Bid
1.59000	.03603	.03685	.04324	.04435	.04829	.04945	.05287	.05409	.05799	.05940	.06166	.06317	.06513	.06676	.06916
1.59500	.03200	.03285	.03968	.04082	.04486	.04607	.04955	.05083	.05479	.05624	.05854	.06007	.06207	.06371	.06616
1.60000	.02816	.02904	.03625	.03743	.04156	.04283	.04635	.04768	.05169	.05318	.05551	.05706	.05909	.06075	.06323
1.60500	.02454	.02545	.03299	.03420	.03838	.03971	.04325	.04464	.04869	.05022	.05258	.05415	.05620	.05788	.06039
1.61000	.02115	.02208			.03672		.04028	.04172	.04580	.04736	.04974	.05132	.05340	.05509	.05763
1.61500	.01802	.01897			.03387		.03744	.03892	.04301	.04461	.04696	.04856	.05066	.05235	.05491
1.62000	.01517	.01613			.03113		.03469	.03621	.04031	.04192	.04432	.04592	.04803	.04974	.05231
1.62500	.01262	.01357	.02163	.02290	.02714	.02859	.03213	.03368	.03777	.03941	.04181	.04342	.04554	.04724	.04983
1.63000	.01036	.01130	.01924	.02050	.02471	.02617	.02967	.03125	.03532	.03697	.03936	.04098	.04309	.04481	.04739
1.63500	.00840	.00931	.01703	.01829	.02242	.02389	.02734	.02894	.03297	.03463	.03701	.03863	.04074	.04246	.04504
1.64000	.00671	.00760	.01501	.01625	.02029	.02176	.02515	.02675	.03074	.03240	.03476	.03638	.03849	.04020	.04277
1.64500					.01831	.01977	.02308	.02468	.02862	.03028	.03262	.03423	.03632	.03802	.04059
1.65000					.01648	.01792	.02115	.02274	.02661	.02826	.03057	.03217	.03424	.03594	.03848
1.65500					.01479	.01620	.01934	.02091	.02470	.02635	.02861	.03021	.03225	.03394	.03646
1.66000	.00231	.00314	.00862	.00976	.01323	.01462	.01765	.01920	.02290	.02454	.02675	.02835	.03035	.03204	.03452
1.66500	.00166	.00250	.00741	.00852	.01181	.01317	.01608	.01761	.02121	.02283	.02499	.02657	.02854	.03021	.03266

Callout (pointing to 1.60500 Jun 16 Ask .02545):

> Below the money
> Buy Jun 16, 2011 1.60500 calls
> Breakeven 1.63045
> Volatility 9.01 % Delta .67

Callout (pointing to 1.63500 Jun 16 Bid .00840):

> Above the money
> Sell Jun 16, 2011 1.63500 calls
> Breakeven 1.64340
> Volatility 8.55 % Delta .36

Figure 3.5 A basic forex options screen

- *Strike price.* The price at which the underlying currency pair
  will be sold or bought if the trader decides to exercise the
  option. On written (short) options, it will be the price at
  which the trader will have to sell the currency pair if the
  option is exercised at expiry.

  Call options will have a higher premium when the strike
  price is lower, while put options will cost more when the
  strike price is higher. On calls, the price of the option
  decreases at each rise in level. The strike price is successively
  less ITM or more OTM, and so its intrinsic value becomes
  smaller. The inverse situation occurs with puts, which go
  from less OTM toward more ITM with every rise of the strike
  price, and their intrinsic value thus gets bigger.

- *IV percentage on bid and ask.* The expected level of future
  volatility, which is based on the actual price of the option and
  includes several other variables concerning how much time
  remains until it expires plus the difference between the strike
  price and the current price of the underlying currency pair. IV
  is usually calculated with the Black-Scholes pricing model.

- *Delta percentage on bid and ask.* The value that represents the
  equivalence of the option in regard to the underlying currency pair. It will be reaching toward 100 for calls and -100
  for puts the more the option is ITM. That would be the maximum equivalence, and the option price would then move at
  the same pace as the currency pair rate (point for point). An
  option with a delta value of 50 would be moving half a point
  when the currency pair moves 1 pip.

  Delta values are positive for calls and negative for puts.
  As for the premium, they will be higher on call options at a
  lower strike price and on put options at a higher strike price.

- *Gamma percentage on bid and ask.* Related to the delta value, a
  percentage that shows how many delta points the option
  will increase or decrease if the underlying currency pair
  moves 1 point.

- *Vega for bid and ask.* The Greek value that indicates how much
  the price is expected to rise or fall in regard to a 1-point
  increase of IV. It is better to buy options when this value is low.

- *Theta for bid and ask.* The Greek value that indicates how much of the option value is going to be lost per day until it reaches zero at expiry.
- *Volume.* The number of transactions that have been performed on that particular option in the trading session. Options that show large volumes usually will have tighter spreads, as there is much competition going on to acquire calls or puts on them.
- *Open interest.* The values that show how many contracts (pending options orders) are opened but not yet in the market for any given option.

C H A P T E R

CONTRACTS FOR DIFFERENCE 101

Contracts for difference, or CFDs, have been used for more than 20 years, but they did not become popular with retail traders until the last decade. Essentially, a CFD is a derivative—its value is based on the performance of an underlying financial instrument, such as stocks, mutual funds, bonds, commodities, currencies, and market indexes—used to speculate on the future value of an asset by taking either a long or short position.

The investor, or "buyer," and CFD provider, or "seller," agree to pay the difference between the current asset price and its value on the contract date. For a long position, the seller would pay the difference to the buyer if the asset price rises, and the buyer pays if the asset price goes down. For short positions, those results are reversed.

THE HISTORY OF CFDs

London traders created the first CFDs as a way to hedge risk when trading equities without paying a U.K. tax applied to stock transactions. The CFD served as an equity derivative that enabled investors to speculate on stock movements, up or down, without owning the actual shares. CFDs exploded in popularity when brokerage houses allowed them to be traded on margin and packaged them with electronic trading platforms that provided investors with real-time price information and enabled live trades. Using the leverage of margin trading, investors had the potential for higher returns (and losses), since they only put down a small percentage of the underlying asset's actual value.

Brokerage houses jumped into the market with CFD products. Initially limited to equities on the London Stock Exchange, their offerings soon expanded to include the commodity, bond, and currency markets. The most popular CFD products are those based on the major worldwide indexes, such as the CAC in France, the DAX in Germany, the FTSE in Great Britain, the Dow Jones, and the NASDAQ markets.

The U.S. Securities and Exchange Commission does not allow trading in CFDs under its regulation of the OTC market. The derivatives are traded in many other countries, including Australia, Canada, Germany, France, Ireland, Italy, Japan, New Zealand, Norway, Poland, Portugal, Singapore, South Africa, Spain, Sweden, and Switzerland.

CFD TRADING

Trading of CFDs occurs between individual investors and CFD providers—typically, large brokerage houses. Contract terms for CFDs are not standardized among the different providers. Each provider can dictate its own terms or change those terms for any particular CFD. However, almost all CFD contracts contain a number of common elements.

The CFD contract is initiated by the investor taking a position in a particular financial instrument through an opening trade. The position is only closed when the trade is reversed with a second transaction—the contract has no expiry date. At closing, the profit or loss is determined by the price differential between the opening and closing trade. The CFD provider may assess several fees or charges on the trade or open position, including account management fees, bid/offer spread, commissions, and overnight financing.

Because the CFD never expires, if a position is left open overnight, it is rolled over and the profit or loss is credited (or debited) to the investor's account after any finance charges are deducted. Most markets allow CFDs to be traded on margin. As with other margin trading, the investor must maintain a qualifying account balance.

Modern brokerage technology constantly calculates the required margin in real time and provides a Web interface for the trader to view his or her account balance, margin balance, and trading profits and losses. Of course, if the trader's account balance drops below the minimum level required, he or she can be subject to a margin call. If the account balance is not quickly increased to the new minimum level, the brokerage house can liquidate the position.

CFD COSTS

Most CFD providers charge a daily financing fee for long positions left open overnight. The fee is typically based on an established benchmark, such as the LIBOR in the United Kingdom or the Reserve Bank rate in Australia. If the investor takes a short position, he or she may receive a daily fee in lieu of deferring transaction proceeds, so that the CFD is still settled upon the closing trade for the cash difference with the opening trade. A CFD that controls equity shares is also usually charged a commission based on the size of the position. The trader does have the option with most CFD providers to forgo commissions in favor of a larger market maker (MM) bid/offer on the equities.

THE USE OF MARGIN TO INVEST IN CFDs

A CFD trade provides two types of margin: initial and variation. The initial margin requirement can typically range between 3 and 30 percent for equities and between 0.5 and 1 percent for other instruments, including commodities, currencies, and market indexes. The rate depends on the quality of the financial instrument's contracted and perceived risk. For example, following the collapse of the U.S. brokerage house Lehman Brothers in 2008, initial margins rose precipitously across all markets in response to the volatility the collapse caused.

Variation margin is required if the CFD position moves against the investor. For example, if the trader bought 1,000 shares of a stock at $1 per share and the price lowered to 90 cents, the CFD provider would deduct $100 in variation margin (1,000 shares × −10 cents) from the client's account. These calculations are all marked to market in real time. The effect of variation margin on the trader's account balance is ongoing and occurs instantly; however, initial margin is deducted from a customer's account at the time the contract is purchased and then is recouped at settlement when the trade is closed.

Many investors think of initial margin as a deposit toward the CFD's purchase price. The margin percentage depends on the broker's policies and the trader's relationship with the broker. Margin can also be low for the most popularly traded stocks and high for stocks that are less liquid.

CFDs AND STOP-LOSS ORDERS

Like other trades, CFDs can be controlled with a stop-loss order that triggers a closing transaction if the underlying security's price reaches a predetermined level. Once triggered, the sell order is executed according to the CFD provider's business terms and with consideration for market liquidity. If market liquidity is insufficient, the stop-loss sell order may not be executed, and the investor's position will remain unchanged.

Be aware that the stop-loss order is only a target price—the market actually has to trade at that price to trigger the stop loss. If the price moves past the stop-loss order price in one step, the order may be executed at the next price traded, or it cannot be traded if that's the CFD provider's policy. That scenario does not often happen with highly liquid instruments such as market indexes and currencies but can be a problem with thinly traded equities. If the stock market is closed, it can also be problematic because the price difference between one day's closing price and the next day's opening price can be significant.

To mitigate that risk, many CFD providers offer a guaranteed stop-loss order (GSLO) that ensures that a stop-loss order is executed if triggered. The trader pays a premium for GSLO, and there are usually other restrictions. For example, most providers do not allow the GSLO to be more than 5 percent below the current price of the security.

CFDs are typically bought OTC through a brokerage or through an MM, and that choice will affect the price of the contract. The CFD provider dictates the terms of the CFD contract, specifies its margin requirements, and lists the financial instruments available for trade. MMs are the most popular source of CFDs. The MM provider sets the price for the CFD and accepts the risk of all payouts. Most MMs hedge their positions, either by buying or selling the underlying security, by using portfolio hedges, or by consolidating their clients' positions and then offsetting their long and short positions.

ACTS BY THE CORPORATION ON EQUITY-BASED CFDs

Corporate acts, such as the payment of dividends, stock splits, and rights issues, affect the corporation's share prices and, therefore, the price of a CFD for those shares. However, because the holder of a CFD position does not actually own the underlying shares, he or she would not receive those dividends, split shares, or rights issued. Instead, the CFD provider pays an equivalent sum to the holders of a long CFD position and deducts that sum from short positions. In general, any corporate act that has an economic effect on the underlying security is applied to the CFD; however, the holder of a CFD never receives noneconomic benefits, such as voting rights.

CFD RISKS

Trading in CFDs comes with a number of risks, including charges, fees, and loss of principal. The following is a summary of the primary risks traders in CFDs face.

Market Risk

The obvious risk is that the market will move in the opposite direction of the investor's contract. The same market risk that traders of any security face increases with CFDs because they are traded on margin. Margin leverage increases potential gains and losses.

However, it is that risk/benefit that motivates most CFD traders, as a way to either increase profits or hedge positions to minimize losses on other trades. Market risk can be mitigated with the use of stop-loss orders.

Liquidation Risk

CFD providers require investors to maintain minimum variation margin, and if the price of the underlying asset moves against the trader's position, additional margin can be required. Investors that cannot provide that margin quickly risk having the provider liquidate their CFD contract at a loss to them. The investor is then liable for paying that loss.

Counterparty Risk

CFD counterparty risk is the potential for financial instability or insolvency on the part of a counterparty to the CFD contract. If the counterparty cannot meet its financial commitment, the CFD will have little or no value regardless of the paper value of the transaction. Counterparty risk exists in many derivatives traded OTC. Counterparty risk can result in severe losses to the CFD investor even if the underlying security's price moves in the trader's predicted direction. Providers of OTC CFDs are required by market rules to separate client funds from their own accounts in order to protect clients in case the company becomes insolvent.

CFD RISK COMPARED WITH THAT OF OTHER INVESTMENT OPTIONS

CFD providers promote the contracts as an alternative to other investment products, such as direct investments in equity shares and other derivatives including futures, options, and covered warrants. Because CFDs are traded outside of the exchanges, no firm statistics are available on their use; however, it is estimated, for example, that CFDs account for between 20 and 40 percent of the volume of the London Stock Exchange. Among those alternative investments, CFDs are most closely associated with futures and options.

Futures

For most professional traders, futures are the preferred investment vehicle for trading in indexes and interest rates because they are traded on the exchanges. On the other hand, CFDs have advantages over futures in that the contract can be smaller in size and its pricing more transparent because it mirrors the underlying financial instrument. The price of futures contracts tends to decay as they reach their expiry date.

Interestingly, CFD providers often use futures to hedge their open positions. To protect against price decay, traders typically roll over their CFD positions into the next future period as liquidity for the futures option dries up in the last days before its expiry.

Options

Professionals also like options because, like futures, they are exchange-traded and centrally cleared. Options can also be used by traders to hedge risk or speculate on markets. The primary advantage that CFDs have over options is the simplicity of their pricing structure and diversity of financial instruments that can be controlled through the CFD. Like the pricing of futures, the pricing of options is complex and decays as the option nears its expiry date. However, CFDs are not suitable for use in risk reduction, as options are.

Covered Warrants

Like trading in options, trading in covered warrants has increased in popularity in the last decade as an inexpensive strategy for speculating market movements; albeit CFDs offer a wider range of investment asset options. Compared with those of covered warrants, CFD costs are usually lower.

Exchange-Traded Funds

As with CFDs, exchange-traded funds are popular vehicles for making short-term bets on market movements and can be bought for a wide range of financial instruments, including commodities, indexes, and shares on foreign markets.

CFD TRADING STRATEGIES

The two most popular CFD trading strategies are those based on technical analysis and on financial news. CFDs can be used as a pure market direction bet, although investors looking to make such a bet are typically employing a more advanced strategy.

Applying technical analysis and observing market indicators improve the investor's probability of correctly calling the market direction. Combined with the availability of leveraged CFD trading through margin, an investor can earn impressive gains. Technical analysis is critical for the short-term trader, who should consider when key support and resistance levels are broken and should also take into account other indicators, such as moment indicators, moving averages, and trendlines.

Financial news can also predict market direction. Earnings reports, insider trading reports, mergers and acquisitions, and executive turnover are all news events that could foreshadow changes in the value of associated financial instruments. Of course, early access to the news is important. The market reacts quickly, and if you don't hear news until hours or days later, the chances are that the valuations have already changed.

Still, even if one correctly assesses each indicator, trading CFDs is not risk-free. No trading strategy works all the time, and so investors need to plan their CFD positions carefully to maximize their chances of success. Predicting short-term price fluctuations can be hugely profitable, but investors need to keep in mind that valuations react to many influences. Systematic trading can override market indicators, and any stock can be affected by unexpected news. Other variables that can affect markets include agricultural reports, forex rates, inventory data, unemployment figures, and weather forecasts.

Investors should establish a trading plan that determines entry and exit points, ensures risk mitigation, and applies sound money management principles to maximize trading success. Consider a trial period using the various trading systems available to identify the one that works best for your trading style.

CHARACTERISTICS OF A SUCCESSFUL CFD TRADING SYSTEM

There are many trading systems that have been devised and promoted. Some are inflexible; others allow for some subjectivity by the trader. Whichever system you choose or design for your own trading, it should have several characteristics to ensure success. The system should identify potential investments that offer a positive reward-to-risk ratio. It should have a methodology for determining a good entry point into the investment and safeguards that trigger an exit—whether for taking profits or cutting losses. Finally, it should make a rational decision regarding the size of the position so that you can benefit if it moves in your direction, yet not lose significantly if it doesn't.

Those characteristics are even more important when trading in a leveraged CFD. Your system should identify an entry signal that strongly suggests the position will become profitable immediately. It should determine where your stop loss should be set, whether based on a predetermined value or percentage or on the support level of key market indicators. And the trade's potential reward should be indicated, and it should be at least two to three times the potential loss for the risks to be justified. Finally, your system must ensure an exit is made while the trade is profitable and not allow the price to swing back into negative territory before you close the trade.

WHEN SHOULD YOU INVEST IN CFDs?

The flashy brochures offered by CFD providers list the benefits they claim you receive by investing in CFDs. Obviously, the providers have a vested interest in convincing you to trade, but when should you really invest?

The first thing potential CFD traders must determine is whether CFDs are even an appropriate investment vehicle for portfolios. By their nature, CFDs are designed for short-term trades, and the investor must compare the costs of speculating through the CFD versus trading the underlying asset directly.

In the United Kingdom, where CFDs originated, the cost of direct trades includes the stamp tax that CFDs were designed to avoid. The trader must calculate the savings gained by not paying the stamp duty and compare those with the additional finance costs of the CFD. Setting aside any commission costs for the moment, calculating the breakeven point between the two investing options is easy.

The funding cost incurred by a CFD comprises the additional cost of taking a CFD position compared with that of making a traditional direct stock purchase. A typical funding charge is about 3 percent applied to the 80 percent of the position that is margin-financed by the CFD provider. Comparatively, a traditional stock trade can incur an immediate stamp duty—in the United Kingdom, that fee is 0.5 percent. The breakeven point will occur when the CFD's funding costs exceed the savings it provides on the stamp tax.

In the U.K. example, the CFD funding costs match the 0.5 percent tax on the transaction value in about 11 weeks $[(0.5/0.8) \times (365/3) = 76$ days]. Thus, if you expect to hold the position for less than 11 weeks, using the CFD to speculate on the asset incurs lower costs than trading the stocks directly.

Obviously, this is a simplistic calculation, and other ancillary costs are incurred; however, it is useful as a general comparison. And for the shortest-term trades and day trades, which have zero financing costs, the argument for CFDs is overwhelming. The economy of the CFD trade increases as the position is traded more than you may initially have anticipated or as your exit price is reached more quickly, as the stamp tax's dilution of net returns is avoided and financing costs are lower than expected.

THE ADVANTAGES OF CFDs

While the decision to trade CFDs should consider many factors carefully, in general, the following characteristics of CFD trading provide an advantage to traders:

- *Liquidity.* The CFD price directly mirrors the underlying market for that asset, which means you benefit from the market's liquidity and that of the CFD provider.

- *Margin trades.* Most providers offer CFDs on margin so that investors need only deposit a small percentage of the trade value to control the entire asset value. Margin leverage enhances the investors' potential return. For a lower cost per trade, margin allows you to gain 10 times the potential return (or more) versus a direct trade.
- *Tax-efficient trades.* CFDs deliver tax benefits because their investment costs, such as interest payments, are usually tax deductible. Also, rather than locking in a taxable capital gain through a direct share position, the investor can sell the CFD to manage how the capital gain is realized.
- *Lower transaction cost.* Broker costs are typically much lower than direct share purchase through full-service brokers. Also, in some jurisdictions, the stamp duty assessed against long stock positions does not accrue to the CFD, since the investor never actually owns the underlying asset.
- *Transparent execution.* CFD trades are no more difficult or complex than trading shares. All transactions offer complete transparency.
- *Long and short trades.* True speculation is enabled, as CFD traders can profit from a down market. CFDs trade on a financial asset's price movement only—the investor does not own the asset. Therefore, selling is as simple as buying. Prior to the introduction of CFDs, shorting a share typically incurred an additional brokerage fee. With CFDs, the provider usually pays interest to the investor on short positions.
- *Ability to trade multiple markets from one account.* Through CFD derivatives, investors can speculate in many markets through the same account of record. CFD providers offer products that trade in international markets, commodities, indexes, oil, precious metals, bonds, and many other asset classes
- *After-hour trades.* Providers extend their hours of operation so that investors can trade in the more active markets (such as the FTSE or Dow) after close of business on those exchanges.
- *No predetermined expiry.* Traders can speculate across any time period.

- *Flexible contracts.* The quantity and the value of the CFD are at the investor's discretion. Any number of shares can be traded.
- *Less complex valuations.* Unlike comparable investments, such as options and warrants, the price of CFDs is a direct reflection of the underlying market.
- *Dividends received sooner.* CFDs pass the dividend to the investor on the share's ex-dividend date, which can be up to a month sooner than the dividend's actual payment date. Over the long term, this feature of CFDs offsets financing charges.
- *Benefit from corporate acts.* CFDs reflect the underlying market and, therefore, receive the benefits that corporate acts, such as share splits, dividend increases, and rights issues, provide.
- *Access to stop-loss order, GSLO, and contingent order protections.* Investors can execute sophisticated trading systems by locking in risk.
- *Ability to hedge an existing portfolio.* CFDs are an excellent hedging tool. For example, the investor can hedge a long position using a CFD to short the stock.

THE DISADVANTAGES OF CFDs

Conversely, CFDs are not for every investor, and these characteristics may represent the disadvantages of CFDs to many traders.

- *Losses magnified by margin leverage.* Just as margin leverage can exponentially increase your trading profits, it magnifies your losses.
- *Higher risks.* If the market moves in the opposite direction, you can lose more than your actual margin investment. If you have to meet a margin call, other assets may have to be sold, reducing those profits or locking in losses. Investors in a short position are exposed to huge potential losses.
- *Too low capital requirements.* Low margin requirements encourage undisciplined investors to overtrade.

- *Daily finance charges.* Positions held overnight incur a financing charge typically based on a leading index (LIBOR, U.S. prime rate, etc.) and applied as a percentage of the position value. Those interest payments add up and increase for long positions held for an extended time to the point that they roughly equal the value offered by margin leverage after six months in many cases.
- *Interest charges.* The CFD trader pays interest on the entire contract value, as opposed to traditional margin lending for direct share purchases that only charge on the actual investment.
- *Collateral requirement.* CFDs are marked to market, and losses are applied to your account balance in real time. This can result in margin calls for additional deposits to your account or liquidation of the position.
- *Provider inflexibility.* CFD providers determine the margin level for each contract. Traders are expected to set that level and manage their money around it. Many providers also reserve the right to adjust the margin level of open CFDs. You may be forced to deposit more money to avoid having the position closed out.
- *No shareholder rights.* As a CFD owner, you do not have shareholder rights because you do not own the underlying asset.
- *No broker transfers.* Again, you don't own the underlying asset; you have purchased a two-party contract and must deal with the provider that opened the position for you. Your position cannot be transferred to another provider or broker.
- *Dividend liability.* The owner of a short CFD position is liable for payment of any dividend issued if the position is maintained past the dividend record date.

In general, the disadvantages of CFDs are very apparent, understandable, and foreseeable to even nonprofessional traders. The risks are higher, as they are for all other margin trading, but it can be expected that most investors will buy with eyes wide open.

SUMMARY

The popularity earned by CFDs in the retail markets since 2000 has provided liquidity to CFD providers that has allowed the market to expand beyond equity shares to offer traders a wide range of investment opportunities. CFDs have been a major source of funding to the forex and index markets. Traders executing a short-term investment strategy or longer-term hedging see clear advantage in the risk profile of CFDs, and individual investors want the opportunity to speculate without paying high fees.

5

SPREAD BETTING

SPREAD BETTING

Spread betting isn't exactly rocket science. It is basically a simple process, but similar to the way people often feel about driving a car, many people decide that it is very difficult—even without trying it out.

You can't start spread betting without understanding the basic rules. People manage many risky things—it's all about following the rules and practicing your skills before you can be successful.

So let's begin understanding what spread betting is all about. It is always advantageous to learn how to enjoy a safe bet at any sporting event. We can start by understanding what spread betting is.

WHAT IS SPREAD BETTING?

Spread betting is a category of gambling that might be used as a substitute for regular trading. Just as you can in regular trading, you can place spread bets on many stocks of the same market. It is a lot like binary betting, but it doesn't have fixed odds, because your profits or losses will depend on price movements.

HOW IT WORKS

You can enter or exit spread betting at any time. These bets can be placed at a certain stake that is equal to the tick value (actually, the point value) used in regular trading. Let's take an example. If a long spread bet is placed on the FTSE 100 stock index using a stake of £20, the profit or loss of the spread bet would change by £20 for each point that moves in the FTSE 100 price.

Spread betting is actually speculating on the stock market without buying any stock.

The *spread* is a range—it is the difference in two prices that are concerned with shares or stocks. Out of these two prices, one is offered by the market when you want to buy stock, and the other is what you get when you want to sell it.

A spread betting company decides on its own spread, and thus the spread of any stock depends on the spread betting company you are dealing with.

The high price is known as the *offer* price—the price that you get when you want to buy stock. The low price is known as the *bid* price—the price that you get when you want to sell stock.

This follows in real-life trading as well, but there is a difference. In spread betting, you do not buy or sell any stock—you only gamble on the way it will move. The real-life markets determine the result of the bet depending upon the values you placed.

In real-life trading, you can bet that a certain value will increase or decrease. This is known as taking a position. So if you think that the value of a certain stock is going to increase, you will assume a long position and "buy" the stock.

If you owned stock in real-life trading and you thought that it was going down in value, you would want to sell it before you lost money. This would be a short sell, and it would mean that you are going to "sell" the stock and buy it later.

If things happened in just the way you predicted, you would make a profit by buying back the stock at a lower price later.

But in spread betting, you can take a short position when the value of the stock is going to decrease. If the stock value falls below the price at which wagers start, you will win the bet. Long positions make a profit when stock values rise.

What do you win? The amount depends upon the stake you placed. We already saw an example earlier. Let's take another one. Let's say you placed £15 per point. You assumed a long position at the offer price of 4002 on the stock, and the values shot up to 4020. Now you can "sell" (it means to conclude the bet). So your winning would be £15 × (4020? 4002) = £270.

Now let's consider another case. Let's say that the stock value decreases at the end of the bet. In that case, you would lose money. For example, if it fell from 4002 to 3995, your loss would be £15 × (4002? 3995) = £105.

This math is pretty simple, and it's easy to find out how much you gained or lost.

THE BEGINNING OF SPREAD BETTING

Different people have different views about when spread betting began, and a number of financial historians map out the origin of spread betting to the United States and the unfettered bucket shops that flourished in the initial years of the twentieth century.

But it was in 1974 when Stuart Wheeler came up with the idea of giving investors a chance to bet on the ups and downs in the gold market. This was the first official case of spread betting, and thus it was born that year.

Wheeler had an idea to make an index to give investors a chance to bet on gold market movement without actually buying any real gold. This new company was named Investors Gold Index, but later the Bank on England raised an objection to that name, and so it was changed to IG Index.

The premise for the whole idea was simple yet brilliant. By breaking the traditional barriers and opening up the surroundings, Wheeler helped a new bracket of investors to assume their positions in the market without going through heavily regulated channels.

But that was then. Scenes have changed now. With all the improvements that have been taking place in the betting arena, now you can bet even via your mobile phone. And since the markets are always open, you can bet at any hour.

Plus there are many other types of spread betting. Now you can select from bungee to binary bets, as the industry is forever innovating.

Before we move on to delve deeper into the subject, it is important to realize that while spread betting can give you magnified profits, it can also result in big losses.

WHAT YOU NEED TO KNOW

Thoughts about big losses can turn into nightmares. Don't let risk factors bring you down. Do sufficient research on spread betting before you begin this new and lucrative journey. Here are some quick pointers for you. Go through them, because if you want to start something in spread betting, these points will help you a lot.

1. Where Money Is

Spread betting is essentially gambling and not investing. You are betting on the future movements of a commodity or a share price. Keep in mind that the odds of winning are mostly in the company's favor, and there is a great risk of loss.

2. Tax Break

Since spread betting is gambling, whatever profits you make are free of any capital gains tax. But that is attractive only if you are making money.

3. A Few Practice Shots

Most companies will allow you to go for a practice run before you touch the actual market. They will provide you with an online simulator for trading. The biggest players in this market are Cantor Index and IG Index.

4. Pain Barrier

Create a stop-loss barrier for yourself. This limit should be used to close your trade at some level if prices are moving against you.

5. The Right Timing

There are some spread bettors who close their trade daily, but if you want, you can leave positions for much longer. There was a woman who took two bets on Google shares at £1 and £2 for a point each and held her position for almost two months. She made a profit of £27,000.

6. Technical Support

If you wake up one fine morning and decide on betting on some shares, this wouldn't be a successful strategy. Many successful spread bettors use charting tools that show how stocks have performed. This is better than using your gut feeling to bet on things. There are many tools available these days to help in betting.

7. The Katrina Effect

Oil speculations were going up after the occurrence of Hurricane Katrina. Currencies are also famous for trading, and forex is one of the most common areas. In fact, trends have been shifting from stocks to forex.

8. The Golden Touch

Apart from forex, people are also betting on gold. So if gold excites you, this might be your spread betting niche.

9. Risk Reduction

Many investors use spread betting to protect their positions. The general risk warnings apply here as well.

For instance, let's say someone who has £5,000 invested in an FTSE 100 tracker is worried about a stock market fall. The person could protect, or hedge, the position by selling it on a spread bet. If the given index closes at, say, 5,386, the investor can sell it at £1.86 for a point (£5,000/5,386). So for every point the FTSE 100 falls, the investor will make £1.86 to cover the losses in the tracker fund.

TYPES OF SPREAD BETTING

Spread betting can be done on any kind of activity. It can be financial, sporting, social, or political. Spread betting started with financial companies, and it was later followed by sports betting companies. Plus the Internet has bestowed innumerable capabilities to the spread betting world, as you can see many online spread betting companies.

The four main types of spread bets are:

- *Future style.* This is the default style. When people talk about spread betting, this is the one they are talking about. In this type, you bet on the future price of a commodity.
- *Daily bets.* These are straightforward bets, and they expire as the day ends. Since they offer tighter spreads, traders like them a lot.
- *Rolling dailies.* These bets do not expire as the day ends. Instead, they roll over to the next day. They are kept open overnight, and so you have to pay extra interest.
- *Binary bets.* These are a bit different from typical spread betting. These bets have only two outcomes (and thus they are called binary).

It's On (Line) 2
IG Index was the first U.K.-based spread betting company. It started in the 1970s and allowed people to bet on gold prices. IG Index was followed by City Index, which was followed by Finspreads. These days, customers can make bets online or on the phone. Over 25 online spread betting companies operate in the United Kingdom. Some companies charge commissions, while others don't.

Financial Spread Betting
This can be explained in one sentence: financial spread betting is betting for a living or maybe for a second income. There is no concept of chance or unpredictability in this definition. Trading in financial markets involves maintaining the balance in probability and finding what to favor to minimize losses.

Spread betting is a good idea for trading financial markets—it is cheap. If you want to set up trades, stockbrokers will charge you. This one is relatively simpler. There is a small set of instructions. Follow the instructions and you can make a spread bet. Plus it is tax-free in the United Kingdom.

Another major plus is that you don't need a lot of cash to start financial spread betting. Keep in mind that the spread would be bigger than what your stockbroker charges you. This is because spread betting companies do not charge you commission.

The spread basically differs from one share to another, and it might be large for some. But you can ignore that and move on to other points. Also, the spread differs from one company to another. So once you gain experience, try to shop around.

Forex Spread Betting

This is one of the hottest areas in spread betting, and people are indulging in it more and more these days. Working with forex is like working in other markets. In this genre, you can bet on currency pairs. For example, you can bet on whether the GBP/USD value is rising or falling.

Forex rates measure the relative value of currencies. You can gamble on the relative value of two currencies that are in a pair. This is forex spread betting. Forex pairs are an important part of a number of investment portfolios, and they are the second highest traded genre in the spread betting business.

Forex markets are very volatile because they are strongly influenced by political and economic pressures.

When you gamble on forex, you can view two price quotes. They are known as bid and offer. In case you think your currency pair is going to move up, you should execute the offer level. Offer is the higher quote. And if you think that the currency you want to gamble on is going down, then you should sell it at the bid level. This is the lower of the two quotes.

Bookies of spread betting make profits from the variation between the offer and bid quotes. The spread is the part that they earn by permitting you to trade via them.

Stop-loss orders are generally not guaranteed to get executed at a certain level unless the guaranteed stop has been paid for. Normal market scenarios will see stop-loss orders that are activated near the prearranged order levels.

Note that major economic data can result in slippage when the bookie hands you the closest price exit at the time of execution. Traders might also face slippage when they hold trades over holidays or weekends. If you want to run bets over the weekend, it is best to place low ones.

If you want to spread-bet on forex, here are a couple of points:

- Traders do not own the currencies on which they are betting. They only bet on price fluctuations.
- Bookies may widen the spread level as the economic data are released.

Sports Spread Betting

Sports spread betting isn't a new concept either. It started when Charles McNeil, a math teacher from Connecticut, invented a different way to bet on sports. He later moved to Chicago and became a bookmaker there.

This idea gained popularity in the United Kingdom in the 1980s and was later followed in North America. The way of wagering in sports spread betting is a bit different. Bettors generally wager that the variation between the scores of two sports teams will be greater than or less than a specified value that was decided by the bookmaker.

When the bettor spread-bets on any game such as golfing, he or she does not necessarily have to select a player that will possibly be the winner. Though this might help, it's not always the winning strategy.

Sometimes this method works because costs show the probability of a player winning. But some players perform well consistently, week after week—which is good.

Spread betting is good for those who prefer betting while using the rules of probability. This makes a bettor able to buy or sell the bets. It depends upon the player—how well or poorly he or she is going to play the game. It is just one among lots of spread markets, particularly on golf. Before a contest starts, every player receives a spread that depends on the mark that the bookies hope to score.

Spread Betting in the United Kingdom

The spread betting industry is now dealing in millions of pounds. There are over 83,000 traders in just the United Kingdom—and the firms are multiplying rapidly. The global spread betting audience is estimated to be about £650 million a year for retail operator revenue, and this number is growing at 20 to 30 percent per year.

There are more than 25 spread betting companies in the United Kingdom, and there is a tough competition that has brought spreads down. About a decade ago, the spread on a benchmark index like the FTSE 100 index was about 10 points. And now it has gone down to 2. There have always been consolidation rumors, but most people believe that there is enough growth in the market that all the spread betting providers can be easily accommodated.

More than 40,000 people in the United Kingdom have spread betting accounts, and most of them are male. But that shouldn't upset the ladies because the number of female bettors is rising too. These spread bettors are usually self-employed people or those who work in the insurance, finance, or IT sector.

Spread betting attracts the same markets as CFDs, i.e., experienced traders who are active in the market and realize the risks that come with gearing and margins. A large part of spread betting is composed of volume-based day trading and short-terms trades that come in and out of their positions.

Experienced traders make spread bets for the reason that if they make £5,000 from spread betting, they can keep the whole £5,000, rather than giving a portion of it to taxes.

As with any other type of gambling, you can make money and you can lose money. On an average, most traders have 6 losses out of 10. But do not be disheartened by this number, because the profits that are made in the 4 winning trades are more than the losses.

If you want to begin spread betting in the United Kingdom, make sure you have a sound income. Spread betting is not for unemployed people or those with low income. You would need a minimum of £100 to begin trading. This is an amount that you should be able to afford to lose. So basically, this dealing is for people who can take small and calculated risks. This is not for the shy and weak. So if you lose money, don't start complaining or writing to TV shows about it.

This market is geared high, so you can win or lose money really fast. The good part is that it is all "zero sum." So the money you make will have to come from somewhere or someone, with someone losing and someone winning.

If you are from the United States, you can't deal in spread betting unless you have an offshore corporation and understand the regulatory guidelines for having and using an offshore corporation. This is because Web sites like Capital Spread are highly regulated by the U.K. government, not allowing them to infringe on the U.S. laws that prohibit American citizens from trading outside the country.

There are many established spread betting corporations in the United Kingdom that are backed by large and reputed bookmakers. If you want to open an account with them, you need a local mailing address. To see a current list of the most widely used spread betting brokers, go to www.jdfn.com.

SPREAD BETTING: IS IT REALLY TAX-FREE?

The simple answer is yes. Spread bettors evade the 18 percent U.K. capital gains tax, which shareholders have to pay on their trading profits. And there is no commission on trades and no stamp duty either. Plus you don't have to pay income tax on dividends that are charged at high rates (sometimes even 50 percent for the high-income group).

But there is an exception: spread betting is tax-free only if it isn't your primary income source. So when you open a spread betting account, do not enter your job description as "trader," because it will be difficult for you to claim the tax rebate later when Inland Revenue queries you about your money.

The sine qua non is that if you pay taxes and you win at spread betting, you are not liable to pay taxes on those profits. But if you have no regular taxable income, then you will be classified as a professional gambler, and thus you will lose the BIM22017 exemption. Keep in mind, though, that HM Revenue and Customs is reluctant to classify people as professional gamblers, because then they can claim relief against spread betting companies and their gambling losses. So as long as you pay PAYE (withholding taxes), you can't be classified as a professional gambler, and thus you don't have to pay tax on your winnings.

Most of the people who indulge in spread betting don't do it for a living, and so, to repeat the point already made in this section, they don't have to pay taxes. And the people who do it for a living get smart accountants who figure out a way to save them from taxes. You can't stop a millionaire trader from having a "subsistence income" from a small business for which he or she pays tax. Get the point?

SPREAD BETTING STRATEGIES AND TIPS

1. Spread betting is easily accessible to new investors, but it is less lucrative because of wider spreads.
2. It is best to start by opening a demo account with any spread betting firm.
3. You will receive a virtual £10,000 to play. You can trade with that money as if it were real. Plan on spending about two to four months to get a basic understanding and to develop your winning strategy. Do not start investing unless you see that you are getting consistent profits each week. If you trade in haste, you will end up in losses.
4. Are you ready to trade using real money? Make sure you start out small. It is a lot harder than it looks. Do not invest huge sums thinking that you have understood it all. Yes, it is enticing, and many people want to start off with big trades, but the results can be painful. You will find many providers that will permit you to start small.
5. Determine what you are going to trade. Different assets have different ways of trading, and they need different skill sets. If you ask me, you should start with simple U.K. FTSE stocks—blue chip stocks if possible. It is also wise to select shares that have less volatility, like bank and insurance company stocks. Forex is also very volatile for starters, and so you might want to practice a bit before you enter the forex spread betting market. Do not deal in volatile markets such as oil. New traders like to deal in oil, since they think it has a lot of prospects, but actually this market is very risky for newbies.
6. When you start, do not begin with trading too many markets at once. Choose a couple of markets and stick to them until you develop more skill and confidence. Of course,

trading in many markets gives more profit opportunities, but it takes a lot of expertise.

7. When you have to use real money, keep in mind that companies will allow you to create an account with £200, but it's best to start with £1,000. This will allow you to take up more losses than with £200 if the bet size is kept to a small fraction. A max risk of 2 percent is best, but since you have a small account, use 5 percent.

8. When selecting companies, make sure you do not begin with more than five companies. Do not short out at this stage, as it is psychologically harder.

9. Do not make wagers in running bets. As you open a fresh spread bet, you should think about the size, direction, and duration of the trade, along with the exit strategy and best entry price. The exit strategy includes two important parts: the initial target for profit and a stop-loss point in case the market moves against you.

10. If you want to make money trading, you need an objective and disciplined approach. So decide the level that you want to trade, and do not fall for the temptation and buy too early. You can also set market orders out of the regular hours to trade more effectively. Plus it reduces the psychological pressures that you might face as a new trader.

11. Before opening each spread bet, write your plan down— why did you opt for this decision, stop-loss level, trade size, and exit strategy. In case you decide not to open a position even after you examined it closely, write down why you did that. When you do enter a trade, note down the fill price and recalculate the risks. If the price hits a level that proves your trade wrong, exit it immediately. It is important to have clear targets—else you will start gambling using your emotions or gut feeling, which does not work. Many new traders take profits too early and stick with the losses, thinking that the trade will eventually improve in the future. When you do not have a plan, you will go by impulse, which is a bad thing.

12. Once you have analyzed all factors and risks, place your bet, but beware that sometimes spreads might not reveal the real market price. They only reflect what the instrument price is, according to the market.

Spread betting is becoming more and more popular overseas and is certainly a way to increase your overall portfolio. I would caution that this may be more risky than other investments that you may be used to. Plan on using only risk capital that you are willing to lose while learning how to spread-bet.

6

FORWARDS AND SWAPS

Among several other interesting financial derivatives (so-called because their value is based upon the value of an underlying asset) that allow investors to manage and reduce their portfolio risks, we can find forwards and swaps.

These are linear payoff derivatives contracts, contrary to options, which have a nonlinear payoff. Forwards and swaps are OTC instruments, thus operating in a nonregulated market and requiring customers to have a banking relationship.

DEFINITIONS

A *forward* is any contract in which liquidation is deferred to a posterior date, defined on the negotiation. Forward transactions are one of the most common derivatives employed in all kinds of financial activities.

This type of contract allows you to purchase a fixed amount of the underlying asset at a fixed price for a specific time period that starts at a future date, independently of the fluctuations that the market can present. Should prices rise, you are protected, as the price you agreed to pay will remain the same for the term of the agreement. A forward contract will allow you to reduce your exposure to price fluctuations, thus facilitating the financial planning of a company's budget.

A *swap* is a contract in which both parties agree to exchange a series of money flows at a future date. Those flows can be based on short-term interest rates, or on stock indexes, or on any other variable. A swap is used to reduce the cost and risk of financing a business or to overcome the barriers of financial markets.

This type of contract is similar to a forward, but the settlement procedure differs. You will agree to purchase a definite amount of the underlying asset at a fixed price and for a specific time period. If the market prices rise, you receive the difference between the agreed contract price and the actual market value; if the spot market price for the underlying is lower, you have to pay the difference. In this sense, swap contracts are equivalent to CFDs. The fixed price allows you to be protected against market volatility, and the exposure to price risk is shared.

CLASSIFICATION OF FORWARDS

Interest Rate Forward

Forward rate agreements (FRAs) are specific individual contracts between two parties who agree to enter an investment at a particular future date and at a particular interest rate, for a theoretical nominal amount. At the expiration date, the difference between the cash market value and the interest rate agreed in the FRA is liquidated.

The FRA is a futures contract used for risk coverage on interest rates. As it is an OTC instrument, its characteristics are not standardized and thus can be perfectly adjusted to the customer's needs. There is no movement of funds between the customer and the banking entity.

The FRA is identified by means of two numbers that refer to the period from the contract date until the liquidation date and at opening; that is the period stipulated in the signed contract. Both periods are expressed in months. For example, FRA 2/5 indicates that this FRA will be liquidated in two months, while the contract period is three months, meaning the contract will expire five months from the contract signature date. The opening of the FRA is the period between the liquidation date and the expiration date.

The FRA helps investors protect themselves against unfavorable changes in the interest rates, and it allows investors to set the interest rate for a loan or deposit prior to the contract date.

You would buy an FRA when you need to be protected from a possible rise in interest rates; you will sell an FRA when you need to guard against a potential decrease in interest rates. Such a contract eliminates uncertainty about the evolution of those rates. The FRA is a coverage instrument, which is not dependent on the financial or investment operation; its contract does not require the payment of any premium.

Forward on Currencies or Exchange Rate

A forward on currencies or exchange rates allows the participants to enter into agreements on forex rate transactions to be realized at specific moments in the future. The size and expiration of this type of delayed contract are negotiated between the buyer and the seller, and the exchange rates are usually quoted at 30, 60, or 90 days or 6, 9, or 12 months from the date on which the contract is subscribed.

Forward over Assets That Do Not Pay Interest or Dividends

These assets are usually commodities that present an anomaly in the delayed price, produced because, among other reasons, the market is not an efficient market. This happens, for example, with oil, where it is impossible to sell short because you cannot borrow the commodity and users that store oil do so because the consequences of a lack of this commodity are terrible, and thus they do not want to lend it to anybody else.

CLASSIFICATION OF SWAPS

Vanilla or Interest Rate Swaps

These are contracts where a party of the transaction agrees to pay the other party an interest rate established in advance, and the second party agrees to pay the first party a variable interest rate over the same nominal value. The only exchange that takes place is the payment of the interests on capital, while the payments that correspond to the capital itself do not participate in the transaction. This type of contract is the most common in the financial markets.

A normal interest rate swap is a contract where one of the parties performing the transaction agrees to pay to the other party an interest rate that has been fixed in advance over a nominal amount, also fixed in advance, and the second party agrees to pay to the first party a variable interest rate over the same nominal amount.

Interest rate swap contracts are financial exchanges where the objects of the exchange are payment obligations, corresponding to loans of different characteristics, which refer to a particular notional value in the same currency. Usually fixed interests are exchanged with variable interests, although only variable interests can also be exchanged over two different reference bases. That means that a swap is not really a loan, as it is exclusively an exchange of interest rate flows and as nobody is borrowing the nominal amount from anyone, meaning that the principal quantities are not exchanged.

Currency Swaps

These are a variation of the interest rate swaps, where the nominal value on which the fixed interest rate is paid and the nominal value on which the variable interest rate is paid come from two different currencies. The traditional form of the exchange rate swap implies a combination of a purchase (sale) on the cash spot market and a compensatory sale (purchase) for the same party in the "forward" delayed market. But this sometimes can refer to compensatory transactions with different expirations or combinations of both.

A currency swap is an agreement between two commercial parties to exchange, for the duration of an agreed-upon time period, two interest flows from two different currencies. This will generally be at the time of expiration of the agreement. The principal amount of the transaction is at an exchange rate established at the starting point, usually the cash spot value for that date. This exchange between parties is what is covered against a nonfavorable evolution of exchange rates.

The simplest types of currency swaps that exist will vary depending on the rates exchanged, where we will have:

- Fixed against variable currency swap
- Variable against variable currency swap
- Fixed against fixed currency swap

One of the advantages of a swap contract is the absence of risk for the principal amount on the contract, as the eventual noncompliance only affects the differential between rates or between prices or the change in the debt structure offered by interest rate swaps.

The disadvantages are the high amount needed for notional principals, the higher costs of intermediaries and setup, and, finally, the difficulties encountered if you want to liquidate the transaction before its expiration because of the low possibilities of finding a counterparty wishing to assume the specific conditions of that particular contract.

Commodity Swaps

This variant makes it possible to separate the risk of the market price from the credit risk, and it allows a commodity producer to run a simple factory that processes commodities without taking any price risks. A typical financial problem is the funding of producers through commodities, as the international commodity markets are often very volatile.

For example, international prices of oil can decrease 30 percent in a few days. For this reason, the companies that produce commodities are generally considered high-risk businesses in regard to credits for investments. Therefore, these types of swaps are designed to remove price risks and reduce the financing costs.

The operation of a commodity swap is very similar to that of an interest rate swap. For example, a three-year-period swap on oil is an exchange of money based on the sole price of oil (there is no physical exchange of the commodity at any moment); thus the swap compensates any difference that exists between the variable market price and the fixed price established by means of the swap. That is, if oil prices fall below the established price, the second party pays the difference to the first party; and if the prices rise, the first party will pay the difference to the second party.

Stock Indexes Swaps

The market of swaps on stock indexes allows you to exchange the performance of the money market for the performance of a stock market. This stock market performance refers to the sum of dividends received, capital profits, and losses.

Through this process, we can obtain the same profitability as if we had invested in stocks, and we can obtain that profitability at the same time the swap transaction is financed; but we can always keep the capital, which can then be invested in other assets.

Exchange Rate Swaps

In this type of contract, one of the parties agrees to liquidate interests over a specific amount of principal in a particular currency. In exchange, that party receives interest over a specific amount of principal in another currency. This is a variation of the interest rate swap, where the nominal amount on which the fixed interest rate is paid and the nominal amount on which the variable interest rate is paid are from two different currencies. Contrary to the interest rate swap, here the principal amounts are exchanged at the beginning and at the end of the swap contract duration.

At the same time, these instruments can be used to transform a loan in a particular currency into a loan in another currency. It can be said that a swap is a long position in an obligation combined with a short position in another obligation. A swap can be considered as a portfolio of contracts at a given term. Presently, financial institutions frequently receive swaps as deposits.

Credit Swaps

This type of contract is used to manage credit risks through the measurement and specification of the prices of each of the underlying instruments: interest rate, period, currency, and credit. Those risks can be transferred to a holder in a more efficient manner, allowing credit access at a lesser cost and adjusting to the relationship between credit supply and demand.

Credit risks are narrowed down to a potential noncompliance risk. There are two modalities of credit swaps: default swaps and total return swaps.

- *Default swaps.* In a default swap, the seller of a credit risk guarantees payment to the other party if the credit status agreed upon in the swap changes in regard to the referenced credit, usually a corporate bond.
- *Total return swaps.* Conversely, total return swaps allow the seller of the credit risk to keep the asset and receive a return, which fluctuates with the modification of the credit risk. The seller pays a total rate of return over a referenced asset. This is generally a bond that includes any price consideration in exchange for periodical payments at a floating rate plus any price reduction.

When these kinds of swaps were invented, they were usually employed solely by the banks to protect banking credits. Presently, they have become very popular coverage instruments, as they allow you to keep the asset while, at the same time, fragment and distribute the risk.

This will allow a bank to free up credit lines and continue lending money to its customers, even if the amount exceeds its exposure limits for that company or industry, using the partial or total discharge of the credit risk through a total return or default swap.

PROFITABILITY

Forwards

A company can settle the parities of different currencies in the future, reducing the exposure to their volatility risks. On a local currency forward, you are establishing the future bid or ask price of a foreign currency in regard to the local currency.

This eliminates the risk of fluctuation of exchange rates, allows you to choose amounts and specific dates for the settlement, and doesn't affect the liquidity of the company because you do not need to have any funds available at the moment of the agreement nor at its expiration.

On a forex forward, you can establish future parities between foreign currencies and perform the contracts in a similar way as described above. These contracts can be agreed upon either with a fixed expiration date or with the expiration within a few days' range.

Profits on forwards are variable, depending on the currencies' interest rates.

For example, a company that exports a commodity to other countries and is therefore exposed to the exchange rate between its local currency and the foreign currencies that are paid for its sales can cover its exchange risk in advance by selling, at a future date, the currencies it expects to receive in the future.

Swaps
In these contracts, you agree upon the exchange of future currency flows for different currencies where both parties decide on the amounts and expiration dates. The contracts allow the physical exchange and holding of currencies or compensation of obligations.

The benefit of operating with forwards and swaps is that you do not require cash flow at the moment of establishing the contract. The forwards don't increase your company's debt levels; and the agreements can be done over the phone, with the bank working with you on the contract privately, which is not subject to any taxes or any commissions or additional costs.

For example, if a company plans to settle its floating debt by means of an interest swap and has uncertain expectancies about the behavior of the rates, it could acquire a selling option on a treasury bond with a similar expiration. This way the interest rates rise, and the option is exercised to compensate the high cost of the swap generated by the rate increase. If the rates decrease, the option will expire worthless, but there will be a profit, as the variable-rate debt has been fixed at a lower value than the actual rate.

RISKS

Forwards

- *Credit risk.*
- *Interest rate risk.* This occurs when there are fluctuations in the interest rates, which affect the final cost of the transactions.
- *Exchange rate risk.*

Swaps

- *Differential risk.* If a swap is covered with a bond and there is a change in the swap differential in regard to the bond, there could be losses (or profits) in the swap profitability.
- *Base risk.* When a swap is covered with a futures contract and there is a difference between the reference rate and the implied rate in the futures contract, a loss or profit can be generated.
- *Credit risk.* There is a probability that the counterparty does not honor its obligations.
- *Reinvestment risk.* This risk is derived from the credit risk when there are changes in the payment dates; it is necessary to reinvest in each rotation date.
- *Exchange rate risk.* There is the possibility that there will be a positive fluctuation of the currency or currencies that are going to be liquidated when the transaction will be effective (purchase or sale). In this case, at the end of the commercial operation, you will have to pay more of your own currency (or any other) to acquire the same amount of the other currency agreed upon in the contract, which affects the final cost of the transactions.

HOW ARE THESE TRANSACTIONS PERFORMED?

Forwards and swaps are usually realized over the telephone or the Internet, and the deal is closed when there is an agreement upon the coupon rate, basis for the floating rate, days, starting date, expiration date, rotation date, application of laws, and documentation.

These transactions are immediately confirmed through a telex or fax followed by a written confirmation. The documentation used in the main currency centers is usually one of two standard forms, the one offered by the British Bankers' Association (the British Bankers' Association Interest Rates and Currency Swaps) or the one offered by the International Swap Dealers Association.

WHO ARE THE INTERESTED PARTIES?

The market of forwards and swaps usually comprises all conventional currency users:

- *Commercial importers of goods and services.* In their normal course of operation, they perform transactions for a specific amount of one or several currencies to be paid at a future date in exchange for receiving merchandise or services from another country.
- *Commercial exporters of goods and services.* Here the transactions are performed for the currency or currencies to be received at a future date in exchange for merchandise sent or services rendered to another country.
- *Companies that owe obligations in foreign currency.* Typically, in this group are businesses that acquire credits in any other currency than their local currency to be paid at a future date.
- *Other agents (private or public companies, institutional investors, particular investors, etc.).* This group consists of those who by the nature of their activities are exposed to the fluctuation of exchange rates or interest rates.

HOW DO THEY ACTUALLY STAND BEFORE REGULATORY ENTITIES?

In March 2011, the U.S. Treasury Department was considering the application of tougher rules for forex forwards and swaps. Nearly $2 trillion a day is employed in commercial transactions. These transactions are essential to multinational corporations and big international investors, as they protect them from losing money due to currency volatility.

This is a seldom-regulated market, and transactions take place in a private environment. Most transactions are between big international banks and commercial parties that agree on a price and execute a contract, the terms of which are also private.

If these transactions were to be regulated, the new rules would require them to be realized publicly on trading platforms, and the need for using a clearinghouse as intermediary would increase the costs. By using clearinghouses and other intermediaries, each party would need to post collateral as a guarantee of the deal, which is not the case in most private deals.

Another risk would be an increase of the exchange rate volatility, as most firms and investors would try to group their buying or selling of currencies at extreme prices in order to control their costs. In addition, a lot of transactions would most probably be redirected outside the United States.

Objections to these new regulations were that unlike other types of swaps, forex contracts are less speculative, as they imply an effective exchange of goods (one currency for another). Also these are shorter-term contracts where market conditions do not have enough time to cause huge changes, which could generate big losses for either party.

On April 20, 2011, the U.S. Treasury Department finally announced that it would exempt forex forwards and swaps from the new rules and from the central clearing requirements of the Dodd-Frank Act. The Treasury concluded that:

> Central clearing requirements will strengthen the rest of the derivatives market, but could actually jeopardize practices in the forex swaps and forwards market that help limit risk and ensure that it functions effectively. The market plays such an important role in helping businesses manage their everyday funding and investment needs throughout the world that disruptions to its operations could have serious negative economic consequences. ("Fact Sheet: Notice of Proposed Determination on Foreign Exchange Swaps and Forwards," April 2011, http://www .treasury.gov/initiatives/wsr/Pages/facts.aspx)

The Treasury Department warned that although exempt from mandatory central clearing, forex forwards and swaps would be subject to new reporting requirements and reinforced business standards. The department stated that plans are in progress that have already started to create a global forex repository. This will allow the expansion of reporting features to the regulatory entities and to the markets, thus increasing the transparency of the overall transactions.

7

TRADING AS A BUSINESS

By now you have taken the next step in your trading. You may be thinking that this is something that you want to do full-time, something that can replace your current income. That may be true, but keep in mind that many have tried before you. I believe that you can, but it will take hard work to make trading a full-time job.

When most people hear that you are or want to become a foreign currency trader, they think of making lots of money and traveling around the world. This can be true, but in all seriousness, if you want to trade full-time as your primary source of income, you are going to be sitting in front of your computer. Now don't take this the wrong way: trading is exciting and can be very lucrative. But it is not a get-rich-quick business.

You will have to take your bumps along the way. I would suggest that you plan on spending a few years dialing in your strategies and money management plans. You can make money while doing this, but you can also lose money. In trading, it isn't how much you lose; it is the simple fact that you make more than you lose. A lot of traders make the mistake of not wanting to accept losses. Losses are okay as long as they are part of your overall money management plan.

Most people don't think about trading as a business, but I learned long ago that the best returns can frequently be made by looking at things differently from the way most people do. If you change your thinking and start looking at trading as more than just investing, but actually as a business that provides income for you and your family, I think you will be pleasantly surprised at the benefits you receive.

In the first place, a small business is about the only great tax shelter still available that the IRS hasn't been able to strip away. Not that it hasn't tried. But Congress has been stubborn in its support of the idea that it is the entrepreneurial spirit that makes this country what it is, and so it has consistently avoided reducing the benefits that businesses offer to their owners. Naturally, it doesn't hurt that most representatives and senators either have small businesses or have relatives who have one, but let's be thankful for the little favors we get, no matter where they come from or in what form.

As you will read in this book and probably already know, trading forex as a business has certainly taken a turn for complication. The many new regulatory reform bills are making it harder for traders to do what they used to do in the spot OTC forex industry. It is still relatively easy to open an account and trade on your own account. But if you are planning on trading someone else's money, then you will have to conform to all the new regulatory requirements.

THE TAX CODE

The tax code classifies people in the securities business into three categories: dealers, investors, and traders. The dealer classification is beyond the scope of this book because it involves people making a market in stocks and other securities for investors. Investors and traders, however, are very important and affect both the way we buy and sell currencies or securities and the deductions we are allowed.

Most people consider themselves investors. They invest and look for a return on their money. Investors, however, don't get any tax benefits, other than the potential of capital gains tax treatment on anything they buy and hold for more than a year.

It is common that in the forex industry brokers do not send you statements you can use for your taxes. Rather, it is left up to you to maintain a record of your trades. Most brokers have a pretty detailed software reporting system that will assist you in running your trading activity, but don't take that for granted. You will need to think ahead about how you are going to report your trading activity on your tax returns.

I personally find this to be somewhat ridiculous. In the equities business, your brokers will send you a year-end statement that they file with the IRS and that you will need to include on your taxes. At least my brokers do. To think that reporting profits to the IRS is left up to the forex trader is unimaginable. And so is the idea that the IRS hasn't closed this loophole.

If, instead of being an investor, you decide to be a trader, here is a partial list of benefits in the form of tax deductions you get:

- The cost of your trading education
- Financial software
- Books and audiotape and videotape courses in investing and trading
- Accounting fees
- Brokerage account fees and commissions
- Office equipment (computers, Internet high-speed connection fees, adding machines, phones, phone charges, etc.)
- Interest on your margin accounts and any other investment-related interest expense
- Financial advice and training
- Tax advice
- Legal advice related to your business
- Entertainment and meals during which business is conducted
- Travel to seminars, trade shows, and other business-related trips anywhere in the world
- Magazine subscriptions related to investing and trading
- Trips to look at corporations you are considering investing in
- The portion of your home expense that qualifies as a home business and a portion of all expenses paid on maintaining the property, utilities, etc.
- Automobile expenses

You can tell the list is rather inclusive and beneficial. Interestingly, as you begin to learn the nuances and combine all the advantages, they add up to a rather tidy sum.

HOW TO BECOME A TRADER

The IRS code does not define trade or business as it relates to the business of trading. The law that has developed comes from court cases and decisions made in the favor of taxpayers who have made this claim. The key elements in the cases were length of holding period, frequency of trades, and purpose for trading, that is, was the person's intent to make money from dividend interest, long-term gain, or short-term trading?

If you are a currency trader, it is pretty easy to show your intent, since that is all you shoot for. If you also trade stocks, you can still make a claim for trader status even if you hold some of them long term, although it is doubtful you will anyway.

While we all hope our business, including our trading business, makes a ton of money, the reality is it won't always do so. The good news is that if trading is a business, then your excess expenses can be used to offset income from other sources just like any other business would allow you to do. It is a win-win situation.

Let's discuss using trader status as it relates to your personal tax return by creating a small sole proprietorship. In this case, you would place your ordinary business expenses on Schedule C, and you would report your income or loss on Schedule D, since it is still considered capital. No self-employment income is calculated on the income, and your trading losses are still limited to $3,000 per year but can be carried over indefinitely. You can also use any losses in the stock market to offset gains in the currency market.

Although the benefits of this strategy are good, there is another way, and often a better way, to operate the business. That is by incorporating the business and creating your own trade corporation.

A trade corporation is your new legal entity in which to conduct your trading. There are near-term advantages, longer-range asset protection, and family financial planning advantages. There will be some extra cost for setup and operation, but as you will quickly see, the advantages far outweigh the cost.

Your first advantage is clarity of purpose. If you form a corporation for the purpose of trading and conduct the trading in the separate entity, there will be no question regarding your trader status, nor will there be an issue about your personal tax return and the deductions you take. This is not to suggest that operating things in the sole proprietorship status is in the gray area of the tax code. It isn't.

Some people like to keep their various businesses separate, protect assets from different creditors, and do estate and financial planning as they go. If you fall into this category of individuals, you should consider using a corporation as the entity to operate your trade business.

I have personally probably taken this to the extreme. It does cost a little more money to be extra careful, but to protect assets, I tend to open separate corporations for each separate business venture I am doing. This way I am not commingling assets, so to speak, among other companies. I primarily do this for the reduction of liability. That way if for some reason you do ever get sued, the lawsuit is basically relegated to the specific corporation in question. Starting a trading business is no different, since your assets in the trading company are not yours personally but the company's.

WHAT KIND OF COMPANY

There are three types of corporations: C, Sub S, and LLC. A C corporation is considered a regular corporation. A Sub S corporation is so named because of the tax code section that gives it benefits. The LLC is structured to overcome some of the structural difficulties of the Sub S corporation. (Interestingly, about the time the individual states got through adopting massive legislation to get around the tax code, Congress decided it didn't want to be outdone and amended most, but not all, of the difficult portions of the Sub S code.)

To be fair to both you as the reader and me as the author, I must now disclose that I am going to make sweeping generalities about which corporations are best and why. The problem is everyone's circumstances are different and volumes have been written about the "best" structure to use. Nevertheless, we will attempt to weed through the tangle of red tape to uncover some solid ideas.

The C corporation is primarily used for public companies, multiple shareholders who aren't interested in distributing profits and losses, but want to build an entity and individual businesses that benefit from a medical reimbursement plan or some types of retirement programs.

For some people, the medical reimbursement can be a great deal because under the current law, individuals and joint filers are limited to medical deductions after a 2 percent limitation of adjusted gross income.

Excepting the medical situation, you will likely benefit greatest in either a Sub S corporation or an LLC. The reason is that both have tax flow benefits at the shareholder level. This means the corporation doesn't pay a separate tax, but the shareholders (in the Sub S) and the members (in the LLC) pay tax on any gain or take losses personally if there are any. This gives you the benefit of a personal tax shelter in years where there is a loss in the company.

It should be noted that if you are going to be the only share holder of your company, then the Sub S corporation is probably the one you should consider. Being a single-member LLC has its complications. The IRS will basically consider you a sole proprietorship if you have an LLC and you are a single member, meaning that you are the only owner. If this is the case, then you will basically be giving up the corporate benefits that you are looking for. So look to the Sub S to provide the corporate flexibility you need.

The benefit to using a Sub S is that it has been around the longest, and so most CPAs and attorneys are comfortable with it. The benefit of the LLC is that you can do some interesting family, estate, and asset protection planning.

Let's take a look at a few examples. Let's say you form an LLC trade corporation. In an LLC, you are allowed to issue multiple types of shares. Because you would like to shift some of your trade income to your children, you issue them a preferred class of stock that has no voting rights but has a preference of income up to a certain level.

This "income-shift" strategy allows you to maintain 100 percent control of your company and all the assets, but shifts dollars to your children, who are in a lower income bracket than you. The children can use the money to pay their bills.

Another twist on this strategy is to pay your children a salary out of the corporation for work they do. The work, depending on age and ability, would give them earned income and allow them to set up an IRA or other retirement program at an early age. While income shifting takes money out of your pocket and puts it in someone else's, you get the deduction; and if you can control what happens to the money, it is the same as having it. Another benefit to helping your children grow an early retirement program is that you may at least have someone to support you if things don't always go as you would like.

LLCs have another advantage; they can be used to protect assets. If you find yourself in a situation where you need to be protected, you can put your assets in an LLC and give, sell, or otherwise structure the share ownership in someone else's name. You can continue to draw a salary from the company and control the operation of the company through special shares, which can be drafted to give you specific rights to do so.

The assets now belong to someone else and are no longer attachable by the creditor, and the income you receive is not attachable because it is a salary. (Some states give certain creditors rights to lien a portion of salary, but this can be adjusted to fit the situation.) Please note, in this example you have actually given up these shares and the assets they represent. This can be a shame. On the other hand, without that happening, you would have lost the assets to a creditor not of your choosing.

By using this structure, you at least shifted the asset to someone you know, and you get income generated from the company in the form of a salary. I would also like to point out that there are laws governing fraud on creditors. These laws do not prevent you from properly protecting yourself and your family, but they are intended to stop what are called shame transactions, where there is no truth or substance to your actions. Since we are only talking about proper planning, these and other strategies should all be available to you and used when needed.

OFFSHORE BUSINESS

Now let's talk about one other method for setting up a business, but in this case we will talk about setting up an offshore business. You hear about it all the time, about people setting up offshore businesses. It is certainly more expensive, but it is also much more secure for liability protection.

A lot of people have set up offshore businesses to protect their profits by paying less in taxes and so forth. Well, this is not why I would recommend setting up an offshore business. I would primarily recommend that one consider setting up an offshore business for asset protection and/or liability protection. The simple fact of the matter is that if you make money, you should pay taxes. Not more than your fair share, but you should certainly be paying your taxes. Furthermore, the IRS is not stupid, so you can be sure that if you think you can get away with not paying your taxes, think again.

Okay, with that said, let's look at some specific examples of setting up offshore corporations and protecting your assets. The best place to set up an offshore corporation is in a country that is still under the Commonwealth (formally known as the Commonwealth of Nations and what used to be called the British Commonwealth). The laws are much more beneficial to your corporation.

Some of the more proactive places to set up an offshore corporation would be Belize, Panama, Seychelles, Cook Islands, Cayman Islands, and British Virgin Islands. There are others, such as up-and-coming Dubai in the UAE, but they are more expensive and a little harder to set up in than some of the other ones I have listed.

The cost to set up one of these offshore companies is a little more than what it would cost in the United States. In the United States, you can easily set up a company for about $150 to $300; for an offshore corporation, you will pay $2,000 to $10,000. If you want to open a U.S. corporation or a foreign corporation or trust, you can go to www.jdfn.com, which offers detailed information and help in finding the right company to assist you. There is also a link to a law firm that I use that can set up a U.S. corporation in any state you want.

So for liability's sake, let's say you open a company in Belize, and to better protect yourself, you create an offshore trust in the Bahamas. You would have the offshore trust own the company in Belize. You would make the beneficiary of the trust someone other than you, maybe a trust you have in the United States has the ownership. You then can be a director of the corporation and open a bank account on its behalf. But if you want to take the liability one step further, you can open your bank account in, say, the British Virgin Islands.

Now keep in mind that if you are a U.S. citizen and you open a bank account in another country, you will have to file the appropriate forms with the IRS, letting the agency know that you have a foreign bank account that you control. Also for tax purposes, if you own a foreign corporation and you are the majority owner of that company, the IRS considers the foreign corporation to be a closely held corporation and will tax the foreign corporation as it would any of your other assets. There may be some additional taxes that go along with that as well. You should talk to your CPA before taking this much more aggressive approach to protecting your assets.

In the example above, we actually don't have any ownership of the company, since we have a trust in the Bahamas that owns the company and we are not the beneficiary of the trust. However, in this example I would still claim the company as closely held, since I didn't set the company up for tax reasons but for liability reasons.

If for some reason someone wants to sue the company, he or she is going to have to sue a company that is domiciled in Belize, that is owned by a trust in the Bahamas, and that has a bank account in the British Virgin Islands. Good luck with that one. But, again, if you're making lots of money and your trading business is really doing well, you may want to consider protecting your hard-earned dollars from unscrupulous attorneys and frivolous lawsuits.

REGULATION IN
THE FOREX

C H A P T E R

8

COMMODITY FUTURES MODERNIZATION ACT

The Commodity Futures Modernization Act of 2000 (CFMA) was signed into law by President Clinton on December 21, 2000. The law represented a sweeping overhaul of the provisions of the Commodity Exchange Act (CEA). The law was prompted due to disagreements between two government regulatory agencies: the CFTC and the Securities and Exchange Commission (SEC).

When the SEC proposed easing its broker-dealer regulations for securities firms that were engaged in OTC derivatives, the CFTC objected, and a power struggle ensued. The CFTC questioned both the legality of derivatives for securities and the legality of oversight under the CEA.

The law addressed some vague areas regarding the status of OTC derivatives and hybrid instruments under the CEA through a number of statutory exclusions and exemptions. In addition, the law also addressed some unclear provisions regarding the status of certain nonretail swaps under the Securities Act of 1933 and the Securities Exchange Act of 1934 by clarifying that while such swaps are not securities under those statutes, specific fraud, manipulation, and insider trading prohibitions would nevertheless apply to certain security-based swap agreements. This legislation received a great deal of criticism in 2001 after the failure of Enron for its treatment of energy derivatives termed the "Enron loophole," and even more criticism followed the rescue of American General Insurance.

What makes sections of this law so important would not be truly felt by all of us until 2008. The effects of the law were well known to large banks, brokerages, and insurance companies, but were very much overlooked by the general public. The issue was credit default swaps, and in late 2008 the public received a crash course in an investment that most people had never even heard of.

A credit default swap is often referred to as an insurance policy that will protect a lender if a borrower (e.g., homeowner) defaults on a loan. When a lender purchases a credit default swap from an insurance company, the liability of the loan becomes a credit that may be "swapped" for cash upon the loan defaulting. The difference between a traditional insurance policy and a credit default swap is that anyone can buy the swap, even those who have no direct interest in the loan being repaid. This type of buyer is known as a speculator. If the borrower defaults on the loan, not only does the lender receive payment by the insurance company, but the speculator receives money as well. Although the lender can be protected by a credit default swap, it is always in the lender's best interest that the loan be repaid by the borrower.

In contrast, the only way for a speculator to profit is if the borrower actually defaults on the loan; only then will the speculator receive credit that, in turn, can be swapped for a cash payment from the insurance company. A credit default swap bought by a speculator is often referred to as a "bet to fail" because of its dependence on a borrower defaulting on a loan.

Credit default swaps have existed since the early 1990s, but the market for them increased tremendously starting in 2003 with a volume of about $3.7 trillion; by the end of 2007 the outstanding amount was $62.2 trillion, falling to $38.6 trillion by the end of 2008 after the market began to collapse. Credit default swaps are not traded on any exchange, and there is no required reporting of transactions to any regulatory body.

During the 2007–2010 financial crisis, this lack of transparency became a huge concern for regulators. They also felt that the massive size of this market and the lack of centralized clearing could pose a systemic risk to the economy. Those concerns were first recognized as being significant when the financial dominos began to fall in 2008; the chain reaction began with the failure of Bear Stearns.

In the days and weeks leading up to Bear's collapse, the spread on the bank's credit default swaps widened dramatically, indicating a huge surge of buyers taking out protection on the bank. This widening helped create a perception that Bear Stearns was vulnerable, which reduced Bear Stearns's access to capital and led to its forced sale to JP Morgan in March 2008.

The next domino fell in September 2008 with the bankruptcy of Lehman Brothers, resulting in close to $400 billion becoming payable to the buyers of the credit default swaps against the unexpectedly insolvent bank. However, since most positions were hedged, the netting of the positions meant that only about $7.2 billion actually changed hands. Next in line that same month was insurance giant American International Group (AIG). It required a bailout from the federal government because it had been excessively selling credit default swaps protection without hedging against the possibility that the reference entities might decline in value; this exposed the giant insurance company to potential losses of over $100 billion and led to the coining of the famous phrase "too big to fail."

Today almost everybody in the world knows about the financial crisis and the actions taken by the U.S. Treasury, the Federal Reserve, Congress, and two different presidents through the Troubled Asset Relief Program and bank bailouts. But these issues also spread around the globe, causing financial emergencies everywhere. So the question is, why would an insurance product cause so many problems?

Most Americans are used to the concept of insurance and the reserves required in order to meet obligations for claims; so why? Because credit default swaps are not actually insurance. I know, if it walks like a duck, quacks like a duck, and looks like a duck, it must be a duck; but in this case it's still not considered a duck—or insurance either. Therefore there are no reserves to back up the potential liability faced by the insurance company.

Now even though buying a credit default swap also resembles placing a bet, and the common term in credit swaps "bet to fail" would certainly give someone the impression that it's gambling, it's not considered gambling because specific wording was put into the law that would keep it from being considered that way and thus keep it from being subject to state gaming laws. These similarities, however, did not go unnoticed by state regulators around the United States.

The law's treatment of credit default swaps has received much attention for the two issues mentioned above. It has been argued by state insurance commissioners that credit default swaps should have been regulated as insurance and that the CFMA removed a valuable legal tool by preempting state bucket shop and gambling laws that could have been used to declare credit default swaps as illegal. In 1992, the Futures Trading Practices Act of 1992 preempted those state laws for financial derivatives covered by the CFTC's swaps exemption; however, a gap in the CFTC's powers prohibited it from exempting futures on nonexempt securities.

This loophole in the law meant that, before the CFMA, the CEA's preemption of state gambling and bucket shop laws would not have protected a credit default swap as nonexempt. The application of state laws to a credit default swap would depend upon a challenge in court, finding that a swap was a gambling, bucket shop, or otherwise illegal transaction. This was an important issue that led to the specific exclusion of credit default swaps and all security-based swaps from being labeled as gambling, which would have fallen under the jurisdiction of state gaming laws or resulted in being classified as insurance products that would be subject to state insurance regulations. The lobbyists did their job well in their claim that they were simply trying to keep business here in the United States, and the stage was set for the largest shell game in history.

There were those who had written that the CFMA was enacted in part to avoid having OTC derivatives transactions move offshore. AIG, which was the poster child for credit default swap abuse, located its controversial derivatives dealer (AIG Financial Products) in London, and it conducted its regulatory credit default swap transactions through a French bank because of the bank regulatory capital provision that allowed banks (not AAA-rated parties) to receive a reduced credit risk weighting for their obligations—including credit default swaps owed to other banks.

These actions helped disguise just how much risk existed in the system, and when those dominos began to fall, we were finally able to see just how big the problem had become. While most Americans believe that the bailouts were to cover bad loans, the reality was that the bailouts were simply covering the gambling debts of large financial institutions.

We can all imagine how different this latest crisis would have been if this legislation had not been passed or had been written with more common sense. We can probably all agree that the likelihood exists that credit default swaps will be remembered as the catalyst to a real estate market bubble and bust that nearly destroyed the world's economy, and had individual states been allowed to regulate this area that had been excluded by the CFMA, our economy would not have suffered so much harm.

9

THE FARM BILL

REGULATION IN THE FOREX MARKET

As mentioned in earlier chapters, the forex market is known as a spot market. You may be familiar with similar markets such as the spot gold or oil market. What differentiates a spot market is the fact that this is a cash market that is normally traded for immediate delivery of the commodity. However, when it comes to the retail forex spot market, no delivery of currencies is taking place, only the opening and closing of positions that are usually placed using a margin account—in other words, purchased or sold using leverage.

In the case of the forex, there is nothing to deliver. Therefore it did not qualify as a commodity. In fact, it simply fell between the regulatory cracks, so that no regulation of this burgeoning industry existed other than the CFTC stepping in when outright fraud was reported. While the lack of regulatory flaming hoops helped this new area of investing get a foothold and grow rapidly, there was a downside, one that always rears its ugly head when it involves people's money—corruption.

Because there was no regulation in this new industry, brokers began appearing everywhere. These companies could make any outrageous claim that they wanted to in order to gain investment dollars because there were very few people around to tell them no. The lack of regulation led to a great many abuses and caught the attention of those responsible for protecting the public. One result of this scrutiny was changes in the laws, and another was the implementation of oversight in this fledgling industry.

The first real change was a law that had been kicking around Congress for years; it was known as the 2008 farm bill, or H.R. 6124. On May 22, 2008, Congress passed the Food, Conservation, and Energy Act (a.k.a. the farm bill), which included the CFTC Reauthorization Act of 2008 (amending the CEA). This legislation reauthorized the CFTC's authority through 2013 and gave it enhanced jurisdiction over forex transactions. The new CFTC forex rules, which include new registration and capital requirements, are a result of this new legislation. Now you might wonder what farming has to do with the forex market, and that would be a very reasonable question. One of the areas covered under the farm bill had to do with commodities, which are a regular part of farming. Commodities include corn, orange juice, wheat, cattle, and hogs, just to name a few; commodities also include resources such as gold, silver, and oil.

Why does all this matter? Because under the new farm bill, commodities also included the spot forex market. Finally this new investment vehicle would face regulation under the CFTC. For the first time, the CFTC would be empowered by Congress to write new rules that would regulate the fast-growing forex market, and those new regulations would begin to clear out those firms that had been abusing the public trust by taking advantage of unsuspecting investors.

The CFTC said that it had seen a very large increase in cases of new investment opportunities coming on the scene, and some of them were very complex in nature and open for abuse. The CFTC specifically claimed that it noticed a significant rise in foreign currency trading scams.

The CFMA, which was passed in the year 2000, gave the CFTC the jurisdiction and authority to investigate and take action against a wide range of unregulated firms that offered foreign currency futures and options contracts to the retail public using counterparties that were not registered as futures commission merchants.

The first major change dealt with the requirement to be a registered entity with the National Futures Association (NFA), which is the self-regulatory organization (SRO) responsible for the oversight of the commodities industry. While many brokers were already members, quite a few were not. The second major shift was in the area of net capital; this refers to the required financial reserves that brokers would need to have on hand in order to protect their clients.

The regulation of financial reserves was implemented in stages, requiring $10 million in net capital beginning 120 days after the enactment of this clause, $15 million beginning 240 days after enactment of this clause, and $20 million beginning 360 days after the enactment of this clause. These single changes managed to push many smaller firms, which could not meet the net capital requirement, out of business.

The changes that were felt most by the investing public were both painful and unnecessary. Prior to these new regulations, margin leverage was available up to 400:1; but the NFA and CFTC believed that customers were at too great a risk and first dropped the maximum leverage to 100:1 and then ultimately all the way down to 50:1. While the argument about protecting customers from harm seemed noble, the fact remained that customers could trade foreign currency futures from commodity firms at leverages that exceeded 300:1. This contradiction did not go unnoticed during the industry's fight to block these new rules from taking effect.

While these new rules certainly had a profound effect on the brokers who acted as counterparties to trades, another matter of enormous change occurred in the regulation of money managers and IBs. The rules added requirements for these groups that had not existed in the past.

Money managers would need to register with the NFA as commodity trading advisors (CTAs); they would be required to hold a commodities license and pass qualification exams that would demonstrate their understanding of this business in which they were trading for their customers. The exams that need to be passed are the Series 3 and the Series 34, both of which are administered through the Financial Industry Regulatory Authority (FINRA). FINRA is the SRO responsible for the oversight of the securities industry.

Under the watchful eye of the NFA, brokers, CTAs, and IBs would no longer be able to make outrageous claims of success or promises of financial returns unless they could actually demonstrate that what they were saying was true. These types of rules would allow the regulatory bodies responsible for the industry to properly police the behavior of both members and nonmembers, thus protecting the investing public from harm.

10

DODD-FRANK WALL STREET REFORM AND CONSUMER PROTECTION ACT

At both the personal and business levels, these constant regulatory changes have created a nightmare for many in the financial industry and even more so in the forex marketplace. For me, the Dodd-Frank Act, yet again, forced me to change my business model and basically eliminated my already changed business practice stemming from the previous regulatory changes.

Just like many others in business, when these major changes took effect, I had to follow along. In some cases, hardworking people lost their jobs, and that was a travesty. I know of many corporate executives that believe the Dodd-Frank Act was the final straw, so to speak, for their businesses. Many business owners decided to move their business offshore completely. In most of these cases, people lost their jobs, and even more, the business services of asset management ceased to operate for U.S. citizens. Most of these now displaced companies are only working for non-U.S. citizens; which speaks volumes about the process of our congressional oversight.

In Chapter 8, we discussed the significant damage caused to our economy by credit default swaps under the CFMA. We now need to discuss the response to the financial crisis that we, as a nation, faced, and the impact that those changes have had on the forex market.

The financial crisis that began in 2007 and continued until 2010 caused a political firestorm throughout the United States and sparked demands for improvements in our regulatory system. In June 2009, despite a wave of criticism from his opposition, President Obama proposed new legislation that would profoundly transform the regulatory structure of the U.S. financial system in ways and scope not seen since the 1930s. The law got its name after being introduced in the House of Representatives by Congressman Barney Frank and in the Senate Banking Committee by then Chairman Chris Dodd. The original proposal from the president that was termed "A New Foundation" and included the following parts as its goals:

- The consolidation of regulatory agencies, the elimination of the national thrift charter, and a new oversight council to evaluate systemic risk.
- Comprehensive regulation of financial markets, including increased transparency of derivatives (eliminating OTC).
- Consumer protection reforms, including a new consumer protection agency and uniform standards for plain vanilla products, as well as strengthened investor protection.
- Tools for financial crises, including both a "resolution regime" complementing the existing authority of the Federal Deposit Insurance Corporation (FDIC) to allow for the orderly winding down of bankrupt firms and a proposal that the Federal Reserve receive authorization from the U.S. Treasury for extensions of credit in "unusual or exigent circumstances."
- Various measures aimed at increasing international standards and cooperation; included in this section were proposals related to improved accounting and tightened regulation of credit rating agencies.

The Dodd-Frank Act, according to the official title, was:

A bill to promote the financial stability of the United States by improving accountability and transparency in the financial system, to end "too big to fail," to protect the American taxpayer by ending bailouts, to protect consumers from abusive financial services practices, and for other purposes.

The law changes the existing regulatory structure by creating a host of new agencies in order to streamline the regulatory process regarding financial institutions, increase oversight of specific institutions regarded as a "systemic risk," and amend the Federal Reserve Act. The law establishes stringent standards and supervision to protect the U.S. economy, American consumers, investors, and businesses. It ends taxpayer-funded bailouts of financial institutions, provides for an advanced warning system on the stability of the economy, creates rules on executive compensation and corporate governance, and eliminates the loopholes that led to the economic recession.

Either the new agencies are granted explicit power over a particular aspect of financial regulation, or that power is transferred from an existing agency. All the new agencies, and some existing ones that are not currently required to do so, are also required under Dodd-Frank to report to Congress at least annually. Some newly created agencies include the Office of Financial Research, the Financial Stability Oversight Council, and the Bureau of Consumer Financial Protection. Changes were also made to existing agencies. The institutions impacted by these new changes include the Federal Reserve, the FDIC, the Securities Investor Protection Corporation, and the SEC.

For those of us involved in the forex market, it is important to note that prior to the passage of the Dodd-Frank Act, investment advisors were not required to register with the SEC if the investment advisor had fewer than 15 clients during the previous 12 months and did not hold itself out generally to the public as an investment advisor. But the Dodd-Frank Act eliminated that exemption, thereby rendering numerous investment advisors, hedge funds, and private equity firms subject to new registration requirements and driving a large number out of the country or out of the business entirely.

Let's break it down for those of you who trade the forex. How does it impact you?

- You cannot engage in OTC foreign currency transactions unless you trade through a government-approved firm. In other words, the firm must be registered with the CFTC and be a member of the NFA.
- The former exemption for money managers or financial advisors who had fewer than 15 clients is now gone. So if they intend to manage forex accounts or offer advice to clients who reside in the United States, they must become member firms of the NFA. This is similar to regulations you might have heard of that make online gambling (such as poker) illegal for U.S. citizens; even if the company you are dealing with is "offshore" and not located within the United States, it is illegal, and the U.S. government can go after the offending firm.
- You cannot engage in spot metal transactions unless you intend to take delivery within the allowed time period. The only nonconspiracy rationale for this particular action could be to inhibit speculation. However, since speculation in metals, through the use of commodity contracts, is still permitted, it is unclear what the true goal of this part of the act really was.

The reductions in margin leverage for the spot market from 100:1 to 50:1 that were written into the CFTC rules that took effect in October 2010 seem to match the perceived intention of these changes. The reason given by regulators was to reduce the risk of using high leverage that customers experience when trading in the spot market. But since the leverage available through commodity firms for both currency and metals is still higher than the previously available leverage in the spot market, one can only surmise that the true intention was to move this trading to the long-established and regulated CME, where the contracts would be traded as futures contracts.

In January 2011, Rep. Michele Bachmann (R-Minn.) introduced legislation to repeal the widely criticized Dodd-Frank financial reform measure that President Obama had signed into law. Bachmann, who made the move shortly after being sworn in for her third term, assailed the law as protecting Wall Street at the expense of taxpayers.

"I'm pleased to offer a full repeal of the job-killing Dodd-Frank financial regulatory bill," Bachmann said. "Dodd-Frank grossly expanded the federal government beyond its jurisdictional boundaries. It gave Washington bureaucrats the power to interpret and enforce the legislation with little oversight."

It appears that the Dodd-Frank Act may be repealed through a piecemeal process. As of May 2011, it is reported that the House Financial Services Capital Markets Subcommittee has passed several bills that would repeal or revise several of Dodd-Frank's more onerous provisions. Among them:

- The Data Collection Relief Act (H.R. 1062), sponsored by Rep. Nan Hayworth (R-N.Y.), would repeal Section 953(b) of the Dodd-Frank Act. Section 953(b) requires public issuers to disclose both the median annual total income for all employees except the CEO and the annual total income of the CEO and to calculate the ratio comparing the two figures.
- The Small Company Capital Formation Act (H.R. 1070), sponsored by Rep. David Schweikert (R-Ariz.), would amend the 1933 Securities Act to exempt securities offerings below $50 million from SEC registration. Currently, the offering threshold is $5 million.
- The United States Covered Bonds Act (H.R. 33), sponsored by subcommittee chairman Scott Garrett (R-N.J.), would create a U.S. covered bonds market.
- The Small Business Capital Access and Job Preservation Act (H.R. 1082), introduced by Rep. Robert Hurt (R-Va.), would repeal Dodd-Frank's requirement that private equity funds register with the SEC.
- The Business Risk Mitigation and Price Stabilization Act (H.R. 1610), introduced by Rep. Michael Grimm (R-N.Y.), would exempt legitimate end users from derivatives regulation mandated under the reform act.

- The Asset-Backed Market Stabilization Act (H.R. 1539), introduced by Rep. Steve Stivers (R-Ohio), would restore credit rating agencies' protection against expert liability under the 1933 act by repealing a Dodd-Frank provision that eliminated the exemption.
- The Church Plan Investment Clarification Act (H.R. 33), sponsored by Rep. Judy Biggert (R-Ill.), would amend the 1933 act to allow church plans to invest in collective trusts.

At a session in early May 2011, in a bill delaying implementation of swaps and derivatives regulations in Dodd-Frank, Frank Lucas (R-Okla.), chairman of the House Agriculture Committee, said:

> Efforts of Dodd-Frank to increase transparency and stability in our financial markets will be for naught if the regulatory process is rushed. We need to acknowledge that Dodd-Frank set *impractically tight deadlines* for the implementation of dozens of regulations that will touch every segment of the economy.

History will tell us if the Dodd-Frank Act survives the dislike that Wall Street has for it and the politics of providing funding that is required from the congressional representatives in Washington, D.C.

11

REGULATORY ACTION IN THE FOREX

In the early days of the retail forex, market abuses of the investing public were much too common, resulting in an initially bad reputation for the burgeoning forex market. In fact, if we go back no further than 2007, we can see case after case in which investors became the unwitting prey of unscrupulous forex firms.

In this chapter, I will discuss some of the older cases. I will not describe these cases in their entireties because they are lengthy; however, what I want to show you are some of the things that are and have been going on in the industry. In the earlier years, most of the improprieties were more related to futures than spot forex.

The CFTC banned many unprofessional brokers in the industry from the futures markets. Some of these individuals moved to the unregulated retail spot forex in the United States.

In many of the scams at the time, the brokers would take their customers' money, trading it in the spot forex and in the futures market, or just not trading it at all—which, in my opinion, is more appropriately labeled as stealing.

You will read that the industry had a bad reputation for customers using the market for illicit purposes such as money laundering.

The cash markets were an easy place to launder money. Criminals were sending in cash to be traded through offshore destinations.

Some of these practices resulted in much stronger and tighter anti–money laundering practices. That coupled with the changes made after 9/11 reduced money laundering within the spot retail forex significantly, as the broker became primarily responsible for knowing where the money was coming from.

CFTC CASE #1

February 11, 2004
U.S. COMMODITY FUTURES TRADING COMMISSION CHARGES FLORIDA FOREIGN CURRENCY OPTIONS FIRM WITH DEFRAUDING CUSTOMERS
Company and Firm Lied When Pitching Foreign Currency Options to Customers. Forex Broker Also Charged.

The CFTC filed a complaint in a Florida federal district court against a Florida corporation and residents of Boca Raton, Florida, and the surrounding area for allegedly defrauding customers they solicited to trade foreign currency options. The complaint also charged a New York–based foreign currency dealer with liability as a principal for the acts of its IB.

A federal district court judge issued a restraining order freezing the assets of the IB and principals. The restraining order also prohibited those defendants and the broker from destroying documents.

The complaint alleged that starting in May 2002, the IB and principals solicited at least 267 members of the retail public to trade foreign currency (forex) options through the broker. According to the complaint, the IB used aggressive, high-pressure sales tactics, including (1) making false promises of large profits, (2) misrepresenting the broker's expertise and track record, and (3) downplaying the risks inherent in trading forex currency options contracts.

The complaint also alleged that the IB failed to disclose that one of the principals had previously been enjoined by a federal court from committing solicitation fraud in connection with options, and that the CFTC had issued a cease and desist order against this person, also prohibiting him from committing options fraud (CFTC Docket No. 94–8, December 9, 1993).

The complaint further alleged that this person was responsible for the majority of trading decisions made on behalf of the IB's customers and that he made deceptive and misleading statements to customers and prospective customers regarding the profit potential and inherent risks associated with trading foreign currency options contracts. The complaint alleged that these actions violated the antifraud provisions of the CEA and CFTC regulations. As alleged, the IB's president, vice president, and compliance manager, were charged in the complaint as the IB's controlling persons.

According to the complaint, more than $3 million of the IB's customer funds was deposited and traded at the brokerage. The complaint alleged that, through an exclusive IB-brokerage business relationship in which the IB acted as the broker's agent, the broker paid the IB over $800,000 in commissions in connection with the customers' accounts that the IB introduced.

This was more of a case where the former futures individuals had previously been in trouble and moved to the forex market.

CFTC CASE #2

Another blatant case resulted in an order from the U.S. district court that the owner and his company would have to pay over $33 million in restitution and civil penalties for engaging in fraud in the sale and solicitation of illegal forex futures contracts and misappropriating customer funds.

The owner was also sentenced to 97 months in prison. The firm solicited customers to participate in a forex fund, and in order to do so the firm misrepresented the profit and risks in forex trading, it issued false account statements, and it used new-customer monies to pay off other customers' fictitious profits on their investments.

This case represented a typical Ponzi scheme, which is an incredibly common theme when it comes to investment scams. On that subject, let's take a brief look at how a Ponzi scheme works and some of the ways to recognize the signs.

What Is a Ponzi Scheme?

A Ponzi scheme is an investment fraud that involves the payment of purported returns to existing investors from funds contributed by new investors. Ponzi scheme organizers often solicit new investors by promising to invest funds in opportunities claimed to generate high returns with little or no risk. In many Ponzi schemes, the fraudsters focus on attracting new money to make promised payments to earlier-stage investors and to use for personal expenses, instead of engaging in any legitimate investment activity.

Why Do Ponzi Schemes Collapse?

With little or no legitimate earnings, the schemes require a consistent flow of money from new investors to continue. Ponzi schemes tend to collapse when it becomes difficult to recruit new investors or when a large number of investors ask to cash out.

How Did Ponzi Schemes Get Their Name?

The schemes are named after Charles Ponzi, who duped thousands of New England residents into investing in a postage stamp speculation scheme back in the 1920s. At a time when the annual interest rate for bank accounts was 5 percent, Ponzi promised investors that he could provide a 50 percent return in just 90 days. Ponzi initially bought a small number of international mail coupons in support of his scheme, but he quickly switched to using incoming funds to pay off earlier investors.

What Are Some Ponzi Scheme "Red Flags"?

Many Ponzi schemes share common characteristics. Look for these warning signs:

- *High investment returns with little or no risk.* Every investment carries some degree of risk, and investments yielding higher returns typically involve more risk. Be highly suspicious of any "guaranteed" investment opportunity.
- *Overly consistent returns.* Investments tend to go up and down over time, especially those seeking high returns. Be suspect of an investment that continues to generate regular, positive returns regardless of overall market conditions.
- *Unregistered investments.* Ponzi schemes typically involve investments that have not been registered with the SEC or with state regulators. Registration is important because it provides investors with access to key information about the company's management, products, services, and finances.

- *Unlicensed sellers.* Federal and state securities laws require investment professionals and their firms to be licensed or registered. Most Ponzi schemes involve unlicensed individuals or unregistered firms.
- *Secretive or complex strategies.* Avoiding investments you don't understand or for which you can't get complete information is a good rule of thumb.
- *Issues with paperwork.* Ignore excuses regarding why you can't review information about an investment in writing, and always read an investment's prospectus or disclosure statement carefully before you invest. Also, account statement errors may be a sign that funds are not being invested as promised.
- *Difficulty receiving payments.* Be suspicious if you don't receive a payment or have difficulty cashing out your investment. Keep in mind that Ponzi scheme promoters sometimes encourage participants to roll over promised payments by offering even higher investment returns.

CFTC CASE #3

In December 2007, the CFTC concluded an action that had been filed in 2005 regarding forex boiler room fraud. That action resulted in $3.4 million in sanctions against a firm and its principal after concluding that they had defrauded customers who lost more than $1.7 million trading in the forex.

The CFTC was awarded a default judgment order against the firm. The judgment found that the firm had fraudulently operated a foreign currency (forex) boiler room, and the judgment permanently prohibited the defendants from engaging, directly or indirectly, in any business activities related to commodity trading.

The original complaint alleged that beginning in December 2001 the defendants fraudulently solicited investments from at least 160 retail customers in forex contracts. During those solicitations, the defendants made false promises of high returns; failed to disclose hidden commission charges; issued account statements that falsely characterized the undisclosed commissions as trading losses; made false representations regarding the risk of forex trading, as well as their experience and past performance in trading forex; and misappropriated customer funds.

In April 2007, the court granted the CFTC's summary judgment motion and ordered penalties, including more than $2 million in monetary sanctions, against the firm, its principals, and employees.

CFTC CASE #4

One of the bigger and more disturbing CFTC cases was resolved in 2009 when the agency obtained an emergency court order freezing assets held by two Minnesota residents and their firms. All were charged by the CFTC with fraud and misappropriation in connection with off-exchange leveraged foreign currency (forex) trading.

The court's order also prohibited the destruction of books and records and provided the CFTC access to such documents. The CFTC charged the defendants with running a massive forex scheme that defrauded hundreds of customers of more than $190 million. The court's order originated from a CFTC complaint, filed under seal in November 2009 in the U.S. District Court for the District of Minnesota, charging the defendants with running a massive forex scheme since 2006.

The complaint also charged that the defendants misappropriated customer funds to purchase property, develop a hotel and casino, buy seven luxury cars, and purchase a houseboat and a submarine, as well as fund their frequent gambling.

The defendants allegedly solicited customers to trade forex by fraudulently claiming that, since 2003, they earned more than 10 percent annual profits and sustained no losses. The defendants also claimed that customers' funds were placed in managed, segregated accounts with a Swiss company that was majority-owned by one of the firm's principals since December 2008.

Instead, defendants misappropriated customer funds and continued to solicit and accept funds until July 2009, even though the Swiss Financial Market Supervisory Authority placed the Swiss forex firm in question into receivership in December 2008 and into bankruptcy in May 2009. The defendants allegedly perpetuated their fraud by providing customers with account statements that falsely depicted their accounts as earning from 10 to 12 percent in annual profits.

CFTC CASE #5

Even firms outside the United States are not immune to the actions of federal regulators. On December 7, 2010, the CFTC announced the filing of an enforcement action in the U.S. District Court for the District of Utah against a private Mexican financial services holding company, and its foreign currency (forex) trading division, with issuing false customer statements and misrepresenting trading results on the company's Web site in connection with the company's foreign currency trading enterprise. This particular group had never been registered, in any capacity, with the CFTC.

The CFTC's complaint alleged that, from at least 2005 to 2010, the defendants accepted at least $28 million from more than 800 U.S. customers for the purpose of trading forex on behalf of customers in pooled accounts. The complaint further alleged that, from June 2008 through April 2009, the defendants reported trading profits when, in fact, they lost approximately $19.4 million.

The defendants allegedly reported trading profits in at least eight separate months, when they actually incurred substantial trading losses, often exceeding $1 million per month. So no place is safe from the CFTC when it sees wrongdoing in the forex markets.

CFTC CASE #6

On January 26, 2011, in its first action since the new rules took effect in October 2010, the CFTC decided to sue 14 foreign currency firms in a nationwide sweep. The CFTC announced that it simultaneously filed 13 enforcement actions in federal district courts in Chicago, the District of Columbia, Kansas City, and New York, alleging that 14 entities were illegally soliciting members of the public to engage in foreign currency (forex) transactions and that they were operating without being registered with the CFTC.

These new regulations require entities that wish to participate in the forex market to register with the CFTC and abide by regulations intended to protect the public. These regulations require that forex dealers take steps to protect investors, including maintaining minimum capital and proper records, which would reduce risk and increase transparency throughout the industry.

In the forex market, entities known as retail foreign exchange dealers (RFEDs) or futures commission merchants (FCMs) may buy foreign currency contracts from or sell foreign currency contracts to individual investors. Under the CEA and CFTC regulations, an entity acting as an RFED or FCM must register with the CFTC and abide by the rules and regulations designed for investor protection, including those relating to minimum capital requirements, record keeping, and compliance. Further, with a few exceptions, such an entity also must be registered with the CFTC if that entity solicits or accepts orders from U.S. investors in connection with forex transactions conducted at an RFED or FCM.

In all but two of the complaints, the CFTC alleged that a defendant acted as an RFED; that is, it offered to take or took the opposite side of a customer's forex transaction without being registered. In the remaining two complaints, the CFTC alleged that the defendants solicited customers to place forex trades at an RFED without being registered as an IB.

In every complaint, the CFTC alleged that the defendants solicited or accepted orders from U.S. investors to enter into forex transactions in violation of the act. The CFTC had moved for preliminary injunctions preventing these defendants from operating unless and until they complied with the CEA and CFTC regulations. The CFTC's complaints also sought civil monetary penalties, trading and registration bans, disgorgement, and rescission.

I strongly urge the public to check whether a forex firm is registered before investing funds. If a company operating in the United States is not a member of the NFA or registered with the CFTC, an investor should be wary of providing funds to that company.

While the CFTC represents regulatory oversight and enforcement actions against forex firms at the federal level, the NFA is an SRO charged with the oversight of its members. In many cases, the end result of NFA-originated actions can be seen in CFTC actions like those I have just discussed. The NFA also has the ability to sanction and bar members. Let's take a look at a few of these cases.

NFA CASE #1

In April 2010, the NFA permanently barred a forex firm, registered as a CTA and located in Illinois, from NFA membership. The decision by the NFA also barred the firm's principal from NFA membership for a period of two years. The firm's principal would have to pay a fine of $5,000 in order to reapply for NFA membership after the expiration of the two-year bar.

The decision that was issued by an NFA hearing panel was based on an NFA complaint filed in August 2009 and a settlement offer submitted by the forex firm and its principal. As part of its settlement, the firm agreed to permanently withdraw from NFA membership and consent to findings that it committed the violations alleged in the complaint without admitting or denying the allegations.

The panel found that the firm used a misleading Web site, as well as misleading customer account documents. As alleged in the complaint, all the U.S. customers with whom the NFA spoke expressed confusion regarding the nonregulated forex firm that they were doing business with, as well as which entities were actually regulated by the NFA.

NFA CASE #2

In October 2010, the NFA ordered a forex dealer member from New York to pay a fine of $320,000 as a result of a complaint issued by the NFA and a settlement offer submitted by the firm and its principal. The complaint alleged that the firm engaged in certain price slippage practices on the MetaTrader platform that were favorable to it and caused disadvantageous trading conditions for certain customers.

The complaint also charged that the forex firm failed to supervise the MetaTrader platform used for its forex business and also failed to supervise the firm's operations. In addition to having to pay the fine, the firm had to provide appropriate refunds to its customers as a result of these asymmetrical slippage practices. The firm and its principal neither admitted nor denied the charges.

NFA CASE #3

At the same time in another case the NFA ordered a forex dealer member located in New Jersey to pay a $459,000 fine as a result of a complaint issued by the NFA and a settlement offer submitted by the firm and its chief executive officer.

The NFA's Business Conduct Committee alleged that the forex firm engaged in abusive margin, liquidation, and price slippage practices that benefited the firm to the detriment of its customers. The committee also alleged that the firm failed to maintain records for certain unfilled orders, failed to adequately review the activities and promotional material of the firm's unregistered solicitors, and failed to supervise the firm's operations. In addition to having to pay the fine amount, the forex firm also had to provide appropriate refunds to its customers as a result of these detrimental margin, liquidation, and asymmetrical slippage practices. The firm and its chief executive officer neither admitted nor denied the charges.

It is clear from these cases that the CFTC and the NFA take the abuses of customers very seriously and will not hesitate to bring appropriate action in order to protect the investing public. With that in mind, it is the responsibility of the members of the investing public to do their own due diligence when choosing a forex firm. Remember the old saying, "If it sounds too good to be true, it probably is."

NFA CASE #4

On June 30, 2008, the NFA issued a complaint charging a broker with failure to implement an adequate anti–money laundering program. The complaint also charged the broker and principal with failure to supervise and failure to implement an adequate anti–money laundering program.

On April 24, 2009, a designated panel of the Hearing Committee issued a decision to the broker and principal after a hearing was held. The hearing panel determined that the NFA did not prove the failure to supervise charge; therefore, Count II was dismissed with prejudice. The hearing panel ordered the broker to pay a $250,000 fine and to retain an independent auditing firm to conduct four semiannual audits to review compliance with the Bank Secrecy Act, the implementing regulations, the NFA's anti–money laundering rules, and the broker's own anti–money laundering procedures.

On January 21, 2010, the NFA's Appeals Committee issued a decision affirming the hearing panel's decision about the broker. In addition, the Appeals Committee reversed the hearing panel's finding that the NFA did not establish that the principal violated NFA Compliance Rule 2–36(e) and ordered the principal to pay a $50,000 fine.

One of the more high-profile frauds was the downfall and ultimate bankruptcy of Refco. Let's take a look at how the Refco collapse has affected the retail forex industry.

THE REFCO IPO AND SCANDAL

One of the more high-profile frauds was the downfall and ultimate bankcruptcy of Refco, Inc., which specialized in forex and commodities. The company was actually one of the main futures brokers on the CME. In 2005, the company started to come tumbling down. Refco was forced into filing Chapter 11 bankruptcy from creditors. News about the CEO's involvement in the company's mass fraud practices was about to break, including the fact that the CEO hid the company's bad debts, which stemmed from loans by Bawag P.S.K, the fourth largest bank in Austria.

The timing of the bankruptcy was ironic, coming shortly on the heels of an initial public offering Refco was involved in. This raised the eyebrows of some of the regulators and, of course, some of Refco's newest investors. By holding the looming revelations from the public, it was evident that the management may have helped inflate the stock's initial offering.

The shares were offered to the public at an initial price of $22 per share through a number of different investment banks; some of the banks were the largest on Wall Street. You can imagine the black eye they were about to receive, since the banks should have done their due diligence on the company's financials in the first place.

A quick review of how the Refco stock did will show that the shares were traded publicly for about two months, with a high of

$30.12 on September 7, 2005. The fraud announcement happened in October of the same year, barely a month after the high. As a result, investors ran for the hills in a panic, sending the 26.5 million shares of the newly public company crashing to just $0.80 a share.

Apparently the CEO was padding the company's financials by hiding $430 million in bad debts through various subsidiaries. This would create a problem for Refco's other companies including its forex brokerage business.

Refco FX, LLC, had just over 17,000 retail customer brokerage accounts at the time that it declared bankruptcy. In the bankruptcy proceedings, Bank of America, along with other major creditors, convinced the bankruptcy court that the customers were actually unsecured creditors. Refco hadn't segregated the customers' funds, even though the company had told the customers it did, causing the customers to become unsecured creditors.

This legal action by the large creditors essentially sealed the fate of the Refco forex customers. They were now treated as unsecured creditors and had to wait in line after the secured creditors got their money. This probably would not happen in today's regulatory environment. But you never know.

Another forex firm tried to come in and actually buy the customers from Refco, but it was unsuccessful in doing so. The customers basically lost anything they had left in their accounts and were able to recover just pennies on the dollar, if anything.

Refco creditors ultimately lost about $2.4 billion in total and recouped about half of that back.

RECENT CASES

Let's take a look at some of the most recent litigation going on in the industry on a retail basis, at the time of writing.

A large law firm in Florida has recently filed a class-action lawsuit against a prominent forex broker alleging fraud and racketeering by the nation's largest forex dealer.

The lawsuit, filed in the U.S. District Court for the Southern District of New York (Manhattan Division), alleges that the broker has bilked thousands of customers out of hundreds of millions of dollars using deceptive and unfair trade practices, including falsely portraying its forex trading platform as a fair, transparent, and true foreign currency exchange when instead it is a "rigged game" designed to systematically separate customers from their money.

The plaintiff brought the action on behalf of himself and all others similarly situated, accusing the broker of fraud by misrepresenting itself as a trading platform that is free from dealer intervention or manipulation. Instead, the plaintiff alleges, the broker used a number of devices and tricks, including software applications, designed specifically to interfere with the customers' trades.

The complaint further alleges that the broker engaged in a pattern of racketeering activity by collaborating with its software developers and programmers to develop a "diabolical" software application that provided the broker with a myriad of tools and system commands in which to interfere with customers' trades, including routing trades to "slow" servers and sending false "error" messages when customers attempted to close out profitable trades.

Finally, the plaintiff alleges in the complaint that the broker lured thousands of customers to its trading platform by promoting a "demo account," which was touted as providing customers with a true market trading experience. Instead, he claims, once "live" trading commenced, the broker deployed specially designed software to manipulate customers' trades.

The law firm believes this will be an important step in bolstering accountability in an industry that has been largely unregulated since inception. The law firm believes, as the complaint alleges, that the broker has taken advantage of the trust placed in it by its customers, causing substantial financial harm to this group of people, and the firm is committed to working to recover those losses.

There is unfortunately a multitude of litigation on the horizon for some of these crooked forex dealers. I would suggest that you simply stay informed about who is doing what and when. You can always go to www.jdfn.com to stay up to date on current litigation in the forex market.

FOREX BROKER SCHEMES

12

BACK-OFFICE SOFTWARE SCAMS

By the time you read this, you should have come to realize that most forex brokers use various tactics to separate you from the deposits in your trading account. But as a trader, it may be difficult to recognize the various tools your broker is using against you. Brokers have very sophisticated and specialized software at their disposal designed specifically for the purpose of trading against your positions. In this chapter, we take a deeper look into what your broker is doing to you, as you will soon realize there is more to the story than your broker just taking a counterposition to your trade.

The advanced software that brokers have in place allows them to "steal" money right from under your nose without your even knowing it is taking place. Have you ever wondered why when using your practice account or demo account, you never seem to have a losing trade? Have you ever wondered why brokers so aggressively push their practice accounts or demo accounts?

There is a reason for this madness, at least from the broker's standpoint; it flows right into the next question. Now that you have decided to trade real money and you have funded your account, why is it you can't seem to place a profitable trade, even though you're not doing anything differently than you were in your demo or practice account provided by your broker?

How could this be? In a demo or practice account, you are receiving straight-through pricing (STP), with your broker's commissions or markup added to it to give you the bid and ask prices. This is pretty straightforward; when you place the trade in the demo or practice account, the price you see is the price you get; however, move ahead to your live account, and this is not always the case. Brokers have a financial incentive for you to lose money as long as they are the counterparty to the trade; the more you lose, the more they make. So let's discuss some of the sinister tools your broker-dealer has leveraged against you to ensure your losses and a financial windfall for your broker-dealer ... at your expense.

VIRTUAL DEALER PLUG-IN

I would like to start by discussing the Virtual Dealer Plug-In; sounds harmless enough, right? The Virtual Dealer Plug-In has a number of ways to take advantage of the unsuspecting customer. It allows the broker-dealer to compete with you and have complete success in comparison with your trade account by manipulating trades with manual execution orders through forex symbols or groups.

The Virtual Dealer Plug-In implements a number of features that leave traders believing they are placing legitimate orders; however, the broker can delay your order fill times by several seconds to allow for market movement against you from the time you placed your trade until the broker fills your order. The plug-in also will check your limit, stop levels, and freeze levels, allowing the broker to make the difference at your expense. Virtual Dealer Plug-Ins also process pending-order activations, stop triggers, and stop-outs; this will allow the broker to literally move the market to trigger your stop and take you out of a trade with a loss.

These plug-ins have the ability to stream prices for instant execution with adjustable slippage rates. This will allow a predetermined number of pips to be added to any entry or exit you place in the market, increasing the broker-dealer's bottom line as you lose money. The Virtual Dealer Plug-In will use automated shift parameters to move the limit, stop levels, and freeze levels according to the preset list of news events and times. And it will disable settings, modifying and deleting pending orders during news events, leaving the trader totally helpless during the market's most active times, often resulting in substantial loss or even liquidation of your trade account.

SLIPPAGE

The Virtual Dealer Plug-In allows the broker-dealer to work your order. All brokers receive a number of prices from their prime bank; however, they only show you an aggregated or average price. Using slippage, your broker can fill your trade at the worst price the market has to offer, fill the trade for itself at the best price in the market, and hold the counterposition to the trade. This is instant profit for the broker-dealer with virtually no risk; the broker-dealer simply makes up the difference from where it filled you at the worst price and where it is holding the trade at the best price—in essence, free money for the broker-dealer.

GAP

This Virtual Dealer Plug-In decreases the likelihood that a market gap will impact the broker adversely. If the market gaps or the price moves beyond the gap spread previously set by the broker-dealer, the broker-dealer can issue a requote to the trader, making the trade you place null and void. However, if the price jumps within the spread, the price will be taken and delivered.

NEWS TRADING AND VOLATILE MARKET CONDITIONS

Brokers can set spreads to widen at a time of volatility, usually around news events or important announcements. Brokers set the Virtual Dealer interface to increase spreads at times when the market may be most volatile, thus penalizing traders for trading when the market is most active and liquid all the while increasing the brokers' profit margin.

To top it off, many brokers trade against you using your own deposits! How can this happen? Very simply; what brokers will do is put all the customer deposits into their prime broker account and allow you to trade margin on your position. However, using the brokers' leverage, you only ever touch a fraction of the deposited amount, leaving a large portion of the account balance untouched in the broker's account. When you place your position at the market, brokers will use the deposits left in the prime broker account as the counter to the trade, potentially using your own money to trade against you and keeping the money they systematically siphon from trades you place as their profit without ever touching any of their own capital.

I was in a situation not too long ago when an acquaintance who works at a major forex broker was bragging to me how much his firm was trading in the forex every day. I thought that was pretty bold considering that the firm was essentially trading customers' money. The firm may trade some of its money, but in reality it is just placing trades against its customer. If it runs a dealing desk, then it is placing trades against its customers. And if it is not running a dealing desk, it is probably placing trades against its customers. Even if it is running STP, it is still getting access to all its customers' money that is free from margin.

These are only a few of the tools and automated systems that brokers have spent millions of dollars to purchase and develop to trade against their customers. As you can see, even if your broker claims not to have a dealing desk, in today's technology-driven environment brokers no longer need a trader at the other end to make the orders. They can rely on complex computer algorithms, dealer interfaces, and software plug-ins to do the job with near flawless execution.

13

SLOW SERVERS AND ERRORS

In this chapter—one of the most important in this book—I will talk about not only what I know from an extensive two-year investigation that I conducted on my own but also what I have learned from personal experience in my trading. Unfortunately, what I discovered was that the devious practices I found are not specific to just one broker but apply to many; we all know brokers who use some of these unscrupulous tactics.

With that said, let me clarify that not all brokers are bad. But I have found, through my own trading experiences, that most of them seem to be that way. As noted above, I spent the better part of two years investigating the brokers in the forex industry. It was a personal crusade. The reason I spent so much time trying to get to the bottom of what was going on is simple. I wanted to know why a perfectly sound and tested trading strategy could go bad all of a sudden, and have nothing to do with changing market conditions. I have witnessed my accounts go down for no specific reason and felt something strange was going on.

During my investigations, I uncovered how brokers use latency to their advantage. Latency, or slow fills, is a benefit to brokers and certainly not something we want to deal with; but when we are setting up our trading systems, we want to make sure that we have the most direct access to the banks as possible.

That means every server you use, including your desktop or laptop, and every broker you employ will slow the transaction down. Every time a broker is between your trade and the bank, things can go wrong. The problem is that we cannot easily go directly to the bank. Most prime banks, such as Bank of America, require very large minimum deposits to trade directly with them. You can trade directly with them as your tier one provider, but they are going to require that you have at minimum $150 million to open your account.

There are other such banks out there that will provide an interim or entry-level solution. They will require much less money, some as little as $500,000, and then they aggregate the balances to basically have their one account with a prime bank. This will help you in your executions, but in the end you have to know what is going on so that you can beat the banks and the brokers at their own game.

Slow servers are something most commonly used by brokers that are trading against your account. The reason they want to slow down your trade execution is so that they can go into the marketplace and get a better price themselves before taking your trade, whether to open or close. Any time you have slow fills on your trades, you should immediately suspect that something is going on.

You will mainly see this happen when you are trading large amounts or if your account has been profitable for some time. One of the things that you can do to help protect yourself is to continually take the profits out of your account. Every time you hit a predetermined growth in your account, you should simply withdraw the excess.

At some point you will be trading the bank's money literally, instead of your money. If you want to keep compounding your profits, open another account at a different broker; that way you can stay off the radar and elude detection as a trader that makes too much money.

During my investigations, I have seen various e-mails that were communications within a brokerage and that specifically talked about providing different servers to different levels of customers.

The different servers each have their own special settings. MetaTrader alone has at least five servers. If you are familiar with trading with MetaTrader, then you know that you can see a multiple of different servers.

In my case, when I was trading one of my most successful accounts, I was using a MetaTrader terminal. About nine months into no month-over-month drawdowns, I received an e-mail letting me know that my broker was worried about my not getting the best fills, and so the firm was moving me to a new server—a better, faster server, according to the company. The funny (or not so funny) thing was that I never had a profitable month again after I was moved to the new server. I was inundated with errors, slow fills, and no fills. The latency was ridiculous; my trades had slippage on what seemed to be every single trade.

Further, reading through the e-mails that I had access to, I was able to find that not only do the brokers that use MetaTrader have multiple MetaTrader servers, but they actually have specific servers for slowing down the trades. In addition, I found that these servers not only slow the trade but also have a myriad, sometimes thousands, of different settings to assist brokers in separating you from your money.

If you asked those brokers about the many servers with thousands of settings, they would say that all those servers and settings are needed for risk management. That might be so, but the risk management they are talking about is managing the risk that you are making money but they are not. So they have to eliminate the risk, at your expense. I know this because that is what numerous brokers did to me, and this is what they said when I confronted them about their slow fills, errors, slippage, etc.

So pay close attention to your trades; if for some reason when you push the TRADE button your order is not going through in milliseconds, then something may be wrong. Put your broker on the spot; use e-mail and find out what is going on. If you find that you cannot get off the slow server, then change brokers.

Use the e-mails as your chain of information and save them for your records. I have found that when you talk to your brokers on the phone, they will say one thing; but when you get an e-mail response, they are much more likely to take a position and stick to it. Keep in mind that the brokers are required to record their calls.

OFF-PRICE QUOTES

You will find the errors of off-price quotes primarily on MetaTrader terminals, but I have seen the error message on other broker platforms as well. This is yet another way to eliminate your chances of making money trading. The "off-price quote" error message will usually come up in fast-moving markets when the broker will have a hard time shopping your order.

When you see this error message, you know that the broker is working your trades. I have been in trades and tried to get out, only to click the CLOSE TRADE button and get the off-price quote error. Worse yet, I have been in profitable trades and attempted to close the trades repeatedly, in some instances 10 to 20 times—and repeatedly got the error message—before I finally got my trades executed, only to find that I lost money on the trades. Bet the broker didn't lose money on my trades.

You can go to your logs on your computer and see the games that are being played. The software trading platforms that you use will normally leave logs of the trades on your system. MetaTrader definitely does. You can sift through these logs and see the errors and when they occurred. Quite frankly, the logs are fairly interesting to read after the fact. You can clearly see patterns of when the brokers are specifically targeting you. Go to www.jdfn.com to see more on how to find and read your logs.

TRADE CONTEXT BUSY

This is an error that is more prevalent using expert advisors or robots on MetaTrader. If you are using robots and happen to be using several on the same currency pair, you will find this error come up. Basically, what is happening is that your individual robots are trying to hit the server at the same time to get in or out of a trade. Your robots can only make one trade at a time. There is also a known setting on the back-office MetaTrader manager using the dealer plug-ins that can allow the broker to reject the order of whomever the broker wants to freeze out of a trade.

WORKING ORDERS

Ah, the working order, what a ridiculous error! I am not even sure my broker knew that this was a trading terminal error. I have personally witnessed this one too many times. In fact, this error came from a software platform from a broker with an employee who swore to me that his firm didn't work my orders.

On more than one occasion, I have tried to open or close a trade, only to place the trade and then, after clicking the TRADE button, wait while the trade would just sit there. The terminal would be flashing "working order." Seriously, can you believe the order screen just sat there flashing "working order," and it would sometimes take up to a minute before the trade would execute. Bet the broker got a better price than I did.

You see, the broker would simply work the order to get a better price and then offer me the higher price. By the time the order was worked, the broker would make the spread on the trade plus the difference in price it gave me for the trade—inexcusable!

Please keep in mind that whenever you have any of these issues, you can call the broker's trade or dealing desk and basically give the person there a hard time. Most people will say sorry, the price is the price on the first go-around, but if you stay persistent, you will ultimately get what you are asking for.

In the end, the broker does not want you to file a complaint with the NFA. Hint, hint . . . don't put up with that garbage. All brokers have software that can tell them exactly what the price was at any given second, including the spreads that were offered at a specific time.

SERVER BUSY

This is another error you will find when the broker is working your trade. All these errors will basically fall under the slow server category, since these are all variations of ways for the broker to slow your trade down and ultimately make money on the trade. You will most likely see this during busy market conditions but not all the time. In the end it comes down to the broker making money—not you.

I have had situations when the "server busy" error message was a huge problem. In one instance, I was trading with multiple trades and lots on the board. The market started moving on me, and I started to close trades. I kept getting the "server busy" message and was canceling the order to get it placed; ultimately what happened was that my orders were closed and the broker doubled up my orders so that I was now in the market on the other side. My trade manager didn't show the open positions, and the next day I found out that I was still in the trade the other way. Lucky for me, I made money, so I didn't have to beat up anyone at the broker's office.

SLIPPAGE AND STOP HUNTING

SLIPPAGE

Let's talk about one of our favorites, slippage. I think all of us who trade find that at some point during our trading we experience slippage. Well, the forex market is certainly ripe for this practice. With the big movements in the forex market, it is easy for the brokers to create slippage. So you need to keep an eye on the unscrupulous brokers out there.

There have been some substantial investigations under way by the NFA on its member retail forex firms. You can visit the NFA's Web site for a current list of registered forex firms. The NFA wants to see whether firms take advantage of small price movements that occur between the time when a customer orders a trade and the time when that trade is executed—slippage. I personally know of several complaints about this very practice that are about to be filed with the NFA on numerous brokers within the industry. For an ever-growing number of retail forex traders, this is something that just isn't common knowledge—the fact that their brokers may be trading against them.

The forex dealer is usually on the other side of the customer's trade, and so it becomes beneficial for the broker to make sure the price has some slippage. Even if the broker is sending your trade straight through to the liquidity provider, it becomes more profitable for the broker to slip the price a bit. This slippage goes right into the broker's pocket as profit on the transaction. Normally in the equities markets, brokers buy and sell stocks for their customers with best-price execution a top priority.

Here is the worst part: In the fine print at the bottom of your customer application when you open your account, you will find language that basically says that the brokers acknowledge the trading conflict; further the fine-print text will go on to say that the brokers may take positions against their customers. It normally states that the brokers can basically offer any price they choose, at any time. You will see some disclosures that reveal that the brokers may even offer different prices to different customers.

This becomes a more significant problem as the retail off-exchange spot forex market keeps growing. Retail forex trades now make up about $300 billion in turnover a day, and this may be a conservative number; the actual number may be far more than that. The overall forex turnover is now on average better than $3 trillion a day, and some estimates put it closer to $4 trillion a day, a significant growth since my first book was released in 2003–2004, which reported that the retail forex turnover was about $1.9 trillion a day.

The forex dealers will have you believe that they are acting within the rules and regulations; these regulations are currently set by the CFTC and the NFA. However, these regulatory agencies have stepped up their oversight on the retail forex industry and are conducting numerous inquiries and investigations, all aimed at creating a fair and orderly marketplace for the retail forex industry. Let's hope they succeed.

Larry Dyekman, a spokesman for the NFA, recently said this about retail forex customers: "They just have to accept that risk if they want to trade." The NFA is the SRO for the futures industry that all retail forex dealers must belong to. Mr. Dyekman goes on to say that NFA rules require dealers to fill a customer's order as close to the asking price as possible. But that asking price is simply the price the dealer has quoted to the trader. There is no requirement that it be based on prices available from other dealers or banks.

I am certainly not a stranger to the practices of slippage. I have had numerous brokers slip my trades. It is interesting to observe; I place a lot of trades and watch as the brokers go through the day. When and how much the brokers will slip your trades will depend on how fast the market is. They don't always slip the price from when you enter it to when they fill it. Add slippage to slow fills, and you start to see where the brokers are really making their money. I have had slippage of 30 to 40 pips before.

The best thing to do when you get a trade that has slippage is take a screen shot and save it; then call your broker and complain. Brokers have a back-office tool that allows them to look back at the prices and spreads by tick. If that doesn't help, then you may need to file a complaint with the NFA.

MetaTrader Dealer Plug-Ins

As mentioned earlier, if you are using MetaTrader through one of the brokers out there, be cautious; some of the dealers use a back-office "dealer plug-in." I have actually seen this from a broker friend of mine that had access. You would be amazed, and actually furious, at what it can do.

There is literally a drop-down menu that the broker can select to create automatic slippage on your account or on any series of customers or groups of accounts the broker wants to add slippage to. Just drop the menu down, click on the number of pips you want to make the market slip, and presto, instant profit for the brokers!

Not all brokers are using the MetaTrader dealer plug-ins. However, you will want to ask your broker if it uses them. I am sure you will be told no way! However, brokers will use them because they have the ability to use them. I have a list at www.jdfn.com that shows brokers that may have the ability to use the plug-ins. This list is not 100 percent accurate, nor is it going to tell you that the broker actually uses the MetaTrader plug-ins. What the list will tell you is which brokers have the plug-ins available to them.

There is one specific third-party MetaTrader provider that does not have the best reputation in the industry. This third-party software provider basically allows brokers to use MetaTrader from the provider's access point. The provider supports the software and gives back-office access and reporting to the forex broker to use. This third-party vendor is the one that uses the MetaTrader plug-ins the most. The list on my Web site will give you some names of brokers that use this third-party vendor. If your broker is on the list, there is a chance that it is using the MetaTrader dealer plug-ins against you. We talked more about this in Chapter 12 on back-office software scams.

If you are using MetaTrader as your trading platform, then you have probably seen some of the changes made, depending on your broker, to the order entry screen. MetaTrader brokers can configure the software with basically unlimited setting possibilities. With the trade servers, one of the settings is the ability to control how your trade is executed. The broker can put you on instant execution or market execution.

Instant Execution

The first method, instant execution, is shown in Figure 14.1. In the box next to "Type," you will see that "Instant Execution" is selected. Now look at the bottom of the figure; you will see that there is a checkbox and the instruction "Enable maximum deviation from

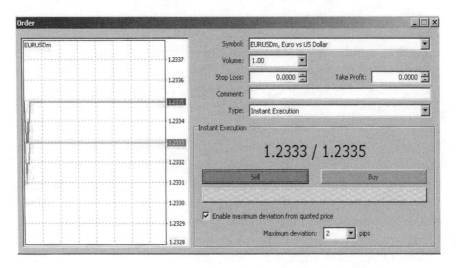

Figure 14.1

quoted price." Below that is another box that will allow you to select your "Maximum deviation" in pips from the price. This allows the traders to select the maximum slippage they are willing to take to get their trade executed.

In this example, "2" is selected. The more slippage that traders are willing to take, the more likely the trade will get executed without having to be requoted or rejected, either of which would ultimately delay the trade execution. Those of you that have used this platform for many years will probably be able to remember that this was the most common setting that brokers used.

Market Execution

The second type of order that brokers can use on MetaTrader is a market execution. In Figure 14.2, as you did for the previous figure, look for the box next to "Type." In this example the box shows "Market Execution." There is no box that traders can check to enable a maximum deviation from the quoted price, nor is there a box in which traders can select the number of pips they are willing to take on slippage to get their trade executed. Now the order is filled at market by the broker and now has a *notice* that says that at order by market execution, the price will be quoted by the dealer.

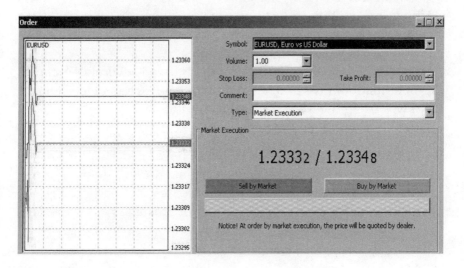

Figure 14.2

This type of order will drastically reduce rejected orders or slippage; however, you now have no control over how much slippage you are willing to take in order to have your trade filled. The broker will just fill you at the next best price. What you will find in this type of order, in my opinion, is a little more latency. The brokers are now going to have the ability to actually work your trade more, meaning go out in the marketplace to their liquidity providers and get a better price before they fill you. Keep in mind that this is done electronically, so when I say "go out in the marketplace," I'm speaking figuratively. The brokers are simply using a back-office software program to look at their liquidity providers and find the best price, a price better than you will be getting.

When I was trading and first saw this trade, I saw my control of slippage go from what I was willing to accept to no control at all, often having 5 to 10 pips of slippage on every trade. And sometimes the slippage was even more and the latency too. I have had orders that would take 30 to 40 seconds to fill with this model.

Brokers often refer to this model as an STP. As well, some brokers refer to this model as an electronic communication network, for which they use the marketing pitch to say that they only act as an intermediary and charge you a commission. I know of one broker that specifically uses this model, and I have discovered some startling information in my investigations about how brokers are able to use slippage order rejects, requotes, etc., to make more money than they make on their commissions.

The CFTC and the NFA have already fined several companies for their manipulative practices within the forex, and at least one of them was using the MetaTrader dealer plug-ins.

Here is a typical complaint:

COMPLAINT: On June 30, 2010, the NFA issued a Complaint against a forex broker engaging in margin and liquidation practices that included slippage practices that had a detrimental impact on certain customers of broker.

DECISION: On October 27, 2010, NFA's BCC issued a Decision accepting an Offer of Settlement submitted by broker in which broker neither admitted nor denied the allegations of the Complaint and agreed to settle the case on the following terms: broker agreed to refund to customers the amount of negative slippage they experienced on the trades that were placed in their accounts between May 1 and July 31, 2009, and which were attributable to the Virtual Dealer Plug-in that broker used on its institutional and retail servers.

OUTCOME: Broker agreed that in the future any and all slippage parameters that broker uses in determining whether a customer's order will be executed or requoted, shall be symmetrical in nature and neither advantageous nor disadvantageous to customer or to broker.

STOP HUNTING

If you have ever traded in the forex market, or any other market for that matter, you have probably had a stop order filled. You typically find the market going against you, and as if by magic, the price hits your stop, takes you out of the market, and then goes right back in the direction you thought the price was going.

Are you one of those traders that think the market has it in for you? That something is wrong because every time you place a trade, the market goes against you? I have felt that way. Most of the time it is simply a flaw in your trading plan; you need to work on the plan a little more, stop chasing the trades, and wait for the right time to enter. This will cut down on the trades going against you every time.

Of course, this won't stop the unethical practices of stop hunting. Let's talk more about that.

Let's look at a typical example:

You think that the USD/CHF is heading up. You have entered a long position at 0.8732 and have set your stop at 0.8632, which is slightly below an obvious double bottom. You set your initial target at 0.8932, giving you a 2:1 ratio of reward to risk. Unfortunately, the trade begins to go against you and breaks down through the support. Your stop is hit, and you're out of the trade. This is why we use good money management; in the event that you are wrong, you won't keep chasing the trade or, worse yet, cost-averaging down, only to overleverage and see your account liquidated, wiped out.

Here is the worst part: You have stayed up for 24 hours watching the trade and hoping it will come back. You have tried everything, and you finally take a step back and the trade hits your stop. Just then the trade turns around and goes right back in the direction you wanted, just as you originally thought it would. As you watch with a sick feeling, the currency pair moves up past 0.9000. Don't start second-guessing yourself. I know it is a bad feeling, and some of you might say, "If only I had set the stop just a little lower." In fact, I have said that, and I have done that only to lose more. Set your money management ahead of time and know where your levels are and then place your trade; do not ever reset your stop. Wait for the trade to level out and turn before you reenter the position.

Keep in mind, though, that your stop being hit was likely not a coincidence. There are stop hunters out there, and brokers use software and technology to automatically look for your stop levels.

The stop hunters and the software can both move the market slightly. By moving the market, they can easily pick off a group of stops. I have been stopped out on the high end with as much as a 150-pip move, instantly. More often than not, you will easily see brokers moving the market 15 to 20 pips to take out stops. The big banks may push prices up or down on a larger level trying to take stops out.

Most amateur traders are predictable in placing their stops. They are using levels, such as round numbers like 0.8700 or 0.8750; while in the equities markets we always say stay away from nickel, dime, and quarter stops: 0.05-, 0.10-, 0.25-, 0.50-, and 0.75-type levels. Add a little to those levels. If you think that a stop is at a certain level, imagine how many other people are going to think that. Stay away from those levels. Don't follow the herd to the slaughter.

There are many ways to continue to trade and stay away from the stop hunters and their tools. One is to use a robot that uses the stop as a market order. The robot will take your stop and store it on your computer; and when the stop is reached, the robot will send it to the broker automatically as a market order. This will help, but more than likely you will still be faced with slippage or order errors, not filling the order right way.

Another way is not to use a stop but instead only trade enough in your account that you are willing to lose in its entirety. If you choose this type of trading, then make sure you are dialed into what you are willing to lose. You can have multiple accounts with either the same broker or more than one broker. By trading this way you can use the margin call as your stop.

You can always trade small so that your account can handle a larger stop. The brokers will see your stop so far out that there is not much they can do. You need to plan on a long-term strategy for this type of trading; sometimes you may be in the trade for weeks.

The NFA has some specific rules on brokers' marketing materials and what their associated persons (APs) can say about slippage and price changes.

NFA Compliance Rules 2–29 and 2–36 deal with all forms of communication with the public by NFA members or APs.

No members or associates may represent that they offer trading with "no-slippage" or guarantee the price at which a transaction will be executed or filled, unless:

- They can demonstrate that all orders for all customers have been executed and fulfilled at the price initially quoted on the trading platform when the order was placed.
- No authority exists, pursuant to the contract, agreement, or otherwise, to adjust customer accounts in a manner that would have the direct or indirect effect of changing the price at which an order was executed.

15

FOREX BROKER MARGIN SCAMS

Scams may not be the right word—when you search the Internet, you will find that people marketing their services, more specifically the forex, love to use the word *scam* because it gets their products and services ranked higher. I have always loved the many sites out there that blast the so-called gurus and scammers. Why? Most of the companies and people bashing the scammers are selling the exact same thing.

Without a doubt, you need to check out those you are dealing with and what they are saying; you may be able to learn something without getting scammed. But keep an open mind. While there are a few bad apples out there, not all brokers are engaging in deceptive practices. Furthermore, most of these practices are not as rampant as they once were now that all the new regulations are in place.

But arming yourself with knowledge will help you recognize if you are in for some trouble.

As has always been the case, forex brokers have offered large leverage to entice prospective customers to trade. That was the allure: put little money at risk for potential huge rewards. However, over-leveraging your account will wipe it out faster than anything else, and the brokers know, or shall I say, knew, that. By offering high leverage, the MM encourages traders to trade extremely large positions. As the trading volume increases, so does the brokers' profits. When this happens, the investor also increases the risk of losing.

Most institutions, like big banks and corporations, use minimal leverage, such as 10:1 or so; the retail side has had access to leverage reaching 400:1. The norm was 100:1 or 200:1 depending on the type of account you had, but the recent regulations have now lowered those levels substantially based on which currency pair you are trading.

A self-regulating body for the forex market, the NFA warns traders in a forex training presentation of the risk in trading currency. The NFA says off-exchange foreign currency trading carries a high level of risk and may not be suitable for all customers. The only funds that should ever be used to trade in foreign currency trading, or any other type of highly speculative investment, are funds that represent risk capital—in other words, funds you can afford to lose without affecting your financial situation.

In July 2009, the NFA found that a broker was conducting abusive margin, liquidation, and price slippage that benefited the broker to the detriment of its customers. In addition, the NFA found that the broker failed to maintain records for all unfilled orders placed prior to May 2009.

The NFA's 2009 audit of the broker found that the firm engaged in leverage and margin practices that were harmful to its customers. For example, the broker adopted a policy whereby, every Friday, it lowered the leverage for all its accounts that were allowed to trade at 200:1 leverage, which included the micro accounts, to a 100:1 leverage. The effect of this weekly adjustment was to increase the margin requirement on these accounts from 0.5 to 1 percent. As a result of the broker's practice of adjusting the leverage-margin levels on Fridays, the accounts of many of its customers became undermargined even though they were adequately margined prior to the leverage adjustment.

In order to bring the undermargined accounts back into compliance with the higher margin requirement, the broker would liquidate the largest losing position in these accounts. However, sometimes the losing liquidated position contained multiple contracts, and the liquidation of only a portion of the losing position was sufficient to satisfy the new margin requirement.

Nevertheless, the broker would arbitrarily liquidate the whole position. This not only would result in the account being overmargined but would preclude the customer from possibly realizing a potential gain on that portion of the position that was unnecessary to liquidate.

The broker did not disclose to its customers in account opening documents, on the firm's Web site, or through any other means that if their accounts traded at 200:1 leverage, they would be subject to these routine weekly leverage-margin adjustments.

The broker claimed that it provided e-mail notifications to its customers every Friday informing them of the leverage-margin adjustments to their accounts. Yet the broker was unable to show that all affected customers received these e-mails. The broker justified the Friday leverage-margin adjustment as a means of reducing weekend market risk for accounts trading at 200:1 leverage, which, as noted above, included all micro account customers.

Furthermore, while promoting micro accounts to small investors and the 200:1 leverage that the micro accounts enjoyed, the broker failed to give micro account customers adequate disclosure of the higher risk associated with the 200:1 leverage, which the broker acknowledged by adopting its practice of adjusting leverage-margin levels every Friday for accounts trading at these leverage levels. In addition to the broker's weekly practice of routinely adjusting leverage-margin levels for accounts trading at 200:1 leverage, when the broker anticipated a significant market move over the weekend due to some important weekend event or potential development, the broker further adjusted the leverage for its customers' accounts by increasing the margin requirement to 2 percent.

This occurred on three occasions in 2008 and 2009: on Friday, December 19, 2008, in anticipation of the potential weekend bankruptcy of GM; on Friday, March 13, 2009, in anticipation of a G–20 meeting that was scheduled for the weekend; and on Friday, June 12, 2009, in anticipation of a G–8 meeting that was scheduled for the weekend. In all three instances, the broker had ample advance notice of the event in question but failed to provide customers with any advance notice of the margin change.

Most of the positions that the broker liquidated on the afore-mentioned three dates, in anticipation of adverse market moves over the weekend, would have experienced minimal gains or losses if they had remained open over the weekend instead of being liqui-dated. However, because of the liquidations that occurred on these dates, affected customers realized overall losses totaling nearly $425,000.

One of the broker's foreign customers had her margin require-ment adjusted to 2 percent on Friday, June 12, 2009, prior to the weekend's G–8 meeting. The broker then liquidated the largest open losing position in the account at a loss of over $25,000. The investor received no prior notice from the broker that it was increasing the margin requirement and liquidating the positions on June 12.

Had the investor received prior notice of the margin increase, she would have sent additional funds to the broker to satisfy the higher margin requirement and thus eliminate the need to liquidate positions in the account.

Yet another customer, this one from the United States, had the margin requirement for his account increased from 0.5 percent to 2 percent on Friday, December 19, 2008, supposedly in anticipation of the potential weekend bankruptcy of GM. The broker then liqui-dated a number of the client's open positions to meet the increased margin requirement, without giving him prior notice of these liqui-dations.

As a result of the broker's actions, the client's account suffered a loss of nearly $15,000. Another troubling aspect of the broker's practice of adjusting leverage and margin levels on Fridays, whether as a routine matter or for special circumstances, was that the broker would wait until late in the day to make the adjustment. As a result, customers would acquire positions on Fridays at one leverage-margin level, unaware that hours, or, in some cases, only minutes, later that same day, the margin required to maintain open positions over the weekend would be increased.

The broker's practice of routinely and repeatedly adjusting lever-age and margin requirements on Fridays, without giving affected customers adequate prior notice of the adjustment, denied customers the opportunity to deposit additional funds to maintain their open positions, or at the very least, select which positions to liquidate, and caused them to experience significant losses in their accounts. As such, the broker breached its obligation to uphold high standards of commercial honor and just and equitable principles of trade.

This is an actual case from the NFA, and you can read more about it online at www.jdfn.com. You can also read more online about how margin can affect the way you trade. One of the biggest things you can do to help protect your portfolio is to practice good money management. Make sure that when you do use margin, it is part of your money management overall plan. That way you can factor in what you are willing to risk and what your drawdown can be.

CHAPTER 16

THE DEMO BAIT AND SWITCH

DEMO ACCOUNT WARNING

I could spend a lot of time on this topic, especially since I have been a victim of it over the years. After spending a tremendous amount of time testing and investigating, I started to discover what was really going on behind the curtain, so to speak.

Traders should take notice that the NFA has specific rules and regulations because of some of the bait-and-switch–type tactics that brokers have used in the marketplace. I know of recent litigation with this specific suspect action outlined in the complaint.

In the forex market, brokers offer customers the ability to use a demo account, or a practice account, to help build their confidence. You can log on, open up your demo trading account, and start making trades. There is nothing wrong with this, and it is a great way to develop your trading plan. Make lots of trades and learn from your mistakes.

I certainly did this and was taught this concept. I was told by the people I knew at various brokerages that trading your demo is no different from trading a live account. The only problem with this is that I was not told everything. I was not told that the brokers do not waste their time with demo accounts; they simply turn them on. There are no special servers to manipulate the feeds or the orders. In some ways, it is more like an ideal forex marketplace. The live market will trade differently from what you are experiencing with your demo account.

The primary reason for this is there is no need for all the gamesmanship in a demo account as there is in a live account. The brokers will not start playing all the games prior to you opening and funding a live account. Only after you go "live" will you make it onto the brokers' secret radar screens of customers that are making money.

THE BAIT

This is certainly not isolated to any one broker, although I do believe the practice is much less widespread than it used to be. The broker will start by marketing the demo accounts as being identical trading to the real thing. You can open a demo account, and you are off and running.

Some brokers allow you to select the type of demo account you can use: a mini account or a standard account. And some brokers will give you the option of selecting the size of the account you want to trade and the amount of margin you want to use. All this is helpful and something that you will want to do regardless of how the differences end up.

Whether the results you experience with your demo account trading will be similar to what you get when you begin to trade live will depend on the games your broker is playing with live accounts. If you are with a reputable brokerage, you may actually be able to have a good idea of what you are going to experience when trading live in the market.

I cannot tell you how many people have come to me to tell me how great they were doing in trading in their demo accounts and how they have made hundreds of profitable trades without a loss. Of course, that is great, but the next time I would see them, what I would hear is how much money they lost when they opened a funded, live account.

There were the occasional traders that said the reason they lost was because they changed the way they were trading from when they traded a successful demo account. They told me they could not do the same thing in their demo account that they were doing in a live account.

Changing strategies doesn't make much sense if you plan to develop a trading plan and test your plan. You will need to make sure that you trade it the same way.

Regardless, though, you are still going to have trouble duplicating your demo trading success with most brokers when you go live. Most brokers are not manipulating the demo account servers or playing many of the games that we have exposed in this book. The same can't be said for live trading.

The NFA has some specific rules in place to govern some of the misleading marketing that brokers make in reference to their demo accounts.

NFA Compliance Rules 2–29 and 2–36 deal with all forms of communication with the public by NFA members and APs. Rule 2–29 covers communications with the public by members who solicit customers to trade on-exchange futures and options on futures, while Rule 2–36 covers communications with the public by members who solicit retail customers to trade forex.

This is primarily why you do not see the older tactics the brokers have taken in the past. They know what they are doing now and just do not tell you how great your demo trading is going. You will still need to pay close attention.

THE SWITCH

So now comes the switch; after all the marketing that the brokers have done to get you in the door and open a demo account, the brokers work on you to open a live account and fund it. There is nothing wrong with that, but the unscrupulous brokers will take it to the next step. When you open your live account, you will start to experience some anomalies, problems that you didn't experience with your demo account.

A few things will start to happen: You will not be able to execute trades as efficiently as you did on the demo account. The dealing desk will now watch your trading, or if your broker does not have a dealing desk, a computer will watch your trades. You may start to see some errors when you place the trade. You will begin to experience invalid prices, slow fills, etc. This alone will change the way your trading plan works.

If you are successful at trading, you will make the broker's "not so good list." This list will either get you blacklisted, where nothing you trade is executed, or get you transferred to a slow server where the broker can slow your trade execution, giving you unfavorable fills and, of course, plenty of slippage.

A recent litigation filed while I was writing this book brought to light some of the very things I am discussing. The plaintiff claims to have lost over $150,000 to the broker over the years. The lawsuit deals with the demo accounts, which serve to attract clients but do not simulate real market conditions; when clients do switch to live, they receive a completely different execution. The lawsuit focuses on the execution itself, where it is claimed that the broker is in fact an MM that actively goes after profitable clients. The main excerpts are below:

> To further bolster customers' confidence in its platform, broker enticed customers to use broker's practice or demo account (hereinafter, the "Demo Account") to simulate a trading experience. But the Demo Account, just like the myriad advertisements, misled customers about the true nature, functionality, and performance of the platform. Once lured into opening an account, customers were subjected to a staggering array of stratagems and ploys, some using extremely sophisticated computer software based upon complex algorithms and high-speed computers, to deceive the customers into believing that their trading was being affected by normal market forces, while in reality broker traded against its own customers.
>
> And the so-called "Demo Account"—which was held out by broker as the sine qua non to persuade prospective customers to trade with broker—was the most cunning

and crippling canard of all. By trading through the "Demo Account" without being at financial risk, the customer was allowed to experience direct market pricing, free from broker-dealer interference or manipulation. The switch pulled by broker on how trading occurs once the customer opens a "live" account and starts trading with real money, is nothing short of a modern-day equivalent of the classic street con game known as "Three-card Monte." Once "live" trading began, direct market pricing was replaced by profound dealer interference and trade manipulation.

FUNDED PRACTICE ACCOUNT

A funded practice account is basically a live trading account in which you place real money so that you can start testing your trading strategy. There are still some brokers that will allow you to trade with micro lots. Most of these brokers are offshore. In any case, the point is to find an account where you can make numerous trades on a small scale, not worrying about what you are risking.

So if you put $1,000 in a small account that allows you to trade micro lots, you can do what I call "dialing it down." Unlike a demo trading account with hypothetical money, you are using real money to trade live in the market.

It is truly amazing how differently you trade when you are using real money. Whether you have $1 or $10,000, you still trade the real cash differently than the hypothetical. When placing the trades with real money, you will start thinking about how much you want to make and how many pips you need. Then all of a sudden you get a trade that goes against you.

Now you have to start saying to yourself, I need to stick to my money management; I need to cut my losses. Don't be afraid to take a loss. When you start trading bigger accounts, do not focus on the dollars; when you look at the dollars, you will have a more difficult time when you have cash on the line.

Percentages are percentages, but for whatever reason, 10 percent of $100,000 looks a lot different from 10 percent of $1,000. So if you get accustomed to using the percentages, and not the dollars, your mind will allow you to take the next step in your trading. You can use pips as well, and so instead of the percentage or the dollar amount, you are simply watching how many pips, up or down, your account is moving. I like to use percentage.

It is good to use funded practice accounts or even the demo account to master this process. The live funded practice account is going to trade differently than the demo trades do; however, no broker games will be played until you begin making money.

17

THE BROKER B-BOOK

It is no secret that in the forex, your broker trades against you. But what does this mean for you, the trader? It means that as you lose money, your broker or bank that acts as the counterparty to your trade makes money. As the counterparty to your position, your broker needs to keep track of you, the trader.

What I want to address in this chapter is something you would be hard-pressed to find searching Google; it is insider information, and it won't make the brokers very happy that I am sharing it with you. In fact, if you ask about it, you will find that most brokers will just ignore you or blow off your question. The book of business, or B-book, is where most brokers make their money. The banks, in addition, have a few other areas in which they can make more money than the average broker.

The B-book is a process. It is the accounting side of the back office where all the decisions are made, and it is essentially how your brokers see you and the deposits in your account. The B-book shows if you are a profitable customer or not; remember, this means profitable for the broker, not for you. If you are making money, then the broker is losing money every time you place a profitable trade.

So your broker pays very close attention to how you trade and if you are making money for yourself or for the broker.

Forex is a zero-net-sum market; this is seen in the broker's B-book as losses or gains. As you make money or lose money in your account, the counterparty to your positions makes or loses the exact opposite that you make or lose. This is called a zero-sum game where the exact gains and losses in your forex account and those of the counterparty to your positions are taken together and added or subtracted to equal zero.

However, when you factor in commissions and spreads, it becomes a negative-sum game, meaning that it becomes possible for the counterparty's B-book to show a greater gain than your actual deposits. I was told during my investigations, by an overseas forex broker running a B-book, that an account will typically yield about 120 percent return on deposits. At least that is what the broker considers your deposit to be worth. So if you put in $100,000, the broker would consider your account to be worth about $120,000, if you lost all your money.

The counterparty to your position uses a number of formulas, tactics, schemes, practices, and software programs to make it nearly impossible for you to make money trading the forex market when you are in the broker's B-book. When all things are equal, you should have a 50–50 chance of making money in a trade. The positions will go either in your direction or against you. It's that simple.

This means that mathematically you should automatically have one winning trade for every losing trade you place in your account. Now let's factor technical and fundamental analysis into the equation. Again assuming that all things are equal and that you understand how to use and apply technical analysis and complimentary indicators to create a technical trading strategy, you exponentially increase your percentages of a profitable trade by using successful trading strategies.

Using fundamentals to help decide the market's direction or trend will further increase the percentage of successful trades you place. Fundamental events are the news events that move the markets. They are the driving force behind the direction in which each currency is going, and they decide the trend and embedded trend of each currency.

When you add your technical trading strategies together with your fundamental analysis and probabilities of 50–50 market conditions, your chances of placing a trade that will move in your direction should be near 70 percent. As any successful forex trader will tell you, money management is a key component to successful forex trading. But this has little to do with the percentage of profitable trades you will place.

According to a recent study by the CFTC, the average forex trader loses $15,000 during the course of his or her forex trading. As we analyze this and dig a little deeper into the workings of your broker's B-book, we can conclude that for each new customer that opens a forex trading account, the counterparty has made it nearly impossible for you to place a profitable trade.

This is done through the broker's risk operations department. The risk operations department sets the parameters for how much risk the broker, or bank, assumes in its B-book. The counterparties' basic strategies start off with a number of simple strategies that target certain groups of traders in order to systematically separate the customers from the deposits in their trade account.

The risk operations department also uses probabilities to determine risk. Just as in your trading, past performance may dictate future expectations, and the counterparty's risk operations department knows this. The department uses a number of various strategies and techniques in a probability model to determine the likelihood that you will lose money in your forex trading account.

Some of the basic strategies used by the risk operations department may include, but are not limited to, holding all forex accounts with less than $5,000 in deposits in its B-book to be the counterparty and assume the risk of that particular group of customers' trades. The risk operations department knows that customers who deposit $5,000 or less are usually new traders and have less experience than more seasoned, veteran forex traders, who have greater risk capital to place into the market. A trader who deposits $5,000 or less will have fewer margins for error. If a trade goes against you with a smaller account balance, the likelihood that your account will get liquidated or stopped out is much higher.

The risk operations department may also hold accounts with higher leverage. If you are using a high degree of leverage, the likelihood that your account will get liquidated or stopped out is much higher than for those customers using low leverage or no leverage at all. These are just a few tactics put into place by the risk operations department and categories it uses to determine risk, or the likelihood that you will lose money in your forex account.

If your broker or bank is the counterparty to your trade, it assumes the risk as the counterparty to your trading position. This means in a net-sum trading account that when you make money, the broker or bank is losing money. In order to prevent losses to the B-book, the counterparty to your positions routes your trade through a dealing desk. All brokers have a dealing desk even if they are running an STP model. Dealing desks are there to provide liquidity and route trades but work as the action end of the risk operations department. A dealing desk, or its equivalent, is seen as a profit center by your bank or broker, and those profits come from your losses!

The B-book side of the business is a closely held secret. That is why you do not see much related to the process when looking on the Internet. Some of this will become more exposed as the market continues to have regulatory changes. Without a doubt, the B-book part of the business is the biggest area where the brokers are exploiting their opportunities against their customers.

Keep in mind that it is not necessarily fraud or a bad practice. I personally don't have a problem with brokers that want to balance their books—meaning if you go long the EUR/USD and I go short, the broker has a balanced book. However, some of the bad brokers will still use some of the tactics we have been discussing. They will slip the process on both sides, making a wider spread and more money. They will slow your execution so they can get a better price from their liquidity provider on both sides of the trade, thus making extra money.

Then you experience trading against you; the broker is going to look and see if it has a balanced book; and if it doesn't, it will make the choice of whether it wants to go into the marketplace and offset the risk. Most of the big brokers will just carry the risk versus hedging on the open market. The broker has the ability to offset its risk, in part or full. So be on the lookout for the broker scams and know that there is a B-book in the background trading against you.

CHAPTER 18

DEALING DESK OR NOT

The question of whether a broker has a dealing desk or not is really one that many forex traders have been asking for years. It wasn't but a short time ago that retail traders (as opposed to broker's traders) started to put the pieces together to determine that the forex brokers were out to get them and that the primary method to separate retail traders from their money was a dealing desk. I have met many broker's traders over the years that have worked for some of the bigger retail forex brokers, and they worked on the dealing desk.

When I first got into forex trading, I was using one of the newer forex brokers. I remember visiting the firm when it moved its offices, which was sort of an upgrade, since it had gotten so big. I was taking a tour of the new facilities, and my "tour guide" showed me the firm's dealing desk (or trading desk, or whatever you want to call it). It was interesting, to say the least; it looked like a control center for NASA, with lots of computer screens and people at their desks.

These people were broker's traders working on the dealing desk for the broker; each trader had his or her own B-book, so to speak. The traders were specifically targeting and trading against the broker's customers for the broker. Of course, the broker's traders were armed with all sorts of sophisticated tools and software to beat the retail traders when they placed their trade, thus the conflict of interest.

With all the recent regulatory changes, many of the big forex retail brokers now claim that they do not have a dealing desk. Well, don't be fooled; they do. They may not call it a dealing desk, but they have something that conducts the same sort of operations, only much faster. Some of the brokers call their old dealing desk operations a trade desk, or they don't even call it anything; they just automate it, and it runs against your trades automatically when you place them.

Most of the brokers out there have some means to sway the trading in their favor. In order to be successful in trading the forex, you have to be smart, stay a step ahead of the brokers, and know how to beat them at their own game. It can be done, and it is done every day; there are still lots of forex traders making great amounts of money. But if you don't arm yourself with the right information and tools, you won't have a chance to beat these brokers.

The broker's traders that are watching your trade on the dealing desk are specifically getting paid to make the broker money. The way they make money for the broker is to cause you to lose money. The broker's traders will use their trading terminal to view the broker's liquidity providers' pricing. The broker's traders will have a B-book that they are responsible for. When the customer trade appears on a broker's terminal, the broker's trader—we'll call him Dave—gets to work.

Dave decides to buy the EUR/USD at 1.4022 by 1.4025. He will quickly look at the bid and ask available through the broker's liquidity providers. Dave will match the trade and find a better rate for the broker than what is being offered to the customer. The arbitrage, or the difference in this spread and these trades, is what the broker makes as a profit. Now add in some slippage, and the broker makes a lot more.

Let's take this a step further. Say the broker wants to make more money. The best way for the broker to do this is to take the other side of Dave's trade. When Dave places his trade, the broker simply holds the trade and does not lay the trade off to the broker's liquidity providers. The broker will act as the counterparty to the trade by taking the other side. If Dave buys, the broker sells.

The broker will hold the trade until the customer loses. The broker will also deploy some other tricks to ensure the broker's profitability. Some of these tactics include slippage, off-price quotes, and widening of the spreads. And these are just a few tricks that the broker can do. In deploying these tactics, the broker only has one thing on its mind, beating you out of your hard-earned money.

As I have noted in this book already, during a recent civil court action through discovery, I read an e-mail written by a forex broker's trader, a trader that was working on the broker's dealing desk. In the e-mail, the broker's trader said, "I have identified what the trader is using. I can definitely beat this customer." The broker's trader went on further to say, "I can find others and beat them." If you are using something easy to place trades, the broker will find out and simply use the same thing to trade against you.

AUTOMATED DEALING DESK

Just because brokers tell you they don't have a dealing desk, don't believe it. In most cases the brokers have simply automated the process. They do not need a dealing desk or a human trader. In fact, humans are too slow compared with computers and servers. The brokers will use sophisticated software and programming to trade faster than the customers. The brokers can slow the trades down, creating slippage. In essence, the brokers can simply do whatever they want to without you knowing.

I think it is important to say that brokers have to make money; that is why they started a business to begin with. As you can see, though, it is unfortunately too easy for them to do the wrong thing in an effort to enhance their bottom line. What would be fair? The smartest and fairest way for brokers to offer their services to customers is to use an STP model where the brokers simply take your order, match it with their liquidity providers at the best price, and then add a markup.

PROFESSIONAL DEALING DESK

Professional dealing desk—I think that is an oxymoron. There is one broker that claims that it runs its dealing desk in a professional manner. The broker acts as the counterparty to your trade, which means it takes the other side of your trade using your money. That doesn't seem professional to me.

I will let you call around and ask the brokers which one has a professional dealing desk. When you find the one, take note. This is the same broker that is responsible for the internal e-mail noted above, saying that the firm uses slow servers and other tools to beat its customers out of their trade, including recognizing the customers' trading patterns and using those patterns to trade against them.

In contrast, another broker I am familiar with acts as an MM, meaning that the broker runs a dealing desk. The broker does say that its operations are 100 percent automated; it simply adds a markup and takes the other side of every trade. The broker uses a process that takes the customer's trade, automatically looks at the broker's liquidity providers for the best price, matches that best price to the customer's order, and then executes with the broker's markup.

TRUE ECN TECHNOLOGY

The future will see true ECN technology become commonplace in retail forex trading. Forex retail traders need to have the ability to participate in the overall forex marketplace by providing increased liquidity and additional forex currency prices.

Something much like the level II–type technology of the mid–1990s would work. If customers were able to offer currency pairs at their own price, it would create a deeper pool of liquidity with a wider availability of prices without all the manipulation. There have been some efforts in the past to do this, but not with much success; and some brokers claim to be ECNs, but they are not in the true sense as far as I am concerned.

Right now, the problem with allowing retail traders to participate in the counterparty side of forex trading is one of regulation.

Rules state that only registered entities can be counterparties to a trade, thus making it difficult for the retail trader to offer currency pairs as an MM. But this will change soon.

One such broker that claims that it is an ECN, and that it was the first to offer true ECN technology to the retail forex industry, is full of it. This broker is one of suspect integrity. I knew of one of the broker's previous owners who used to brag about how much money he could make trading against his customers. He would carry his laptop around, making hundreds of thousands a day just by opening his laptop and using his back-office software to move the market or slow-fill customers, among other sinister-type techniques he had at his fingertips; there was no real ECN technology available to his customers.

In the end, you will need to utilize all the strategies and training you can so that you can beat the brokers at their own game.

HOW TO TRADE AND WHERE TO TRADE

19

TRADING STRATEGIES TO BEAT THE BROKER

As we begin this chapter, let's take a few moments to understand how we can successfully trade the forex market after what we have learned goes on behind the scenes.

Not all forex brokers are stealing your money and not all forex brokers are bad. You simply have to read up on them, conduct your own due diligence, and ultimately open a demo account to see for yourself how the broker's pricing feed and executions work. Keep in mind, the demo account will not be representative of the live account you will ultimately be activating with real money. However, opening and using a demo account will give you an idea of what to look for when you do fund your live account with the broker. Once you open your live account, start small and test the broker to see what kind of fills you are getting.

I have tested many brokers over the last 12 years; some were terrible and some were fine, but I have yet to find the great broker, and I am still looking; but to trade in this market you must have a broker. I think it is prudent to mention that with all the recent legislation aimed at the forex market, most of the big brokers have started to conform. They are not doing what they once did.

The entire landscape of forex is not dissimilar to what happened when the stock market moved toward automation with NASDAQ. There were many years when retail traders where in the dark and always behind the moves, and don't think for a minute things aren't still happening in the equities market that are aimed at getting the small retail trader. Trading equities and using an equities broker is no different from trading on the forex market. You still need to be careful and watch your fills very closely.

There are many strategies out there that can help you stay ahead of the brokers. Many of the strategies that you will want to use will require you to stay off your broker's radar screen. Here are a few: Don't let your broker see your stops and limits. Don't let your broker see you holding on to large amounts of profits. Withdraw your profits periodically and keep your trading account relatively small. You can also use big stops and limits, so long as you are well within your money management plan.

TRADE BEFORE THE NEWS STRATEGY

Getting in ahead of the move is crucial to making money in any trade, but the key is to know the precise time to trade and the direction the market will move. One of the essential factors for any forex move involves news events, or what I like to call the "fundamentals of trading." We can use fundamentals to find the market direction and then use our "technical indicators" to time the precise entry and exit points.

One of the biggest market-moving events is the announcement of interest rate decisions. I am going to provide you with a simple mathematical calculation for deciding if any central bank is going to raise interest rates, lower rates, or keep rates on hold before the announcement goes public.

Let's start off by examining a formula often used by traders to predict the target rate for a central bank's short-term interest rates. Proposed by John Taylor in 1993, the Taylor rule is widely accepted by economists today as a gauge for appropriate interest rate levels in conjunction with current economic conditions. We are able to predict how much, if at all, a central bank should change short-term rates as real inflation or real GDP diverges, respectively, from the target inflationary rates or potential GDP. To find the short-term rate target, you take the central bank's target interest rate and compare it with GDP growth expectations and inflationary figures:

$$i = N + 0.5(Y - Y)^*) + 0.5(P - P)^*$$

where i is the short-term nominal interest rate
N is the neutral rate subtracting the short-term interest rate with target GDP and inflation at the mean
Y is the GDP forecasted growth rate
Y^* is the observed GDP growth rate
P is the forecast inflationary rate
P^* is the targeted growth rate

When this formula to forecast future expectations suggests that the GDP growth rate or forecasted inflation rate is above trend target levels, the short-term rates should be increased by half the difference between the forecasted inflation rate and target trend levels. If the forecasted GDP growth rate or forecasted inflationary rate is below the trend and target levels, the short-term interest rates should be reduced accordingly.

You can also factor in

$$i = N + a(P - P^*) + b(u - U^*)$$

where i is the target short-term nominal interest rate
N is the neutral rate
a is the inflation gap coefficient
P is actual inflation
P^* is the inflationary target
b is the unemployment gap coefficient
U is the actual unemployment rate
U^* is the nonaccelerating inflation rate of unemployment

Remember to use Taylor's model in conjunction with the current unemployment rates and inflationary numbers for forecasting future interest rate decisions. This will help you understand the market's direction before the move takes place and allows you to get in ahead of the announcement, thus making your trade less reactionary and more calculated.

The success of any trading strategy depends on a number of key elements, from timing your entry and exit points precisely to entering at or near the beginning of any run or move that is setting up. Understand that with any market there is always a trend, whether it's an uptrend, downtrend, or a sideways trend. There are also embedded trends or trends within a trend. You can see these smaller trends setting up on lower time frames.

As a forex trader, the key to beating the brokers comes when you learn how *not* to play their game! How can this be done? You might be trading in smaller time frames, and the broker is taking a small piece of each trade through its various means of systematically stealing from you. Then your profits are much smaller, which will mean that your losses will seem much larger, ultimately making it appear that you have poor money management or emotional trading habits. So how can an individual combat these scandalous tactics put into place by the broker? First, by practicing good money management.

MONEY MANAGEMENT FORMULA

Here is one of the formulas I use for my money management:

Account balance times the percentage of acceptable loss, which gives you the amount of money you are willing to lose in a trade, which is then divided by the number of pips in your stop, which equals the number of lots you can trade

This is really is a simple calculation, but there are a few simple rules to follow:

1. *Amount you are willing to risk.* To determine the most you should risk at any one time, take your account balance and multiply it by no more than *0.05 (5 percent). Example:* $5,000 mini account times 0.05 equals $250.
2. *Number of pips you are willing to risk.* This is determined by the price at which you are getting into the trade and where your stop is placed. Add the spread times 2 to limit "head fakes" in position.
3. *Lots you can trade.* The number of pips per trade is determined by the difference between the dollar amount at risk and the number of pips in your stop loss.

Note: If you have an account balance of $5,000 and you're willing to risk 1 percent of your account balance on this trade (5,000 × 0.01 = 50), this gives the dollar amount of your account balance you are putting at risk on this particular trade—in this case, $50. *If* the stop loss is *25 pips* away from your entry price (including 2 times the spread), you divide the dollar amount by the number of pips in your stop (50/25 = 2,) and this now gives you the number of lots you can trade:

$$5,000 \times 0.01 = 50/25 = 2$$

When you combine good money management with your trading strategies, this will help you increase the odds of placing not only a profitable trade but a successful trade as well. One way to beat the brokers at their own game is to trade longer-term strategies. Look for swing or position trades. These are trades that you may hold for a single day or up to several days, thus utilizing the overall trend of the market and minimizing the impact the brokers will have by taking the counterposition to your trade. When the brokers determine your trading strategies and style, they will begin passing the trades off as STP to the banks to avoid the losses to their account.

Here's a strategy you can use for swing trades; note that this is a trade I look to hold for a minimum of 60 minutes up to several days or until the trend reverses. First, I use a daily chart; on the daily chart I will add a 50, 100, and 200 simple moving average. These moving averages are often areas of support and resistance and are universally recognized in determining crosses of fast and slow for major trend reversals.

I will also look for channels or the overall trend of the market using a linear regression channel, making sure that I am at or near levels of support and resistance in conjunction with the channel so that I can take advantage of the larger moves in the market. If the market is trending, I will add a Fibonacci extension to predict where the market is heading. If I am entering on a correction or pullback, I can use the Fibonacci retracement to determine where the market is heading on the pullback.

Next I use a 120-minute (2-hour) chart. I use the chart to find the near-term trend. This trend should match the overall trend from the daily chart. On the 120-minute chart, I add a linear regression channel and areas of support and resistance. Make sure you are trading with support and resistance.

For your entry time, use a 60-minute chart. You will need to add a parabolic stop and reverse (SAR), a Commodity Channel Index (CCI) indicator, and a triple exponential moving average (TRIX) 10-length 9-signal smoothing line. You should place the trade when the complimentary indicators line up together. Look for a cross of the TRIX at the same time you see the parabolic SAR reverse the trend direction. The trade should be entered when the price crosses the SAR in the direction of the new trend.

You will need to confirm that the trade still has room to go; this can be confirmed with the CCI. If the CCI indicator is below 100, it has more room to the upside for a long; and if the CCI is above 100, it has more room to the downside for a short. All three indicators must line up within three candles in the same direction in order for this to be a successful trade.

Last, take a look at a 15-minute chart for volume; you are looking for increasing volume to confirm that there is enough trading taking place in the market for the move to continue. If volume is falling off, the move may not have enough momentum to continue. If volume is increasing, look for this as confirmation that the market is moving and a price correction might be taking place. This will allow you to trade with the overall trend of the market, and it will allow you take a larger profit with more accuracy and eliminate the broker's impact on your trades.

Regardless of some of the less than flattering things about brokers I have written in this book, there will always be individuals trading in the forex. It's an exciting market, it's the largest financial market in the world, and it's only getting bigger. If you use good money management and ignore your emotions, you will be one step closer to making positive trades in the forex. Try using some of the strategies in this book, including the ones noted above, to beat your broker and stay ahead of the forex game.

20

WHICH BROKERS TO TRADE WITH AND WHY

The subject of this chapter is difficult, to say the least. The question of what forex broker to trade with and why is hard to nail down because it is basically a moving target. I have traded with many forex brokers over the years, and I can only imagine how many I will trade with in the future.

In this chapter, I will try to cover what brokers are out there and what information I have on them at the time of this writing. The best way for you to stay on top of what broker I am using and what brokers other traders are using is to go to my Web site at www.jdfn.com; I will always have up-to-date information on various forex brokers posted, whether the information is from me or from visitors to the site.

With all the recent legislation and regulatory changes, most of the big forex brokers are better off financially than they had been in the past, and the smaller ones either are gone or have been acquired in order to meet the increases in net capital requirements.

FINANCIALS

You can go to the CFTC Web site to see where the forex brokers stand on net capital: http://www.cftc.gov/marketreports/financialdata forfcms/index.htm.

FCMs must file monthly financial reports with the CFTC's Division of Clearing and Intermediary Oversight within 17 business days after the end of the month. Selected financial information from these reports is shown in Table 20.1. The most recent month-end information generally is added within 12 business days after FCMs file their reports (but occasionally information may be added later). For example, the seventeenth business-day filing "due date" for, financial reports completed for the end of February 2011—the date February 28, 2011, to be precise—was March 23, 2011. The target of 12 business days for posting these data was April 8, 2011.

The reports will list the type of registration for brokers as either FCM, BD, or RFED, as well as other information such as adjusted net capital and net capital requirements.

I will include on my Web site, www.jdfn.com, the data for the brokers that I am talking about in this chapter as of the end of May 2011. One of the things that my team does is constantly test execution platforms of various brokers, looking for the best executions. When brokers claim to make changes for the better, I will go back and retest and include those results on the Web site too.

FUNDAMENTALS

Besides looking at the financials for the brokers, think about the brokers' fundamentals, things that really matter—the business model, their long-term goals, customer opinions, etc. Conduct your own due diligence.

Consider your relationship with the firm. What are you expecting? What is the firm expecting? Yes, we all know that the plan is to open an account, trade the forex, and, the hope is, make money, but is that all you expect? What about when things go wrong? The best way to know how the good times will be is to get an idea of how the broker will treat you in the bad times. After all, it's not always going to be smooth sailing; occasionally you will need your broker's cooperation to correct issues; so what will your broker do?

Table 20.1   Brokers (all numbers are in millions)

FCM, Retail Forex Dealer	Registered As	DSRO*	As-of Date	Adjusted Net Capital	Net Capital Requirement	Excess Net Capital
FXCM, Forex Capital Markets LLC	RFED	NFA	05/31/2011	73,732,988	26,304,344	47,428,644
FX Solutions, FX Solutions LLC	RFED	NFA	05/31/2011	38,509,672	20,383,010	18,126,662
FXDD, FX Direct Dealer LLC	RFED	NFA	05/31/2011	24,396,671	21,382,649	3,014,022
MB Trading, MB Trading Futures Inc.	RFED	NFA	05/31/2011	24,193,173	21,333,606	2,859,567
Gain, Gain Capital Group LLC	RFED	NFA	05/31/2011	62,623,823	25,066,173	37,557,650
Forex.com (owned by Gain Capital Group), Gain Capital Group LLC	RFED	NFA	05/31/2011	62,623,823	25,066,173	37,557,650

* Designated self-regulatory organization

To find out, for example, how brokers handle bad fills, take a look at customer reviews online. While it is true that most people who post complaints do so because they're unhappy with a situation, keep in mind the fact that people who are content rarely post. So when you look at complaints, just imagine that for every unhappy person there are 100 content people who never said a word. Although angry complaints can at times be misleading, look at the resolutions and examine the situation if you have enough information to do so. I have done this on many occasions when evaluating a broker by using charts to see if the information posted by the customer matches the reality of the charts. To be honest, I have found that some of the complaints were not ultimately supported by the facts of the charts, which makes it difficult to hold the broker responsible for something that it didn't actually do.

I have also seen situations where the trader was completely in the wrong, and yet the broker corrected the situation in favor of the client even though it had no obligation to do so. Some brokers know that the individuals who made unfounded complaints were well aware of who really made the mistake, but these brokers understand that customer service gestures can go a long way, especially when it comes to word of mouth—and these are the brokers you should be looking for.

Call the broker on the phone and ask some stupid questions. Why? Because good businesspeople know that there are no stupid questions when it comes to your clients, and if you are treated badly for little things, you probably shouldn't expect much better for bigger issues.

Open a new account. Nobody says that you have to fund the account, but just go ahead and open one. The reason is simple; by opening an account you get to see how the broker will handle its first interaction with you. Is the broker efficient, or does the broker lose documents over and over again? Are the people you are dealing with friendly, or do they treat you like your business doesn't matter? Do they follow the regulations about knowing their customers, or are they willing to bend the rules?

Why this is important can be answered by asking yourself a few questions. Do you really want a broker that loses documents to have access to your secure information and to hold your money? Do you want a relationship with people who appear to have no interest in you or treat you badly? Can anyone who is willing to bend or break rules or regulations be trusted with your money? These are all important questions, and a little homework on your part can help you narrow the field. The relationship that you have with your broker needs to be mutually beneficial, and so if the broker appears to be giving away too much in order to get your business, then beware; brokers are in business to make a profit, and so too many freebies might indicate that they know they will get it back from you later.

So what else can you do to help level the playing field? Well, one thing you can do is consider an IB.

IBs

First let me explain that IBs are firms that "introduce" customers to one or several forex brokers. IBs basically act as marketing companies, but they usually offer training, support, or other services to the clients that they introduce. In most cases, the IBs are compensated by the brokers out of the spreads that the customers already pay, and the customers are not charged anything additional for trades placed in their accounts.

Many people think that they're better off going directly to the broker, but there are advantages to using an IB. For example, consider what we just discussed regarding due diligence. The IBs already did their due diligence before they decided to form a relationship with the brokers that they introduce their customers to because they don't want to have problems with a broker any more than you do.

In addition, consider for a moment the scenario of a bad fill on one of your trades; rather than you attempting to plead your case to the broker, an IB can act as an intermediary on your behalf and fight for you by using its contacts at the broker to make things right for you. An IB will carry a little more weight than an individual customer fighting alone because the IB represents many of the broker's customers. An IB can also help when paperwork is missing, as well as be there to give you an opinion when you have questions about placing trades or using trading strategies.

As a retail forex trader, you will be relegated to some of these forex brokers listed in Table 20.1. Some are better than others. The brokers in the table are all fairly large. You will probably see some consolidation within the forex industry, but not necessarily among the ones in the table.

If you were truly committed to trading the forex and had the means to take the next step, you would be looking to open your account with a more direct route to the liquidity provider. Some banks such as Citi offer a more institutional access point for you to trade foreign currency. If you go this route, you will circumvent the forex brokers and their games.

Don't get me wrong. The banks play the same games, but at a much different level. The problem with using a larger bank such as Citi is that most of these banks require a lot more money in your account to get started. You can find some banks that will require a minimum of $25,000 to $50,000 to open a live trading account. I was speaking with a prime bank the other day that requires a minimum of $100,000 to open a foreign corporate account and $500,000 for a personal account to use its prime banking services.

If you want to trade the forex, you will need to have a trading account and most likely at a retail forex broker. The ones listed in Table 20.1 have their pros and cons. There are other big retail forex brokers in the United States that I have not listed, and you can give them a try as well. The funny thing about all these forex brokers is that when you read the reviews, you will always find someone that likes them and others that don't. So ultimately you will have to make your own decisions about what broker you want to use. I would suggest that you open a demo account and then fund a live account with a small amount of money that you are willing to lose. Then, after making many trades in both your demo and live account, you can make the determination of which broker is right for you.

FOREX TRADING STRATEGIES

21

THE SIMPLE S/R PRICE ACTION STRATEGY

The support and resistance (S/R) price action strategy is a trading method mostly based on price action and its behavior at key levels, which are principally the main horizontal and diagonal S/R zones.

Horizontal zones are confirmed by areas of accumulation or tight ranging, which I also call "decision zones," where buyers and sellers enter a relationship of relative balance. Diagonal zones are determined by trendlines. Another set of horizontal S/R zones is defined with Fibonacci retracement and extension levels.

I analyze the price action of a currency pair by observing the particular candle patterns at those levels and around the decision zones and by paying attention to the successive cycles of accumulation, distribution, and trending. Accumulation is manifested by price moving inside a tight range after a break, and it is usually followed by a period of distribution, which takes place within a much wider range above the previous break and is characterized by a predominance of strong moves in the direction of the main trend.

S/R levels get stronger the more the price attempts to break the level and fails. Also, stronger S/Rs usually test both sides, and price will tend to respect such a level. If Fibonacci levels, daily pivots, and trendlines coincide, the zone will be stronger and able to sustain a high-probability trade.

I have used this strategy as an alternative to my main trading method (which is basically contrarian and short term and presently is circumscribed to the AUD/USD) for the last two years to broaden my choice of currency pairs. I place trades with a longer-term approach because it is very simple and can be applied to any pair with similar results. The strategy elements that follow are used to confirm the trading plan.

STRATEGY ELEMENTS

Indicators
I use S/R levels, daily pivots, price action (chart and candle patterns), Fibonacci levels, and trendlines. Also, I take into consideration the psychological levels and round numbers at 00, 20, 33, 50, 66, and 80 ending pips.

Trading Style
This ranges from day trading to medium term.

Time Frames
I use 4-hour and daily charts to set the global S/R levels:

- 1-hour charts as the main trading time frame
- 15-minute charts for the entries

The strategy can be adapted to longer periods using weekly and daily charts for supports and resistances, 4-hour charts as the main time frame, and 30-minute charts to pinpoint the entries.

Type of Orders
Stop and market orders are used most often. Sometimes limit orders are used when expecting the retest of a confirmed level.

Timing of the Entry
When waiting for a specific candle pattern to be confirmed, and using direct market orders, entries are decided on the close of the

hourly candle and are taken on the 15-minute charts for more precision. There is no specific timing when using stop orders.

Analysis Hours
These occur from London open to U.S. open, usually one or two hours before the opening of the U.S. markets.

Trading Hours
The best session time to trade this strategy is when the London and U.S. markets overlap—usually from 9 a.m. to noon, eastern time.

Distance in Pips from the Trigger Levels
On stop orders, the distance used as a buffer from trigger price levels is 5 to 7 pips, depending on the currency pair.

Instruments
My preferred instruments are the majors: EUR/USD, GBP/USD, EUR/GBP, USD/CHF, AUD/USD; second are yen pairs: EUR/JPY and USD/JPY. This method can be used on any currency instrument.

Risk-to-Reward Ratio
Where possible, this ratio should not be less than 1:3. Some trades between 1:2 and 1:3 can be taken if the probabilities of success are high.

MONEY MANAGEMENT

Risk parameters are set at a maximum of 2 percent of the equity for high-probability trades ("A" trades) and at 1 percent on lower risk-to-reward ratio transactions ("B" trades). Position size and true leverage will depend on the currency pair chosen and the size of the stops. Here are some examples:

Total equity = $10,000
Maximum risk
  A trades = $200
  B trades = $100
EUR/USD trade (pip value = $10 per standard lot) and 20-pip stops

A trade: $200/20 = $10/pip allowable = 1-standard-lot position size, with true leverage at 1:10

B trade: $100/20 = $5/pip allowable = 0.5-lot position size, with true leverage at 1:5

EUR/GBP trade (pip value = $16.66 per standard lot) and 15-pip stops

A trade: $200/15 = $13.33/pip allowable = 0.8-lot position size, with true leverage at 1:8

B trade: $100/15 = $6.66/pip allowable = 0.4-lot position size, with true leverage at 1:4

Note: If you are going to trade several different currency pairs, it is best to use an Excel spreadsheet to calculate the exact lot size for pairs where the quote currency is other than the U.S. dollar. The amount of maximum allowable lots is obtained by dividing the maximum allowable value per pip by the actual pip value for a standard lot.

As per the above examples:

EUR/USD and other XXX/USD pairs = $10/$10 = 1 lot
EUR/GBP = $13.33/$16.66 = 0.8 lot, and successively

EXIT RULES

The stop-loss rule for this strategy is based on relatively tight stops in regard to the expected profits. These would be the primary exits if the trade goes against the direction chosen.

Depending on the main time frame and the trader's ability to monitor the trade actively, three exit methods can be used:

1. A target profit level set according to S/R and risk-to-reward projection
2. Trailing stops set above or below significant resistance or support levels
3. Partial locking of profits in half the position at the projected take-the-profit level and stops to break even on the remainder

BACK-TESTING

This strategy has been extensively back-tested on EUR/USD, GBP/USD, AUD/USD, NZD/USD, EUR/GBP, EUR/JPY, and

USD/JPY, with 100 trades taken on each pair over a three-year period (2007–2009). It has been forward-tested on a real trading account from February 2010 to April 2011, giving similar results in both backward and forward tests. The average win/loss ratio to be expected is 60:40, which is very good given the high risk-to-reward requirements. It is possible to find approximately two or three good trade setups per currency pair in a month.

A Few Charts and Trade Examples

The two EUR/GBP trades shown in Figure 21.1 were taken at the beginning of the second trading week of April 2011. As the S/R levels were very clear, I didn't use Fibonacci retracements in the analysis.

A few days before, the price had already broken both the higher hourly trendline and the daily trendline, retesting the break at 0.87956 and falling back to the lows from where it bounced back again to the upside. On Sunday, the tenth, after the weekly open, I decided to wait for price action around the previous resistance at 0.88519.

The resistance was pierced. However (as we will see in Figure 21.2), the price confirmed a pin bar candle and was rejected back below the resistance level; and although it had returned back above the daily trendline, I thought there was an opportunity for a

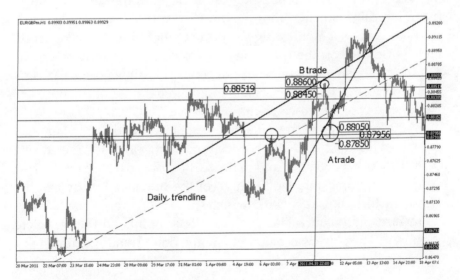

Figure 21.1   EUR/GBP—April 10 and 11, 2011

Figure 21.2   A B trade—short market order at 0.8845

short-term countertrend trade, given the rejection reaction at both the horizontal resistance and the diagonal continuation of the previous hourly rising trendline.

Being in a countertrend position, I placed a pending stop order with tighter stops (15 pips) to be filled at 0.8845 (5 pips below the psychological level and round number 0.8850; see Figure 21.2), with the target profit set 30 pips below, at the level of the second hourly rising trendline starting from the lows on April 7 (0.8815).

Because I was monitoring the trade at that time, the take-profit level wasn't set on the trade, since I would be watching the price action at the rising diagonal support line. This allowed me to eventually perform a partial close, leaving the remainder of the position running in case the move went much lower.

After reaching the trendline level, the price made a pin bar, and I decided to close half of the position at the initial target profit (0.8815), banking 30 pips, and to move the stops to 0.8835 on the rest of the position, just above the high of the previous hourly candle. This way the risk was covered with a small profit above the 1:1 risk-to-reward ratio (equivalent to 5 additional points on the complete position). The price was again below the daily trendline, thus with bearish potential.

Although I generally don't take many countertrend trades with this strategy, I thought there was a fair possibility for prices to move in a range and revisit the lows of the previous week, with small risk (1 percent of equity as this was a B trade) and a reward potential of at least twice the risk taken.

The price again crossed the hourly trendline but was contained by the strong support area at 0.8790–0.8796. I exited the second portion of the trade at 0.8795, obtaining 50 pips on the remainder of the original position, with a net pip amount of 40 on the complete trade and 2.66 percent yield on equity (1 percent × 2.66).

I simply could have closed the whole position at 0.8815, getting a complete 1:2 risk-to-reward ratio; but in the end I got a slightly higher profit, attaining a 1:2.6 risk-to-reward ratio. If I would have been stopped out in the second portion, the risk-to-reward ratio would have ended at 1:1.3.

The decision to take a countertrade was a little bit off the rules; however, the trade was managed as per the strategy in regard to risk levels, position sizing, and overall control of the position, as it was being closely monitored.

As soon as the previously described short was closed, I entered another market order at 0.8805 (5 pips above the round number and 10 pips above the support line) after seeing the bounce (see Figure 21.3). The projection for this trade was much higher, targeting the next round number at 0.8900.

This trade was taken as a high-probability position because the previous highs had pierced the former resistance level at 0.88516 and the overall behavior of the market was still showing bullish momentum on hourly charts, despite the temporary break of the daily trendline. The previous correction proved to be a retest of the support line at 0.87956 and bounced back swiftly.

The stop loss for this position was set at 0.8785, 20 pips with a 2 percent risk on equity, about 6 points below the recent low (0.87912). The target profit was set at 0.8900 as the projection point, a little below the 138.2 percent Fibonacci extension (0.8912 extension point on the swing high from the previous week's lows at 0.8712 to the recent high at 0.8857), because of the proximity of the round number.

Figure 21.3   An A trade—long limit order at 0.8805

The charts show a TP1 level, which was not used to close a portion of the trade, but instead was used as a mark to start trailing the stops. The first mark was set at 0.8820 (15 pips of locked profits) as soon as the price went 45 pips above the entry, reaching the formerly pierced resistance. The second mark for trailing was set at 0.8850 as soon as the break candle closed, and a third trail was set at 0.8872 on the next hourly close.

The price barely touched 0.8900 twice, and the trade didn't close until the fifth candle that broke the level. I was tempted to close manually, but as the profits covered already amounted to a 1:3.3 risk-to-reward ratio, I decided to give it a chance to come to completion by itself and left the trade alone.

Total pips made on this trade: 95 pips for a 1:4.75 risk-to-reward ratio and a 9.50 percent yield on equity (2 percent × 4.75).

EUR/USD—May 4, 2011

Figure 21.4 shows a trade I was finally able to enter, after thinking I had missed the boat the previous day at the time I first spotted the interesting working area and formation. This is an example of a short position entered with a limit order, set at the lower price level of the resistance area.

Figure 21.4   EUR/USD—May 4, 2011

I spotted this opportunity on the four-hour charts while checking on another trade I was monitoring on the AUD/USD, about one hour before the New York markets closed. The pair was already trading at around 1.4825, and so it was too late to enter as per the rules, or the risk-to-reward ratio would be very small, given that the stops had to be placed above the range and upper line of the resistance area (1.4900) and the additional spike up to 1.49386 had added more than 30 pips to the risk.

The euro-dollar had been in a wide 100–120-pip range, with a steady resistance area between 1.4900 and 1.4880. The ideal entry price for a short was just below the range, at 1.4875, with a 2 percent risk (despite being a countertrend trade, the previous price action indicated it was a high-probability A trade) and 30-pip stop loss at 1.4905 (only 5 pips above the round number).

If this level broke to the upside again, it would have meant that the bulls were back for a further rise for a projected target at the other end of the range (1.4770, the higher level in the support area between 1.4770 and 1.4753).

I traced a Fibonacci retracement on the previous swing high from the April 26 lows to the tip of the spike and pin bar, confirming

1.4770 as the 38.2 percent retracement and adding to the probabilities of success. I placed a limit sell order at 1.4875 after the New York markets closed, just in case there was another opportunity to step into the markets, with a stop loss at 1.4905 and target profit at 1.4770. I did this, since the trade development was most probably going to happen while I was sleeping and I'd rather be on the conservative side of the picture, although the next support at the 50 percent level was attainable and beyond, as it proved to be later on.

Figure 21.5 shows how the situation looked on the daily charts: the daily candle was trading near its close price one hour later, and I had to wait for it to close under the broken trendline for confirmation of the bearish tone of the move. The open price on May 5 was lower than on the previous day.

On 30-minute charts (the entry time frame), we can appreciate the coincidence of the Fibonacci levels with the projected entry. The stop loss used was very tight in regard to the previous high at the top of the spike. However, as I said previously, the price chosen was the level at which I would consider the trade to have failed if surpassed, given that the highest top of the range of the resistance zone was at the round number 1.4900 (see Figure 21.6).

Figure 21.5   EUR/USD

Figure 21.6   EUR/USD

The trade was triggered when I was sleeping, and I had a nice surprise to see my profits banked when I reopened the trading platform the next morning. The total profit on this position was 105 pips, giving a risk-to-reward ratio of 1:3.5 and a 7 percent return on equity (2 percent × 3.5). Not bad for a set-and-forget trade.

If I had been able to actively monitor the trade, I would probably have taken partial profits (one-half or two-thirds of the trade) at the set initial conservative target profit, to let the remainder run to the next support level. However, I considered the risk-to-reward on this trade to be fair enough, and the purpose was to be as safe as possible while minimizing the overall risks.

It is better to leave some pips on the table than aim too high and miss the point, just to see the trade come back and blow out your initial stops. In hindsight, this trade could have yielded a 1:8.75 risk-to-reward ratio and a 17.5 percent return on equity! (The price fell below the 261.8 percent extension on the previous swing low.)

NZD/USD—April 27, 2011

Figure 21.7 presents one of the typical setup patterns sought in this strategy: a trending pair that breaks a key resistance or support

Figure 21.7   NZD/USD—April 27, 2011

level, followed by accumulation and then distribution in a wide range before resuming the trend or reversing.

As shown in Figure 21.8, a previous trending phase had ended on a V-type chart pattern, reaching the lower part of the R/S area at 0.7995; it then bounced back to touch the rising trendline and again reached and pierced the resistance area at the round number at the 0.8000 level. It then made another smaller (fractal-type) V pattern before breaking the level frankly and started its accumulation period.

Let's zoom out on 30-minute charts to have an even better picture of all the previous activity:

We had two strongly respected levels during the accumulation phase, one at 0.7990 and the other at 0.8005. I thought this was a good price for a long stop entry, just above the round number and in the direction of the main trend; and after seeing the double bottom (which you can clearly see in Figure 21.9) that had formed the day before, I got my trigger confirmation.

The trade was entered by opening a buy stop order 5 pips above the round number, at 0.8005, with a 15-pip tight stop at 0.7990 and risk level 2 percent of equity. The target profit was set a little below the 138.2 percent Fibonacci extension on the previous swing high

Figure 21.8   NZD/USD

Figure 21.9   NZD/USD

(from the lows at 0.7820 to the high at 0.8006), expecting a 0.1:4.66 risk-to-reward ratio.

The trade was triggered during the night and lasted 17 hours until it reached the target. Almost at the end of the trade, after the

New York markets closed, when the trade already had 50 positive pips and had reached the 127 percent extension level, I moved the stops to 0.8045, securing 40 pips, just in case there was a sudden reversal. Finally, the target was reached, banking 70 pips, which represented a 9.32 percent return on equity (2 percent × 4.66).

There have been many other different trade setups in all the pairs under test; however, this last pattern is what I would consider the most perfect situation among them all.

22

THE CONTRARIAN BB STRATEGY

The core philosophy that I profess about adopting a contrarian point of view on the forex markets is based on two premises: the first is that the majority will most often be going in the wrong direction, and the second is that prices will always tend to regress to the mean.

If you watch the microstructure of price action on any currency pair closely, you will notice that in normal conditions, price exhibits a relatively stable behavior and seems to hover around and come back to a precise value time after time. This is what I would call the "fair value" for that instrument.

People are buying and selling in a short range, which shouldn't change the average value much. Each buyer needs to have a seller and vice versa. Then, at a certain point, external forces seem to enter the market, and both buyers and sellers can become overly enthusiastic or fearful, initiating a crowd behavior that will attract other market participants. As a result, an excess of supply or demand will take place, bringing the currency pair ratio to an overpriced or underpriced condition.

Shortly after, the market comes back to normal operation once more. The price is back to its "fair value" again, which will have slightly appreciated or diminished, depending on the strength, direction, and fundamental support of the previous extreme market sentiment.

The contrarian point of view looks to spot those extreme moves and tries to be ahead of the majority: the market starts to climb, after a while everybody is frantically trying to buy, and this is when the contrarian will start thinking about selling.

Of course, I have to be aware of the subtle signs of market exhaustion before throwing myself blindly into the fire of the action, as sometimes the extreme moves extend over a longer time span. However, every currency pair moves in cycles, and those can be easily measured and understood, provided we dedicate some time to perform a thorough study of a particular couple of currencies.

This strategy has proved to be excellent to work short term on ranging markets, as trades can be taken on both directions successfully; trending requires more waiting time for price to reach the appropriate buying or selling zone.

STRATEGY ELEMENTS

Indicators

- Three 20-period Bollinger Bands (BBs), with 1.5, 2, and 2.5 deviations;
- 34-, 100-, and 200-period simple moving averages
- Daily pivots
- Fibonacci retracement levels
- Trendlines
- S/R levels
- Psychological levels (ending in 00, 20, 33, 50, 66, and 80)
- Price action (chart and candle patterns)

I also use a stochastic indicator with settings at 5, 3, 3 exclusively on the 1-minute charts to spot immediate divergences for extremely short-term trading.

Trading Style

My trading style is basically day trading and short term, with some "scalping" trades eventually.

Time Frames

Short term (less than 1 day) and extreme short term

- Daily charts to evaluate the main direction
- 30-minute charts to evaluate the shorter-term trend
- 5-minute charts as main trend
- 1-minute charts for entries and stochastic divergences

Day trading (1 day to 1 week)

- Daily charts to evaluate the main direction
- 4-hour charts to evaluate the shorter-term trend
- 30-minute charts as main trend
- 5-minute charts for entries

The strategy can be adapted to longer periods using weekly and daily charts for S/R, 4-hour charts as the main time frame, and 30-minute charts to pinpoint the entries.

Type of Orders

These are mostly limit orders, especially on longer-term setups. Both market orders and limit orders can be used on short-term positions. Use only market orders on scalping.

Timing of the Entry

On market entries, I wait for the coincidence of the three lower time frames (trend, main, and entry) and the price coming back from the 2.5-deviation through the 1.5-deviation BB. I will wait for one candle to close inside the middle area (between the 1.5 deviations) and the next one to open in that same area (on the smaller "entry" time frame) before entering the trade.

On scalping entries, the entry will be triggered by a clear divergence spotted on the 1-minute stochastic.

Limit orders will be planned according to specific support, resistance, and Fibonacci retracement levels, jointly with the successive steps of the "route map," which is defined by all the indicators used.

Analysis Hours
I do this daily, just after the New York close. During the weekend, I examine the daily, weekly, and monthly charts to draw the most important levels of support and resistance. I will employ an additional reassessment period about 2 hours before the New York markets open, depending on the previous price action and if there are trades still open.

Trading Hours
Australian/Asian sessions are useful for quiet ranging price action and shorter-term trades. I make use of the 3-hour Europe/London and London/United States overlap, depending on my own time availability. Total trading time is split in two or three parts.

Distance in Pips from the TriggerLevels
Limit orders will be set at 5 pips above spread (for long positions) or 5 pips below (for short trades). Use the psychological levels 00, 20, 33, 50, 66, and 80.

Instruments
This strategy has been tested only on the EUR/USD and AUD/USD with the actual parameters. Although I have been using it for general analysis on other pairs, the settings for the smaller moving average and the three BB periods and deviations would need to be slightly adjusted to match the particularities of other currency pairs.

Risk-to-Reward Ratio
The risk-to-reward ratio is from 1:1 to 1:3. The lower risk-to-reward ratio is compensated by the higher win/loss ratio.

MONEY MANAGEMENT

Risk parameters are set at a maximum of 2 percent of the equity for high-probability trades (A trades) and at 1 percent on lower risk-to-reward ratio transactions (B trades).

Position size and true leverage will depend on the currency pair chosen and the size of the stops, which in turn will depend on the main trading time frame used (see the "Money Management" detailed examples in Chapter 21).

EXIT RULES

Stop losses are set below the 2-deviation BB level, with similar parameters as entries in regard to psychological levels and round numbers.

Depending on the main trading time frame and the trader's capability to monitor the trade actively, these three exit methods, first presented in Chapter 21, can be used:

1. A target profit level set according to S/R and risk-to-reward projection
2. Trailing stops set above or below significant resistance or support levels, as per the route map, psychological numbers, and Fibonacci levels
3. Partial locking of profits in half the position at the projected take-profit level and stops to break even on the remainder. You may want to consider using this variant only for high-probability and swap-positive longer-term trades.

Risk Management

On longer-term high-probability and swap-positive setups, entries can be split in two or three parts for doing averaging-in. The risk (maximum loss allowed) per total position remains the same, but there can be several reentries based on recurring price waves inside a range before a definite impulse in the direction chosen.

Exits and Loss Management

When a longer-term, three-part trade is momentarily going against the original direction, the first position can be partially closed (scaling out the losses one-tenth at a time) starting if and when it reaches 100 negative pips. Meanwhile, the other trades are balancing the loss with their profits, trying to keep at least a 2:1 ratio or higher until the original direction of the trend resumes and all parts can come to completion at the target level that has been set.

An emergency stop loss is set at 2 percent total risk.

Example

Let's assume the following: equity $10,000, total allowable loss
2 percent = $200.

I will usually set a distance for the second trade at 50 pips from
the first entry and the same for the third entry.

When the price goes 50 pips against my direction, I open the
second trade. If the price goes another 50 pips negative, I open the
third trade. The first trade is now 100 pips negative; the second
trade is 50 pips negative. This is a total maximum 100 pips on the
first trade and 50 on the second. The emergency stop is set for all
trades at a 15-pip distance from the third entry (total risk = 115 +
65 + 15 = 195, roughly 200 pips).

My value per pip has to be $1 to meet the risk requirements.

The third trade goes into positive 30 pips but comes back
against the direction. I exit the third trade with 20 pips, giving back
one-third of the profits, and close one-tenth of the first position
[equivalent to 8 pips = (100 − 20)/10].

Net pips = 12

I look to reenter the third trade at the same price as or at least at
a better price than the exit. The entry gets triggered, and the price
goes in my direction 60 pips. The second entry is 10 pips positive. I
close both, banking 70 pips. The first trade is now 40 pips in the
negative.

Net pips = 12 + 70 = 82

I reassess the levels and reenter the second position at either the
previous price or 10 to 15 pips farther from the first entry—in any
case, always at a better price than the exit.

During the process, key levels are moving around and are used
to determine the probable exits as long as the price hasn't recovered
up to the first entry.

The second entry gets triggered 10 pips lower than before. The
first trade is 60 pips in the negative; the price retraces a little bit
and again goes in my direction for 30 pips, and it is at a 20-pip distance from another key level in shorter time frames. The price goes
further, and I close the trade with 40 pips, looking to reenter the

second position, as always, at the same as or at least at a better price than the exit. The first trade is 10 pips negative.

Net pips = 12 + 70 + 40 = 122

The price retraces 20 pips below the exit and hits a key level, and I reenter the second trade at a 30-pip distance from the first entry. The price continues past the first entry and is heading toward the original target level. At the first entry price, I am already 30 pips positive on the second trade. I break even on the first, and I am 112 pips above due to the previously closed positions. Plus the eventual positive swap is added daily to the account.

Only two-thirds of the total position is open; I have banked 142 pips, which represent a 1.42 percent return on equity (pip value = $1)—and the trade is just starting to develop. The target profit is set at a key level with a 1:2 risk-to-reward ratio.

Let's do a comparison with the original scenario at 2 percent risk and average 50-pip stops:

The first position stopped out minus 50. The second position stopped out minus 50. The third position trailed to the entry of the first position = positive 100 pips. The trade would have remained at breakeven: −2 percent −2 percent + (2 × 2 percent) = 0. With this variant, there is an advantage on traditional entries (when the direction is absolutely correct) due to the cyclical nature of the markets and the positive swap. Should the trade be totally wrong in the end, the loss would be only 2 percent or less (thanks to the partial covering and exiting of negatives) and would have conformed to the risk policy.

(*Note:* The above is a hypothetical situation to explain the process; a detailed description of a series of variant trades taken on my real account is included at the end of this chapter.)

BACK-TESTING

This strategy, as well as its variant, has been back-tested exclusively and extensively on the EUR/USD and AUD/USD over a short 3-month period in late 2008. Given the excellent results, I decided to launch the forward-test in my live trading account, and I have been using it as my main strategy since February 2009 up to now (May 2011). The average win/loss ratio to be expected is around 80:20. There are plenty of trades to be taken daily on shorter time frames.

CHARTS AND TRADE EXAMPLES

The Basic Setup: Indicators

Indicators are no more than what their name suggests: a signpost on the road, a call for alertness at a certain point in time and price.

Prices evolve in waves or cycles and most of the time are bound within a range. That range can be flat or horizontal (sideways market) or move inside diagonal boundaries: slightly ascending (bullish) or descending (bearish). After thousands of hours watching the charts, either trading live and forward or using the visual tools of the simulator platform, I have observed that price action exhibits a recurrent behavior when reaching or getting near those particular signposts.

The whole setup uses a multi–time frame approach, because I have also noticed that when a key level is broken on a smaller period, the action will continue on the next upper time frame (see Figure 22.1).

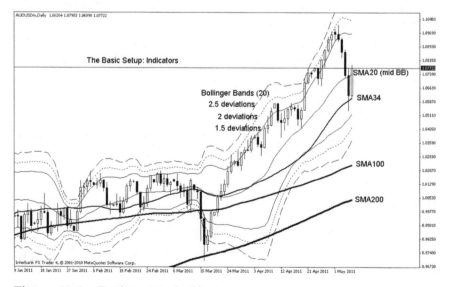

Figure 22.1   Basic setup indicators

A Short Description of the Cyclic "Route"

The following is roughly what can be expected at every level in any of the major or minor route maps.

1. BBs, 20 Periods, 2.5 Deviations

Price is coming to one of its extremes and can either break this level to the outside (which signals a high probability for a continuation of the current direction) or come near and reverse back to the lesser deviation level.

2. BBs, 20 Periods, 2 Deviations

This is the standard setting for BBs. It's not really needed on the charts but kept there as a visual aid to compare the behavior of the other two deviation levels.

3. BBs, 20 Periods, 1.5 Deviations

This is the key level that signals a reverse move to the middle line or even all the way through to the other side of the bands. When a candle closes "outside" this level (below the upper 1.5-deviation band for a short position or above the lower 1.5-deviation band for a long trade) and the next candle also opens outside, the price will almost invariably continue to at least the middle line or the 34-period simple moving average, or SMA34 (whichever comes first depending on the position of the moving averages on the chart). Most of the time (about 80 to 85 percent) and especially on shorter time frames, the price will walk back through the whole set toward the opposite group of bands.

4. Middle Line of BBs (20-Period Simple Moving Average, or SMA20)

This line signals the exact mean of the range; however, it is usually weaker than the following moving average (SMA34). Here the price will almost always bounce back at about halfway through the distance that separates it from the 1.5-deviation BB line if the markets are ranging. On strong trending or corrective price action, this level can be overlooked, and the price will prefer to react on the next, especially when this line comes before the 34-period moving average line.

5. 34-Period Simple Moving Average (SMA34)

This is a key level especially in trending markets for EUR/USD and AUD/USD currency pairs. This level might have to be adjusted to match other instruments.

The price here will practically *always* bounce back *once* for a retest either to the middle line of the bands, if it comes second to it, or to the 1.5-deviation band line, and this occurs independently of the direction of the trend. This is the exit level I mostly use for countertrend trades, as the price will tend to stick to it and react as if it were a trendline. When broken, this level will also almost invariably be retested at least once.

The conservative level to use in these cases is some point between the middle line of the bands and the SMA34, not the exact price level of the indicator. To determine this with further accuracy I will need to examine other elements in play such as S/R, pivots, and Fibonacci levels.

6. 100-Period Simple Moving Average (SMA100)

After the price has clearly broken and retested the SMA34, this is the next key level that is almost always tested or pierced once; then the price is rejected and can come back to cross through the level later if it has been clearly pierced. The other elements I will use here to determine further price action are its position in regard to the psychological levels (price ending in 00, 20, 33, 50, 66, and 80) and Fibonacci retracement zones, along with key supports or resistances.

7. 200-Period Simple Moving Average (SMA200)

This is the ultimate key level to determine a trend reversal, especially on longer time frames (4 hours and higher). This level is usually tested once or twice before being effectively crossed. Therefore, we can expect the price action to bounce back for significant corrections on the previous moves, and this on a higher time frame can yield a significant pip amount.

When the Action Has Progressed on a Lower Time Frame, It Has to Be Followed Up on the Next Upper Time Frame

Multi–time frame assessments are to be done both ways. I will first analyze the charts from the higher period down to the smaller time spans to see the overall action and to be able to enter at the best possible price. Then when a trade is in progress, I will be watching successively how the price behaves in regard to the above-mentioned steps or signposts, from the lower time frame (1-minute charts) upward. The key to switch to the next period is the price behavior around SMA34 and the middle line of the bands.

When this area is clearly broken on the 1-minute charts, I will then watch the price location on the 5-minute charts. Should I also be above (or below) the SMA34, I will step to the 15-minute, 30-minute, and so on and evaluate in which precise time frame is the present action really occurring (waves within waves).

I once constructed a multi–time frame BB indicator for analysis with all three deviation levels on the four key time frames of the strategy, but the resulting chart looked quite cluttered. It was, however, very interesting to be able to see at a glance the exact point in which the price was related to the global picture.

Figure 22.2 provides a snapshot of a simplified version of such an indicator, only showing the two deviations, 20-period BBs for three time frames (daily, 4 hours, and 30 minutes) from the point of view of the 4-hour chart.

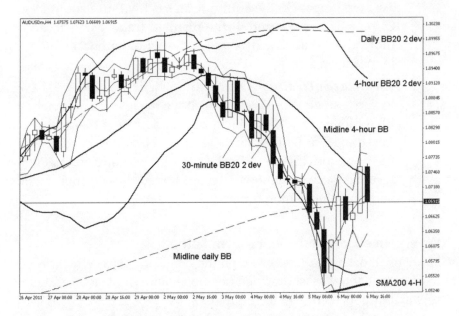

Figure 22.2   Multi–time frame assessment chart

Short-Term Time Frame Setup

The daily chart is the main analysis time frame for any of the styles used (short term, day trading. or longer). Additionally, weekly and monthly charts can be used to determine key S/R levels, but their setup behavior is not taken into account.

If we examine the set of charts in Figure 22.3, we will see the following:

- *Daily chart.* The price was rejected from the key level SMA34 and has slightly crossed back through the middle line of the bands. We have to wait for the close of the candle to see if it might consolidate between those two levels or if it is going back to the upper bands. The trend is bullish.

- *30-minute chart (overall trend).* The trend here looks bullish, but the price has reached the SMA200 and bounced back. Watch out for a retest of the support and the convergence of smaller moving averages.

- *5-minute chart (main trading chart).* The main trading time frame is the one that will be used to calculate the appropriate stop levels and trade targets according to that period's average range. On the 5-minute charts I will use about 20 to 25 pips as a maximum. If the planned trade seems to need more than that, I will reassess the whole scene using the longer-term setup parameters.

- *1-minute chart (entries).* On the entry chart, the price will have to successively close and open above the lower 1.5-deviation BB for longs and below the upper 1.5-deviation BB for shorts. The trade can be taken on the second opening candle; or if the price goes higher too fast, I can set a pending order at that level while waiting for a retest, provided the direction is still valid on higher time frames.

Divergence Extremely Short-Term Setup

I only use stochastic divergences on the 1-minute charts when I want to enter fast and very short-lived positions, with tight stops and narrow exit targets (about 10 to 15 pips).

Figure 22.4 provides an example of a trade taken about 1 hour ago.

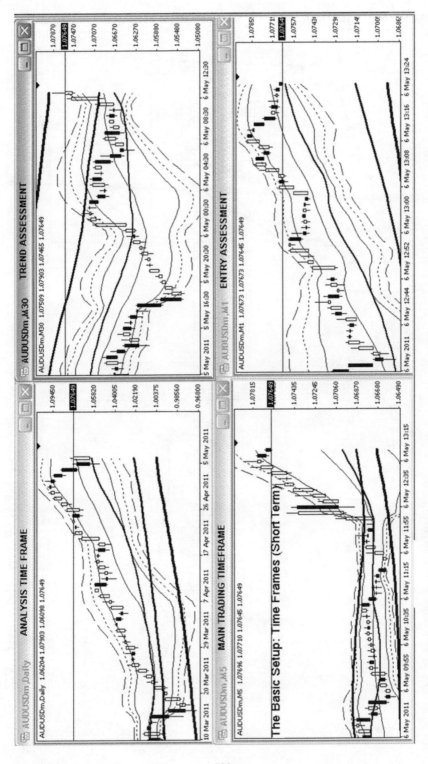

Figure 22.3   Short-term time frame setup

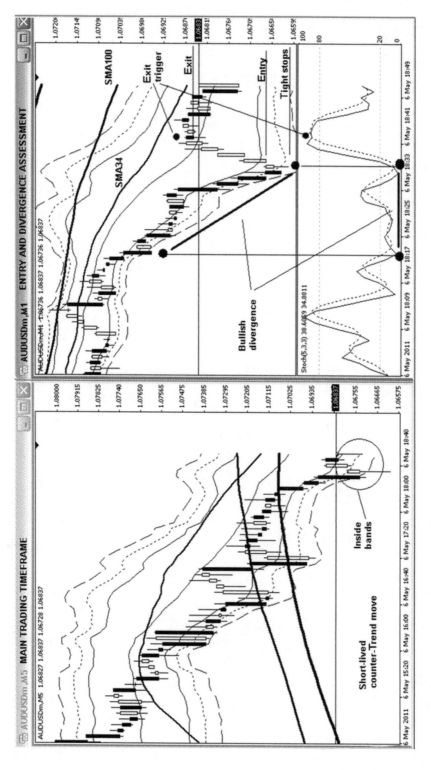

Figure 22.4   Divergence extremely short-term setup

This trade was manually entered at 1.0668 (1.0666 bid + 2-pip spread) on the next 1-minute candle after the stochastic cross up, with stops set at 1.0658 (2 pips below the previous low) and exited at 1.0685. As this style of trading requires full-focused monitoring, the actual stop exit would be triggered sooner than simply letting the price blow the stop loss, which is only set as emergency protection.

The risk allowance used was 1 percent, as we could consider these positions to be B-type trades. The trade yielded 17 pips for a 1:1.7 risk-to-reward ratio and 1.7 percent return on equity. Not bad for an overall 5-minute trade duration plus 1 minute for assessment.

Although I prefer the less stressful method of placing pending orders and allowing the markets to come to my positions, this was the original basic setup when I started testing this strategy, averaging 50 to 70 trades per day. Of course, the enormous expenditure of quality focused time was utterly draining, and after a month or two I started envisioning a more tranquil version with higher potential returns. However, sometimes I will dedicate an hour here and there to this scalping style, especially during slow and ranging times, to keep attuned to the market's pulse and to gauge and update my reaction skills.

Technically, the risk-to-reward ratio here is barely 1:1; however—and as said above—this is only a small part of the whole strategy that fits into my own reaction training. Relatively "large" stops (10 pips) are only there to take care of eventual unpredictable situations (power outages, server disconnections, etc.). Should the position go against my direction, I usually don't allow more than 4 or 5 pips (2 times the spread at most) before exiting, as these are very short-lived moves, especially when countertrending.

Day Trading or Medium-Term Time Frame Setup

The same as for the shorter-term setup, the daily chart is used as a main analysis time frame. In Figure 22.5, we can see the following:

- *Daily chart.* This is the same scenario as above. The price has been rejected from the key level SMA34 and has slightly crossed back through the middle line of the bands. We have to wait for the close of the candle to see if it might consolidate

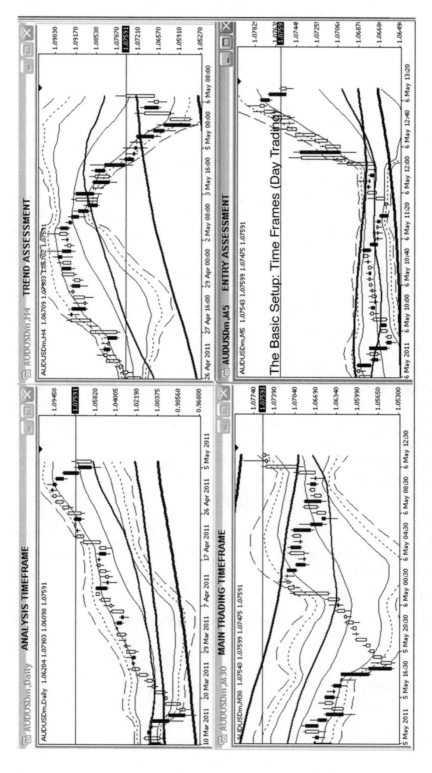

Figure 22.5   Day-trading or medium-term time frame setup

between those two levels or if it is going back to the upper bands. The trend is bullish.

- *4-hour chart (overall trend).* The chart shows we are into a correction phase after a bearish trend. The price is still above the SMA200, but the smaller moving average is turning while the SMA100 is nearly flat. This could be signaling a consolidation phase soon.
- *30-minute chart (main trading chart).* The main trading time frame is the one that will be used to calculate the appropriate stop levels and trade targets according to that period's average range. On the 30-minute charts I will use about 50 to 60 pips. If the planned trade seems to need more than that, I will not take the position.
- *5-minute chart (entries).* On the entry chart, the price will have to successively close and open above the lower 1.5-deviation BB for longs and below the upper 1.5-deviation BB for shorts. The trade can be taken on the second opening candle; or if the price goes higher too fast, we can set a pending order at that level while waiting for a retest, provided the direction is still valid on higher time frames.

ANALYSIS TIME FRAME: THE DAILY CHART

The most important part of this strategy is to evaluate, as accurately as possible, the actual position of the price on the daily route map in relation to the indicators. The beauty of this setup is that, at least for the EUR/USD and the AUD/USD, the settings will work for any time frame you decide to look at. As Figure 22.6 shows, price action exhibits a recurrent behavior more than 80 percent of the time at each step of the route, and market waves become almost predictable.

SHORT-TERM TRADING

Trend Assessment: The 30-Minute Chart

As you can see from Figure 22.7, the main trend is down but presently inside a corrective move; however, it is still trading below the SMA200. Expect a retest of the recently broken resistance and

Figure 22.6   Analysis time frame: the daily chart

Figure 22.7   Trend assessment: the 30-minute chart

confluence of smaller moving averages to the middle line of the bands. Watch for price action and on the opposite side of the bands, should the price revisit the lows.

Main Trading Time Frame: The 5-Minute Chart

In the case of Figure 22.8, we would wait for a retest of the middle line of the bands for an eventual move further to the upside. The stop levels needed would be too wide for this time frame; therefore either we wait for a short position, if the price revisits the highs and comes back below the upper BB 1.5 deviation, or we wait for a fall to the previous lows and the confluence of moving averages. However, we have another support at the SMA34 level, and the price could regain bullish strength. Take no trades in the middle of the action on this time frame; stops shouldn't be wider than 20 to 25 pips, at most.

Figure 22.8   Main trading time frame: the 5-minute chart

Entry Assessment: The 1-Minute Chart

Look at Figure 22.9. The best entry point for long trades here would be around the 1.0690–1.0700 level, provided the higher time frames confirm the direction. The lower support zone is at 1.0670, where the price has been respected on both sides in the past. It is too late to envision a short entry (we should have entered, in any case, when the price came back down, opening below the upper 1.5-deviation BB) because the stops would have to be at least above the second previous highs and upper 2.5-deviation BB and because the next support

Figure 22.9   Entry assessment: the 1-minute chart

level at SMA100 is at a smaller distance, making the basic risk-to-reward ratio less than 1:1.

DAY TRADING OR MEDIUM-TERM TRADING

Trend Assessment: The 4-Hour Chart

You can see from Figure 22.10 that the price has just made a correction to the SMA200, which it did not pierce, and is coming back up toward the SMA34, having closed above the middle line of the BBs. There is a strong resistance area here, which has been respected on both sides.

The trend is still bullish, but we need to watch closely the price behavior should it reach the upper level, as it could briefly spike to retest the highs area at the upper bands and come back stronger to the downside. Looks like we might have a tighter ranging action around the present levels, as bands are starting to curl and converge.

Main Trading Time Frame: The 30-Minute Chart

In Figure 22.11, the price is climbing and has almost reached the SMA200, then being rejected, but it is still inside the upper bands. The situation looks bullish, but we are into a correction of the

Figure 22.10   Trend assessment: the 4-hour chart

Figure 22.11   Main trading time frame: the 30-minute chart

downtrend. Since the price will probably retest the broken level in the 1.0800–1.0830 zone and the SMA200 hasn't yet been pierced, we could expect a first rejection after doing so.

Shorts would need greater stops and would offer too small a risk-to-reward ratio even at that point, as smaller moving bands are curling up and the SMA34 is about to cross the SMA100. Better to wait for another dip to the lows and plan for longs.

Entry Assessment: The 5-Minute Chart
In looking at Figure 22.12, we would want to wait for the price to come back at least at the 1.0670–1.0690 level for longs, with 50-pip stops a few points below the lowest lows that are visible on the chart. A short countertrend entry can be envisioned if the price climbs back to the upper 1.5-deviation BB and stays below the upper deviation. Watch the price action around those levels.

Figure 22.12   Entry assessment: the 5-minute chart

Also, a variant long trade could be attempted using the same stop level (below 1.0630), with the first entry at 1.0735 just above the SMA34 level and early May resistance. In any case, the price will most likely fall toward the SMA34; and price action, at that moment, will determine which is the best choice to employ.

Variant Real Trade Example and Single-Trade Follow-Up
This real-life example began on January 12, 2011, after the New York markets closed.

The daily charts were showing a strong bullish engulfing candle that had bounced from the SMA100 and had reached the SMA34. The trend was bullish. However, it was too late for an entry at that moment. The SMA100 was around 0.9860 and climbing. I decided to wait for the next candle behavior. On January 13, I could see that the SMA34 was pierced and the price closed above it; the candle looked bearish (sort of a spinning top with larger body).

The 4-hour charts showed a tweezer top at about midday, and the price seemed to be in a wide range. The parity level had also been pierced.

On the main trading time frame (30-minute chart), I could see that the price had retested the broken level at 0.9920–0.9930 as well as the SMA200 early in the day, being rejected strongly and crossing all moving averages, reaching above parity. The SMA200 was flat, and the slope of the other two moving averages was going up.

On the entry time frame (5-minute chart), the price was still too high for a direct entry (0.9978) and was trading at a confluence of nearly flat moving averages.

The lower daily BB (1.5 deviation) was flat at 0.9885. Being that parity was already surpassed and given the previous strong engulfing candle, I believed that the price would go significantly higher, and I was targeting the upper daily BB level and round number at 1.0200, below the previous highs. Given the ranging behavior in the 4-hour and 5-minute charts, I decided to employ the variant, as it was possible to have some fluctuation of the range; and even if there wasn't and only one trade were to reach the target, the risk-to-reward ratio would still have been near to 1:1.5.

As Figure 22.13 shows, I placed a first limit order 20 pips above the lower BB level, at 0.9905, and 5 pips above the round number. I placed the second and third orders, as well, at 0.9855 and 0.9805, respectively. The stop loss for all of them was set at 0.9790, 15 pips below the third entry and 12 pips below the previous lower low (0.9802), which would be the key level where the trade direction would prove to be wrong. The total risk was 2 percent.

The first order was triggered on January 14, a few hours before the opening of the New York markets. The price fell about 30 pips more and recovered, barely to break even +5. It then fell again, 2 pips lower but above the second entry, which wasn't triggered. The price

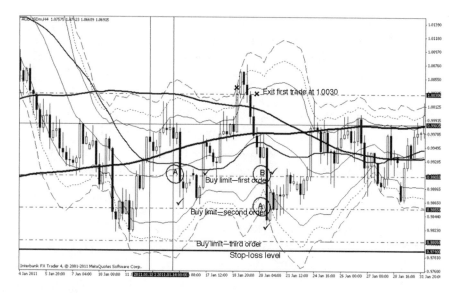

Figure 22.13   AUD/USD

rejected that level and opened the next Sunday above the Friday close
with a small gap, ranged again toward the second entry level making
a higher low, and crossed all moving averages to the other side of the
BBs. I decided to exit the trade at 1.0030 early on day 19, below the
psychological level 1.0033 and near the level of the upper BB deviation of 2.5. The main reasons were that the price seemed to be ranging for a while and that the moving averages were pointing in
conflicting directions, almost flat.

The result: net pips = 125, equivalent to 1.25 percent of equity
(the position size on this triple setup is always at 1:1 true leverage
for these currency pairs and stop levels).

I placed the pending order again at the same level (0.9905), leaving the other two also in place. The first order was triggered again
on day 20 by a 4-hour candle, which broke through the whole set of
lower bands and triggered the second order about 2 hours later.

I exited both trades on February 2, after the price opened outside of the BB deviation of 1.5 on the 4-hour chart, at 1.0115 (see
Figure 22.14).

The result: net pips = 210 on the first trade and 260 on the second
trade for a total of 470 pips and 4.7 percent return on equity.

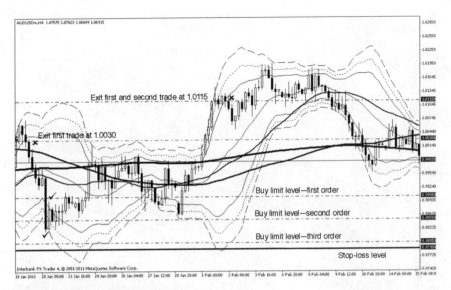

Figure 22.14   AUD/USD

Total net pips on the variant up to now: 125 + 470 = 595 and a 5.95 percent return on equity.

I was now well above the breakeven level, with a risk-to-reward ratio of nearly 1:3. I considered the variant to be one single trade over a longer period of time, with multiple recurrent entries at specific levels.

The direction was still valid, and I kept an eye on those entry levels and final target for a next opportunity as the price was now ranging inside tightening BBs on the 4-hour and daily charts.

Given the subsequent price action and scope of the daily range, along with a new resistance level that formed near my projected target, and knowing the price was rejected, falling to the other side of the range, I then waited to see how the price was going to behave around the formerly respected support zone and psychological levels between 0.9866 and 0.9833.

As you can see from Figure 22.15, the price didn't break at 1.0200, nor did it attempt to reach the previous all-time high (1.0255). Instead, it had made a lower high and a double top (1.0189–1.0199 resistance zone on the 4-hour charts), forming a symmetrical triangle pattern. I decided to close all pending orders and abandon the variant to wait for an impending break, most probably to the downside,

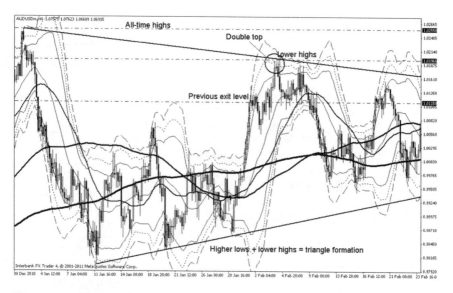

Figure 22.15   AUD/USD

as bearish channels were starting to form, each at a steeper angle than the previous one.

Figure 22.16 depicts what happened next. The price broke the triangle formation, after also piercing the SMA200 and doing an ample whipsaw move to test the critical break zone; then it broke the parity support level and then a key support level at 0.9950, going on to pierce 0.9866 (the level I was watching) and breaking it as in a never-ending avalanche.

As you can see from Figure 22.17, I then placed (on March 16) a Fibonacci retracement/extension indicator on the 4-hour chart measuring the levels on the triangle range of late January–early February (0.9866 to 1.0200). I noticed that the most recent low (0.9702) was below the 138.2 percent extension of the range and that the price was strongly rejected back up. I decided to wait a little more, and it made a retest of the broken lows, getting out of the band zone.

Thinking this was a good level for a return back to the bullish scene, I opened a normal pending order on the next day, at 0.9805 (5 pips above the round number and previous candle low level outside the 1.5-deviation lower BB). The stop loss was set at 2 percent

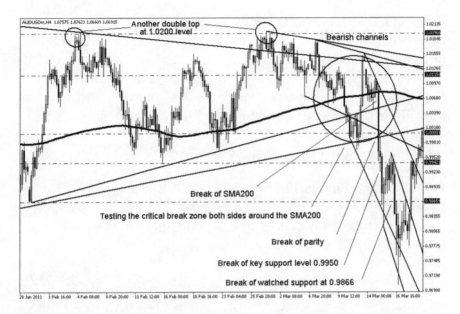

Figure 22.16   AUD/USD

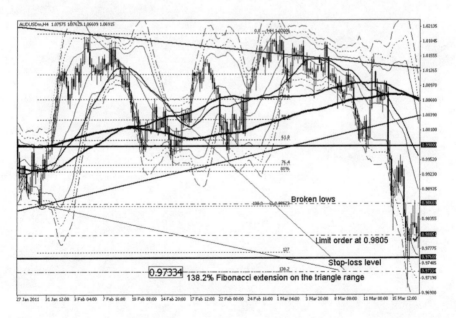

Figure 22.17   AUD/USD

risk and 45 pips, priced at 0.9760 (10 pips below the 1.5-deviation BB level), conservatively targeting 0.9980 (a little below parity just in case) for a 1:3.88 risk-to-reward ratio. I trailed the stop to 0.9930 (locking 125 pips) on that Friday to leave the trade for the weekend. The target was reached on the following Monday, with net pips 175 and a 7.75 percent return on equity (2 percent × 3.88).

ADDITIONAL ANALYSIS TOOLS

I will finally mention that I have used the *Commitments of Traders Report* on several opportunities in net open interest and positions on currency futures to further gauge the potential for a trend reversal at market extremes.

CHAPTER 23

HEDGING STRATEGIES

Every trader's portfolio should include several tools for its protection. Among them, diversification of assets is paramount, and it allows an additional practice: hedging as a means of locking in profits or reducing the risks of loss in the trading account.

In all aspects of my trading, I use various methods of trading. Prior to some of the most recent regulatory rule changes, one could hedge on both sides of a trade. What I mean by this is that you could have gone long on the EUR/USD and short the EUR/USD. This would have given you a perfect hedge. Now, you basically have to find correlated currency pairs to put an effective hedge down. There are, of course, downsides to hedging along with positive attributes. We will talk about that in this chapter.

WHAT IS HEDGING?

Let me start by explaining what hedging *is not*. Many inexperienced traders think that hedging is simply placing a trade in the opposite direction with the same quantity of lots and in the same currency pair. This is not the most effective way to hedge. It won't be long until you get into an impossible situation where you cannot exit one of the trades without compromising the account as a whole, risking or, worse, getting a margin call (account liquidation). So-called hedging on the same instrument only locks in the loss.

Most of the traders I know that use a perfect hedge-type strategy usually trade inside the position to create profits until they can close out the hedge.

Let's briefly look at the basic hedge that most traders are familiar with when trading the forex. This was a prevalent way for traders to reduce risk prior to the regulatory rule changes ... or so they thought.

As mentioned earlier, traders would buy the EUR/USD long and sell the EUR/USD short, thus creating the perfect hedge, simply meaning that regardless of what the trade did, the trader would have locked in the gain or loss. Some traders would use this strategy at the end of the week, so that when the market reopened, they would be protected against a gap in the wrong direction of their trade. And some traders would use the strategy to hedge their open position, so that they did not have to sit in front of the computer.

Traders were so adamant about this strategy that they even considered, in some cases, moving their trading accounts out of the United States to other countries where the traders could still hedge in the same currency pair. Well, this strategy is not all that great. Let's break it down and take a look at a few examples.

If you are up in your trade and want to hedge it, then you will lock in your profit, minus the new spread you have to pay to open the other side of the trade. The same holds true if you are in a losing position but you want to lock in the loss before a big news announcement or the weekend. You will lock in your loss and incur a little more loss because you have to pay the spread on the newly opened lots.

Many traders that use this strategy will often stay in the hedge and simply trade against it, or better said, place more trades. Let's look at that scenario. Let's say you have 10 lots long on the EUR/USD and 10 lots short on the EUR/USD. It doesn't matter if you have the loss or gain locked in or if you are in a breakeven scenario; however, if you are close to breakeven, you may want to just consider closing the trade until after the weekend or a news announcement and take your loss or gain.

Traders will often build into a core position. So before you are hedged and you think that the EUR/USD is going up, you start buying. You buy 1 lot, it goes against you, and then you buy more; you continue to cost-average as the EUR/USD goes down against you. Finally, you have 10 lots open long on the EUR/USD. All of a sudden, the pair breaks down further, so instead of cost-averaging down, you open a 10-lot short EUR/USD trade. Now you are hedged with your loss locked in.

Theoretically you can sit in the trade and lose no more. At this point, you can do a few different things:

You can add lots to either side of the trade—which means you are now long or short and not hedged, making money along the way, picking up pips until you bridge the gap of your locked-in loss on the hedge—and then just close the trade and be done.

Or you can wait until the currency pair, in this case the EUR/USD, reaches a support level and starts to turn up in your direction. At this point you can then close the 10 short EUR/USD lots you had open, leaving you with your 10 long EUR/USD lots open. Many traders will, at this time, add to their position. So let's say you add 10 more long EUR/USD lots to your already open position, giving you a total of 20 long EUR/USD open lots.

Now you only need the price to move half of what you initially needed to break even. This works, and I know traders that only trade this strategy. However, it is risky, as the currency pair might continue to break down and create double the exposure for you. Worse yet, you may not have used proper money management, and now you are overleveraged. If you are going to trade this way, make sure you take into consideration that you might have to double your position. You do not want to be overmargined or overleveraged.

Let's talk about what happens if you are in that situation, because it is not necessarily a good place to be. This example is from a real trade from someone I know that trades this type of hedging strategy.

The trader was long the EUR/USD and was in a significant drawdown. The trader, in my opinion, had actually overtraded the account, and a major news announcement was scheduled for the next day. The trader continued to cost-average down on the trade, which, by the way, can get you in some deep trouble if you don't know what you are doing. So in this case, prior to the major news announcement, the trader put on a hedge on the other side of the EUR/USD.

The trader was now perfectly hedged with a loss locked in until after the news, so he thought. The trader was now watching as the horror unfolded. You see, the banks are not stupid; they see your trades, and in this case, the account was overmargined and the bank knew it. The bank knew that if it pushed the trade, the account would go into liquidation status and be closed.

Yes, the banks will try to take your money. So here is what happened: the news came out, and the bank, in this case, held one side of the currency pair, meaning that instead of a two-wide spread, the bank increased the spread enough that it caused the account to go into liquidation status.

So the bid stayed the same and the ask moved 150 pips away. The banks will actually do this, especially if you have a lot of money on the trade, or you have been making lots of money, or you are overmargined. What a scam. The huge spread resulted in the account going into liquidation, resulting in yet another forex account being blown up. You can avoid this scenario by using good money management and taking this scenario into account if you plan on cost-averaging down. You just have to factor all that in ahead of time so that you know how many lots you can put on.

In my book *Forex Trading Secrets*, I have described one of the fairly common hedging strategies among forex traders, which employs either a basket of currency pairs or just two pairs highly correlated. This true hedging is quite an interesting strategy; however, the degree of relative correlation can vary and is never perfect, thus increasing the risks of wrong proportioning and adding some complication to the picture with the need for closely monitoring the correlations, pip values, and swap rates.

Now, using the same base currency, as is the case with futures options, or even the same currency pair, let's examine a few alternatives based on forex options that you can use to realize a practically perfect hedge to protect your forex trades.

Hedging can be considered as insurance against a potential negative outcome. It will not erase the risk, but the impact of a wrong turn in the markets under unpredictable events can be greatly reduced. The original investment is protected through another investment, the value of which will have to change proportionally in the opposite direction.

It is important to understand that hedging by itself is not a strategy to make money, but an instrument to diminish the possibility of a loss. Risk reduction also implies profit reduction; however, in the eventuality that your original investment loses money, your decision to hedge will help in making that loss much smaller.

Derivatives as futures and options are financial instruments that can be applied to prop up your forex trades, thanks to the development of strategies that allow you to offset the eventual losses in your trading by obtaining profits on the derivative.

Forex options can be used in addition to stop-loss orders or even replace the need for stops. When you buy an option, your profit potential is unlimited if the price continues to move against your forex trade after your stop has been hit. Conversely, your current profits on a trade are locked in as soon as the forex option is bought; and if the prices continue in your original direction, the cost of the option can simply be considered as insurance against a potential reversal.

The outstanding issue with forex options trading is that the risk-to-reward ratio can be very variable, as the cost of the premium will change depending on the strike prices and dates of expiration.

Before attempting to hedge a forex trade with forex options, you need to evaluate carefully if the benefits expected outweigh or at least match the costs. The main purpose of this specific strategy is to protect you from eventual losses, not to make money. Costs can't be avoided, but you can eliminate some of the uncertainty from the situation.

HEDGING WITH CURRENCY FUTURES (GLOBEX)

Long AUD/USD Long Put Australian Dollar

In the charts that appear in this section, you can appreciate how the Globex currency futures prices for the Australian dollar are tightly correlated to the AUD/USD currency pair. This hypothetical example will show how we can benefit from this correlation to apply a protective option to lock in the profits already made on a trending situation.

Example:
Let's say I decided to enter the markets on March 23, 2011, with a long position on the AUD/USD on the next daily candle open at 1.0128, after the rejection from the SMA200 and subsequent break of the middle line of the BBs setup.

As Figure 23.1 shows, the pair breaks to the upside and starts trending nicely, reaching a high at 1.1010 and turning down for a correction. At this point, I could have closed the trade and made 882 pips; however, as I am trading with a longer-term target of 1.1200, I wish to hold on and benefit from the carry.

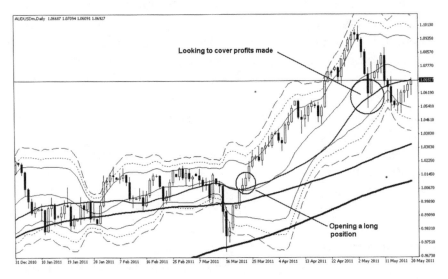

Figure 23.1

On May 5, the pair breaks through the middle line of the bands and pierces the SMA100, also breaking the support zone between 1.7020 and 1.0680. I want to limit the risks while still holding through a possible greater correction, and so I decide to buy a put option on the Australian dollar futures with a strike price at 1.0800 and one forward month expiration date (see Figure 23.2).

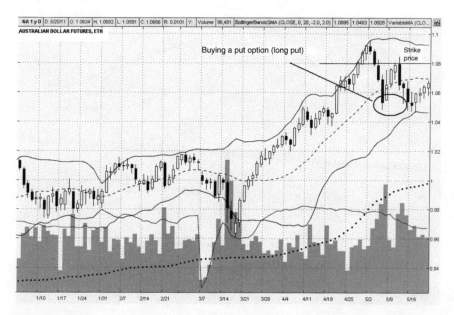

Figure 23.2

The option is currently ITM. My profits are safe minus the cost of the premium and the added possibility that the option turns profitable before expiry, allowing me either to close it as soon as the AUD/USD resumes its trend or to exercise the option and take profits on both the forex trade and the underlying futures if the downtrend continues.

Short USD/CHF Long Put Swiss Franc

Here we have a different scenario in the case of the USD/CHF, as the futures currency we need to use for a hedge is the quote currency (the Swiss franc), which is inversely correlated to the forex currency pair. If it were the base currency, we would be using a long call option to protect a short position, but here we need to employ a long put option again, this time on the Swiss franc futures.

Example:
I decide to open a short position on the USD/CHF after the break of support area below 0.9340 (see Figure 23.3). I wait for a retest of the middle line of the bands and the mentioned broken level, and so I set a limit order at 0.9340, which is triggered on March 8, 2011.

Figure 23.3

The price keeps trending lower and makes several corrections and retests, until it reaches 0.8555 two months later (785 pips). At that point, the USD/CHF does a significant correction, crossing back up through the middle bands and reaching above the most recent S/R level and SMA34.

On May 15, 2011, seeing that the Swiss franc futures are still in a clear uptrend, I decide to hedge my USD/CHF trade with a long put option, also with a higher strike price and being ITM at 1.1600 (see Figure 23.4).

The expected alternatives are similar to those of the previous hedge; profits on the forex trade are protected, and should the USD/CHF reverse its trend, the Swiss franc futures options contract would be further ITM with accrued value.

BULLISH HEDGING WITH FOREX VANILLA OPTIONS

Covered Call

This strategy uses a direct long spot forex position, which is covered by a short call option. It is commonly used to lock in the profits already made on the currency trade.

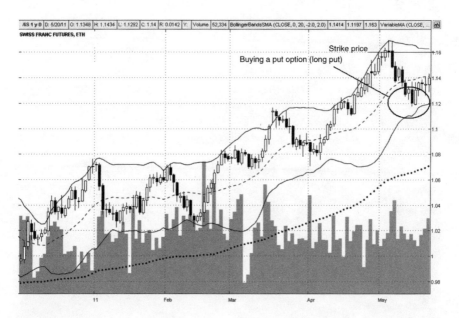

Figure 23.4

The risks are unlimited if the direction changes to the bearish side, while the maximum gain you can expect is the premium received on the written short call option. This usually allows the trader to hold on to a position in a strong bullish trend while periodically generating income from the sold options.

(A variant of this strategy is the protected covered call: this involves adding a long put OTM option to the above. This alternative is intended to limit the risks on the downside should there be a huge fall in the forex pair market's rate.)

Let's look at an actual case.

Example:

On May 16, 2011, I evaluated the 1-hour AUD/USD chart, and seeing that the resistance zone between 1.0620 and 1.0635 had been significantly pierced, I decided to place a covered call on the pullback (see Figures 23.5 and 23.6). I bought 1 lot of the currency pair at 1.0602 and protected the trade with a 1-lot short call with a strike price set at 1.0000 (the premium received was very high, as the call option was deeply ITM).

Order	Order Date (GMT)	Product	Exp. Date	Buy/Sell	Pos. Type	Order Type	Qty	Strike	Filled	Filled Amt	Fees	Total Cost
37828	5/16/11 7:12 PM	AUD/USD	N/A	OPEN BUY	CASH	MARKET	1	CASH	1.06022	0.00	0.00	0.00
37945	5/17/11 7:10 PM	AUD/USD	N/A	CLOSE SELL	CASH	MARKET	1	CASH	1.06135	113.00	0.00	113.00

Net Result

First option entry

37829 **1.0597**	5/16/11 7:13 PM	AUD/USD	May'11	OPEN SELL	CALL	MARKET	1	1.00000	.05969	5,969.00	0.00	5,969.00
37837 **1.0560**	5/16/11 9:24 PM	AUD/USD	May'11	CLOSE BUY	CALL	MARKET	1	1.00000	.05652	-5,652.00	0.00	-5,652.00

Net Result

Second option entry

37838 **1.0560**	5/16/11 9:27 PM	AUD/USD	May'11	OPEN SELL	CALL	MARKET	1	1.07000	.00093	93.00	0.00	93.00
37949 **1.0613**	5/17/11 7:11 PM	AUD/USD	May'11	CLOSE BUY	CALL	MARKET	1	1.07000	.00187	-187.00	0.00	-187.00

Net Result

Net profit = 113 + 317 − 94 = 336

Figure 23.5 Covered call trade example

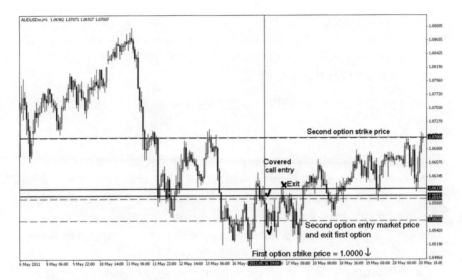

Figure 23.6   Covered call chart

To summarize:

Buy 1 lot AUD/USD on May 16, 2011, at 7:12 p.m. at rate 1.0602
Sell 1-lot call AUD/USD at 7:13 p.m. at rate 1.0597 with a strike
    price of 1.0000 (first option entry)

Nearly $2^1/_2$ hours later I checked the platform and noticed that
the AUD/USD rate had fallen and the option was showing some
profits, and so I decided to close and reopen another short call, but
this time with an OTM strike price.

I closed the first option at rate 1.0560 with $317 profits on the
premium differential. I sold another lot call AUD/USD with a strike
price of 1.0700 (second option entry) at the same rate.

The next day, seeing that the pair had been ranging and didn't
give many bullish signs, I decided to close the whole covered call
transaction and waited until the forex trade was in the positive,
closing it with an 11-pip profit.

I also closed the AUD/USD trade in positive on May 17, 2011, at
7:10 p.m. at 1.0613, with $113 profits.

I further closed the second option with a $94 loss on the pre-
mium differential at 7:11 p.m. at the same AUD/USD rate.

The second option gave me a small loss (as the AUD/USD rate was closer to the strike price, thus raising the premium since it was an OTM contract). This was absorbed by the gains obtained on the first option and on the forex trade.

Net profits made = $317 + $113 – $94 = $336

Protective Put

When you need to protect your position against an eventual market correction, you can employ a protective put. This strategy uses a long spot forex position, which is then covered by a long put option. The maximum loss you can incur is limited to the premium cost paid on the put option, while your profits can be unlimited when the market moves in your bullish direction.

I will employ this strategy when I want to protect my trade against a potential market correction. The risk and reward profile of this strategy is very similar to that of placing a long call.

If there is a sudden sell-off and the currency pair rates fall, the value of the put option will increase and the profits will offset the eventual losses on the forex trade, while the only loss remaining is going to be the premium paid.

If the market rises above the strike price of the put option, this will expire worthless, and the forex position will be accumulating profits. The loss on the option is limited to the premium and all the gains that are being made on the forex trade, as the increase in rates will be much greater than the loss from the option, leaving you with a net profitable transaction.

Example:

I opened the protective put (see Figures 23.7 and 23.8) shortly after I opened the covered call and for the same reasons, also mostly to compare the profitability potential between both:

Buy long position on May 16, 2011, at 7:23 p.m. 1 lot AUD/USD at 1.0600 rate

Open 1-lot long put on AUD/USD

The strategy was also closed the next day and shortly after the previous strategy, because of the ranging behavior of the currency pair. I

Order	Order Date (GMT)	Product	Exp. Date	Buy/Sell	Pos.Type	Order Type	Qty	Strike	Filled	Filled Amt	Fees	Total Cost	Net P/
37830	5/16/11 7:23 PM	AUD/USD	N/A	OPEN BUY	CASH	MARKET	1	CASH	1.06006	0.00	0.00	0.00	0.00 US
37962	5/17/11 8:21 PM	AUD/USD	N/A	CLOSE SELL	CASH	MARKET	1	CASH	1.06233	227.00	0.00	227.00	227.00 US
Net Result													**227.00 US**
													=========
37831 1.0600	5/16/11 7:23 PM	AUD/USD	May'11	OPEN BUY	PUT	MARKET	1	1.04500	.00235	-235.00	0.00	-235.00	-235.00 US
37960 1.0623	5/17/11 8:20 PM	AUD/USD	May'11	CLOSE SELL	PUT	MARKET	1	1.04500	.00021	21.00	0.00	21.00	21.00 US
Net Result													**-214.00 US**
													=========

Net profit = 227 – 214 = 13

Figure 23.7 Protective put trade example

Figure 23.8   Protective put chart

waited until the differential between the profits on the trade out-weighed the loss, so to come out practically at a breakeven point.

I then closed the option on May 17, 2011, at 8:20 p.m. with a $214 loss on the premium differential.

I closed the trade at 8:21 p.m. with $227 in profits:

Net profits made = $227 – $214 = $13

Collar

A collar is another one of the hedging strategies that we can use to limit potential losses on a regular currency trading position. Both risk and reward are limited; the maximum loss is restrained to the difference between the two strike prices minus the net premium (paid or received) and minus the loss on the forex position. The maximum gain will also be limited to the difference between strikes, adding to this the net premium and the profits made on the currency pair trade.

The elements of this strategy are to buy a long position on the currency pair and hedge it with two distinct forex options: one short call and one long put, both OTM. If the net difference between the premium paid and received is positive, it will be added to the difference between the strikes. If it is negative, it will be subtracted.

This strategy is quite similar to a long call spread and is used to increase the profits, adding written call options, and reduce the risks by means of buying the put options.

Example:

I was expecting a bounce from the rising trendline on the hourly chart for the USD/CHF and decided to implement an option hedging strategy (see Figures 23.9 and 23.10). So I bought 1 lot long USD/CHF at 0.8850 on May 16, 2011, at 11:42 p.m.

I opened a short call on the USD/CHF at 11:44 p.m. with a strike price of 0.8800, and I opened a long put at 11:47 p.m. with the same strike price.

[*Note:* This wasn't exactly a standard collar strategy in the end, but instead a long trade doubled with a short synthetic option (see Chapter 24, "Forex Options Strategies"). To be a true collar, the short call should have been set with a strike price higher than the current USD/CHF rate, for example at 0.8900, so it would be OTM. In this case, there is no difference between the strike prices, and only the long put is OTM.]

In the early afternoon of the next day, I noticed that the rate for the USD/CHF was having trouble breaking past the former rising trendline (which it had broken to the downside and was presently retesting). I decided to exit the trade at that level with the small profits made and keep the short synthetic option, as the outlook for the currency pair was now bearish.

I closed the forex trade on May 17, 2011, at 2:12 p.m. with $128.67 in profits at 0.8862.

About 5 hours later, seeing that the premium differential was significantly higher into the positive, I decided to close the forex options.

I closed both options at 7:07 p.m. with a $26.99 loss on the long put and a $221.53 profit on the short call, where the USD/CHF rate was at 0.8806.

Net profits made = $128.67 + $221.53 − $26.99 = $323.21

Order		Order Date (GMT)	Product	Exp. Date	Buy/Sell	Pos.Type	Order Type	Qty	Strike	Filled	Filled Amt	Fees	Total Cost	Net P/S
37840		5/16/11 11:42 PM	USD/CHF	N/A	OPEN BUY	CASH	MARKET	1	CASH	.88507	0.00	0.00	0.00	0.00 USD
37889		5/17/11 2:12 PM	USD/CHF	N/A	CLOSE SELL	CASH	MARKET	1	CASH	.88621	128.67	0.00	128.67	128.67 USD
Net Result														**128.67 USD**
														==========
37841	0.8850	5/16/11 11:44 PM	USD/CHF	May'11	OPEN SELL	CALL	MARKET	1	.88000	.00646	730.23	0.00	730.23	730.23 USD
37941	0.8806	5/17/11 7:07 PM	USD/CHF	May'11	CLOSE BUY	CALL	MARKET	1	.88000	.00448	-508.70	0.00	-508.70	-508.70 USD
Net Result														**221.53 USD**
														==========
37843	0.8850	5/16/11 11:47 PM	USD/CHF	May'11	OPEN BUY	PUT	MARKET	1	.88000	.00273	-308.59	0.00	-308.59	-308.59 USD
37943	0.8806	5/17/11 7:07 PM	USD/CHF	May'11	CLOSE SELL	PUT	MARKET	1	.88000	.00248	281.60	0.00	281.60	281.60 USD
Net Result														**-26.99 USD**
														==========

Net profit = 128.67 + 221.53 − 26.99 = 323.21

Figure 23.9   Collar trade example

Figure 23.10   Collar chart

HEDGING WITH BINARY OPTIONS

Compared with vanilla options, binary options are conditioned by additional factors instead of just the price and the expiration date. They establish specific conditional scenarios that will validate or invalidate the option if they come true. The trader will choose the amount of the payout he or she wishes to receive if the conditions stated are confirmed. The premium cost that has to be paid represents a percentage of the payout.

This alternative, with its fixed payout and up-front risk definition, is much simpler than using vanilla options. There is no spread or commission to worry about, and the options can be easily combined with forex trades using stop losses.

Example:
The GBP/USD broke above the resistance level at 1.6424, and I decided to open a long position on April 21, 2011, at the market open price, 1 lot at 1.6432 with a 20-pip stop loss just below the break at 1.6412 (see Figure 23.11).

The potential loss for this transaction was $200 (20 pips × $10-pip value for the GBP/USD).

Figure 23.11   Hedging with binary options

I wanted to protect my trade in case the price broke back down in the next few days and hit my stop, and so I decided to hedge with an 80 percent payout $250 GBP/USD put option at the level of the previous breakout. This way the cost of the stop loss on my forex trade would be totally offset by the payout if the price went lower than that level: $250 × 80 percent = $200 = zero risk.

To offset the cost of the option, I needed to secure a profit of more than 25 pips (25 × $10 = $250 paid for buying the put) when the forex trade moved in my original direction. If I had thought that the price would end up higher than the breakout level at the date of expiration, I would have hedged with a call option.

Other Exotic Options Strategies: Barrier Options
The additional element in these options is the trigger or "barrier" price where the option will be either validated (knock-in) or canceled (knock-out).

Knock-In and Reverse Knock-In
When this type of option meets the trigger price before expiration, it becomes a normal option. If it doesn't, you lose the premium, and the option is canceled. The additional trigger element makes these

options possess a less expensive premium than traditional options; and when the rate of the underlying forex currency pair reaches the barrier level, the options contract turns into a normal call or put option.

The greater the distance of the trigger price from the actual currency pair rate, the cheaper the premium will be, as there are fewer opportunities for the option to be knocked in before the expiry. The reverse knock-in sets the trigger barrier ITM, while it will be OTM for the knock-in.

Knock-Out

This option will expire worthless when the rate of the underlying currency pair reaches the trigger price before expiry. If it never does, the contract will keep running as a normal call or put option.

Triggers are set OTM, below the actual rate of the currency pair for calls and above for puts. These options will be much less expensive with increased volatility, as more volatility implies that there are more chances for the option to be knocked out before they expire.

The closer the barrier is to the actual rate, the cheaper the options become as the chances for a knock-out increase. A reverse knock-out option will have its triggers set ITM, above the actual rate for calls and below for puts.

One-Touch

If the currency pair reaches the trigger level, a defined payout amount will be paid to the trades. Both risk and reward (premium cost and payout percentage) are limited and known in advance.

No-Touch

Here the amount of the payout will be given to the trader if the currency rate does not reach the trigger before the expiration date. The profit potential (payout percentage) gets smaller as the trigger is at a greater distance from the actual currency pair rate, and chances of not touching the trigger increase.

Double One-Touch

This type of option includes two barriers and two distinct payout profit percentages. The double one-touch is usually employed when there are highly volatile market conditions but no clear direction of the market. It would be similar to employing long straddle or long strangle vanilla contracts. The price is expected to break out of a given range.

Double No-Touch

Inversely, these options are chosen when traders expect the market prices to keep moving inside a range, with low volatility. They can be very profitable during consolidation periods. The double no-touch options also include two trigger levels and a specific payout percentage for each one of them if the rate of the underlying currency pair does not reach the barrier.

All can either be used as stand-alone strategies or be combined with one another or even with other option types, to reduce the overall risk scenario of a particular trading situation.

Delta Hedging: Hedging a Forex Option with Cash Positions

This strategy applies the inverse concept; this is where you will want to hedge an options contract with a spot forex position counterpart. Some forex options brokers automatically include the availability of delta hedging on their platforms, but it can also be calculated provided you have the delta value of your actual call or put option. The aim of this method is to reduce the risk of price movements of the underlying currency pair and offset those through a contrarian position, based on the volatility index of the forex option position.

A long call on the EUR/USD would be delta-hedged by means of a short position on the EUR/USD. The value of the delta will determine the size of the forex spot position to keep the balance in the hedge ratio relationship between the forex option premium value and the trade.

For example, a call option with a delta value of 50 percent will have its premium value rise half a point for each full-point increase of the rate of the underlying currency pair. Thus the delta-hedged spot forex position size would have to be half the size of the option position:

A 1-lot long call EUR/USD delta 50 percent hedged with a 0.5-lot
   short EUR/USD trade

This way the forex option is fully hedged, and the variations in the
premium will correlate to the increase or decrease of the EUR/USD
rate in the same proportion as that of the delta.

24

FOREX OPTIONS STRATEGIES

Forex and options can be a highly profitable combination because of the high level of volatility of most forex currency pairs. A basic forex options strategy will always start with vanilla options: buying a call or a put, which expresses the bullish or bearish views of the trader in regard to the potential direction of the exchange rate of the currency pair. This is the easiest strategy, and it can be used by itself when the direction of a particular market is clear and trending.

For example, in front of a clear reversal candle pattern, which could be a double top, we can simply buy a put option, since we are looking to short the currency pair. The potential loss is limited to the premium we have paid, and its profit potential is unlimited. However, we plan the exit at a convenient support, just as we would do with a regular forex trade.

What can we do when the trend is not clear at all or when we are in an obvious sideways market situation? Beyond the simple vanilla calls and puts, we have a vast array of complex combinations available that will allow you to fit an options strategy to the particular conditions of the currency market at a given time.

For example, if we expect that the currency pair will perform a strong move, but we don't know if the rates will go up or down, we could use a long straddle, which is a simultaneous long put and call with the same strike price. Conversely, if we think that the markets will remain stable and inside a clear range, we can build a long condor, which holds four distinct options: both long and short, ITM, and OTM in a precise setup, which will be described in detail later in this chapter.

Some combinations—for example, call and put backspreads—will even yield profits in whatever direction the market evolves, while also including a directional bias. Finally, some of them can have several different strike prices and expiration dates, for example, the calendar spreads or call and put time spreads.

OPTION COMBINATIONS

Debit Spreads

Also known as call bull spreads or put bear spreads, these options allow us to maintain the bias we might have in a particular direction, thus reducing the risks: the maximum loss will be the difference between the premium paid on long options and the premium received on short options.

The bull call spread is the options strategy to employ when the options trader is bullish on the underlying security and would like to establish a vertical spread on a net debit.

The bear debit spread is useful when the options trader is bearish on the underlying security; a vertical spread can also be established on a net debit by implementing the bear put spread options strategy.

Credit Spreads

Similar to the debit spreads, credit spreads differ in that, instead of paying the premium, the trader looks to make a profit from the premium received for the short options while keeping the market bias. This is the case for put bull spreads and call bear spreads, which are appropriate to implement when you are bullish in a bearish market or vice versa. Also, in addition to the profits that can be earned on the option itself, you avoid the risk of using real cash to set the strategy in place, thanks to the received premium.

Both debit and credit spreads are good to implement when there is a directional bias, either with the trend or with a contrarian point of view.

Straddles

Straddle strategies allow you to capture potential breakouts after consolidation periods, when the market has been moving in a relatively tight range and there are strong expectations of a short-term change in volatility. It is very important to set the same strike price and expiration dates on both options, as different conditions would increase the costs of the strategy, thus decreasing its potential profitability. In this case, one of the options will expire worthless, and the other will allow it to be traded for profits.

Exotic Options

Among these, you will find Asian options, based on average prices; barrier options, where the payout depends on the rate of the underlying currency pair reaching a specified price level or not; currency baskets, where the payout will depend on more than one currency pair; binary options, where the profits are defined by a percentage of the premium paid; lookback options, in which the payout is based on the maximum or minimum price reached along the duration of the options contract; compound options, where you can set options upon options with multiple strike prices and different expiration dates; spread options; chooser options; and several others. These kinds of options can be adapted specifically to the trader's needs, and so these contracts are highly variable and are evolving over time.

HOW TO CHOOSE THE RIGHT FOREX OPTIONS STRATEGY

Identify the Trading Opportunity

Prior to making any decision, we need to have a clear panorama of the market situation and direction for the specific currency pair we want to trade (for example, long AUD/USD or short USD/CHF or ranging market on EUR/GBP) in order to identify the proper option among the numerous options available, which will give the best optimized balance between potential returns and premium to spend.

Evaluate the Available Options
Evaluate the available options under the criteria of estimated volatility of the underlying currency pair and the subsequent potential future value of the option, including the Greeks if you are trading spreads or other strategies that are neutral in regard to the market direction.

Choose the Strike Price
There are three alternatives among which to select the appropriate strike price; ITM, ATM, or OTM.

If the option is ITM or close to that level, the premium will be higher because of a higher delta value, but in return, you will have a greater probability of ending ITM. High gamma levels (when the options are near the money) will also have higher premiums, and generally an OTM option will yield higher profits when your directional potential is strong.

How can we choose the best strike price, and what is the optimal distance this strike has to be from the current rate of the currency pair? To evaluate this, we need to check to see whether the volatility is high enough, and we also need to take into account any fundamental events that could lead the forex pair to a certain level; finally, we also need to consider its potential for a reversion to the mean.

As soon as an option is ITM, its value moves toward delta parity with the rate (1 point for 1 point), with the exception of the time value, which decreases with the proximity to the expiration date. The risks of losses are limited to the premium paid, and there is no other possibility of drawdown, independently of the behavior of the currency pair rates.

The use of forex options also reduces or substitutes itself for the need to set up a stop loss; the more distance the rate evolves from the strike price, the more the value of the option will diminish. But if the rate recovers, the value will also reevaluate; this way our equity remains safe in front of short-term price action.

ITM, ATM, and OTM

When the strike price is lower than the actual market price, a call option is ITM, while a put option will be OTM. Inversely, a call option will be OTM when the strike price is higher than the current market price, and a put option will be ITM in that same situation. Finally, both types of options are said to be ATM when the actual market price is the same as or very close to the strike price.

Though most platforms indicate the status of an option in regard to the relationship between the market price of the underlying currency pair and its strike price, Table 24.1 can also serve as a reminder to help you identify if an option is ITM, ATM, or OTM.

Table 24.1

Market Price	Option Type	Strike Price	Status
AUD/USD 1.0580	Long call or short call	1.0500 (< market price)	ITM
1.0580 (= market price)	ATM		
		1.0650 (> market price)	OTM
Long put or short put		1.0650 (> market price)	ITM
		1.0580 (= market price)	ATM
		1.0500 (< market price)	OTM

Choose the Expiration Date

An expiration date that is far away increases the probability for an option to be profitable, but in return the high theta level will increase the premium value.

We need to perform calculations and analyze them to determine our estimate of the potential future volatility of the rates of the underlying currency pair; we do this to see if there are fair chances for the rate to advance far enough to make the option be ITM before or at the expiry.

Volatility is 1 standard deviation price change at the end of a 1-year time period, expressed in percentage. For example, if the

AUD/USD rate is at 1.0000 and has a volatility of 15 percent, during a 1-year period it should be trading in a range between 1.1500 and 0.8500 about 70 percent of the time (1 standard deviation) and in a range between 1.3000 and 0.7000 about 95 percent of the time. The Black-Scholes formula assumes a normal and mostly symmetrical distribution, to which we need to add our own directional bias.

Vanilla Options Strategies

I have already described the four basic bullish (long call and short put) and bearish (short call and long put) strategies in Chapter 3 ("Forex Options"). The previous chapter about hedging included some of the options trading methods that are performed matching vanilla options and direct spot forex trades. There are many more combinations that do not involve forex trading but instead use the power of options by themselves.

Let's look at their characteristics and the general conditions in which they are usually employed, including some trading examples and results.

BULLISH STRATEGIES

Long Synthetic

This strategy is built by placing one long call option and one long put option at the same strike price. Both risks and rewards are unlimited. The position is equivalent to buying the underlying currency pair. The position should be used when your views on the market direction are bullish. The outcome is also similar to the outcome you get from buying the underlying currency, but buying the options will be less expensive than placing the forex trade.

Example:

On May 11, 2011, after seeing the EUR/USD rate pulling back to the recently broken resistance, holding above 1.4100, I decided to place a long synthetic option on this pair (see Figures 24.1 and 24.2).

> Long call EUR/USD (rate 1.4110) on May 11, 2011, at 11:38 a.m.
> Short put EUR/USD (rate 1.4109) at 11:39 a.m.
> Strike price 1.4050

Order	Order Date (GMT)	Product	Exp. Date	Buy/Sell	Pos. Type	Order Type	Qty	Strike	Filled	Filled Amt	Fees	Total Cost	Net P/S
37755 1.4110	5/16/11 11:38 AM	EUR/USD	May'11	OPEN BUY	CALL	MARKET	1	1.40500	.01230	-1,230.00	0.00	-1,230.00	-1,230.00 USD
37775 1.4171	5/16/11 1:12 PM	EUR/USD	May'11	CLOSE SELL	CALL	MARKET	1	1.40500	.01514	1,514.00	0.00	1,514.00	1,514.00 USD
Net Result													284.00 USD

Order	Order Date (GMT)	Product	Exp. Date	Buy/Sell	Pos. Type	Order Type	Qty	Strike	Filled	Filled Amt	Fees	Total Cost	Net P/S
37756 1.4109	5/16/11 11:39 AM	EUR/USD	may'11	OPEN SELL	PUT	MARKET	1	1.40500	.00515	515.00	0.00	515.00	515.00 USD
37777 1.4163	5/16/11 1:13 PM	EUR/USD	May'11	CLOSE BUY	PUT	MARKET	1	1.40500	.00428	-428.00	0.00	-428.00	-428.00 USD
Net Result													87.00 USD

Net profit = 284 + 87 = 371

Figure 24.1 Long synthetic trade example

Figure 24.2   Long synthetic chart

I exited the option when the price of the currency pair reached near the next resistance level at 1.4180.

Close long call at 1:12 (EUR/USD rate 1.4171) with $284 profits
Close short put at 1:13 (EUR/USD rate 1.4163) with $87 profits
Net profits made = $284 + $87 = $371

Call Backspread
You will need three elements to construct this strategy: sell one call option ITM and buy two calls that are OTM.

The maximum loss potential is limited to the difference between the two strikes plus the net premium, which in this case should be a positive amount. The profit potential is unlimited if the rate of the underlying currency pair rises, and it is limited if it falls.

It is better to employ this method when you are expecting great volatility and are also bullish on the underlying market. You will also be able to obtain profits when the rates fall, but those will be much greater on market upside moves.

Example:
Expecting a substantial price rise for the USD/CAD after the price broke above 0.9670, I decided to place a call backspread on this pair on May 19, 2011 (see Figures 24.3 and 24.4).

Order	Order Date (GMT)	Product	Exp. Date	Buy/Sell	Pos.Type	Order Type	Qty	Strike	Filled	Filled Amt	Fees	Total Cost	Net P
38391 **0.9682**	5/19/11 4:37 PM	USD/CAD	Jun`11	OPEN SELL	CALL	MARKET	1	.96000	.01448	1,492.12	0.00	1,492.12	1,492.12 U
38683 **0.9797**	5/23/11 3:24 PM	USD/CAD	Jun`11	CLOSE BUY	CALL	MARKET	1	.96000	.02295	-2,342.35	0.00	-2,342.35	-2,342.35 U
Net Result													**-850.23 U**
38392 **0.9684**	5/19/11 4:39 PM	USD/CAD	Jun`11	OPEN BUY	CALL	MARKET	1	.97000	.00975	-1,004.71	0.00	-1,004.71	-1,004.71 U
38681 **0.9802**	5/23/11 3:18 PM	USD/CAD	Jun`11	CLOSE SELL	CALL	MARKET	1	.97000	.01537	1,568.71	0.00	1,568.71	1,568.71 U
Net Result													**564.00 U**
38393 **0.9684**	5/19/11 4:39 PM	USD/CAD	Jun`11	OPEN BUY	CALL	MARKET	1	.97500	.00774	-797.58	0.00	-797.58	-797.58 U
38679 **0.9802**	5/23/11 3:18 PM	USD/CAD	Jun`11	CLOSE SELL	CALL	MARKET	1	.97500	.01215	1,240.07	0.00	1,240.07	1,240.07 U
Net Result													**442.49 U**

Net profit = 564 + 442.49 – 850.23 = 156.26

Figure 24.3 Call backspread trade example

Figure 24.4   Call backspread chart

Short call USD/CAD (rate 0.9682) on May 19, 2011, at 4:37 p.m.
with strike price at 0.9600

Long call USD/CAD (rate 0.9684) at 4:39 p.m. with strike price
at 0.9700

Another long call USD/CAD (rate 0.9684) with strike price at
0.9750

The USD/CAD rates effectively went to the upside, and I closed
both long calls on May 23, 2011, at 3:18 p.m. (USD/CAD rate 0.9802)
with $564 and $442.49 profits, respectively. Then I closed the short
call at 3:24 p.m. with an $850.23 loss.

Net profits made = $564 + $442.49 − $850.23 = $156.26

Call Bull Spread

The components of this contract are a long call option with a low
strike price doubled with a short call option bearing a higher strike
price.

This is a very cost-effective bullish strategy, as the maximum
risk you incur is the value of the premium paid on the long call
minus the premium received on the short call. However, this will
also limit your potential profits to the difference between both
strike prices less the net premium amount paid for the spread.

You can employ this method when you are bullish on both market direction and volatility. As the value of this contract is limited to the difference between the two strike prices, the wider the distance from each other, the more profits can be made; but ITM calls will be more expensive, thus increasing the loss potential if the rates go in the opposite direction.

Example:

This call bull spread options contract is still open and expires on June 16, 2011. I am expecting the USD/CHF rates to rise at least to a 161.8 percent extension on the previous daily swing high and to reach 0.9190–0.9200 (see Figures 24.5 and 24.6).

Order Date (GMT) ▼	Product	Buy/Sell	Expiry	Strike	Type	Order Type	Qty	Filled
5/19/2011 4:25 PM	USD/CHF	SELL	Jun 2011	.89000	CALL	MARKET	1	.00731
5/19/2011 4:24 PM	USD/CHF	BUY	Jun 2011	.88000	CALL	MARKET	1	.01320

USD/CHF RATE = 0.8832

Figure 24.5   Call bull spread example

Figure 24.6   Call bull spread chart

On May 19, 2011, I placed a long call at 4:24 with a strike price of 0.8800 and a short call at 4:25 p.m. with a strike price of 0.8900. The USD/CHF rate at the moment was 0.8832.

Potential loss = $731 (premium received on short call) − $1,320 (premium paid on long call) = −$589

Potential profits = 100 (difference between 0.8900 and 0.8800) × $11.20 (point value) − $589 = $531, which gives a risk-to-reward ratio of nearly 1:1

Put Bull Spread

The payout for this strategy is the same as for the call bull spread, but here we will be using put options instead of calls.

Place one long put option at a lower strike price and a short put option at a higher strike price.

The risk potential is limited to the difference between both strike prices minus the net premium received, while the profits that can be made are also limited to the net amount received for the spread (the premium received on the short option minus the premium paid on the long option).

Put spreads are also a bullish strategy and can be chosen instead of call spreads when the implied volatility is higher for the call options that are ITM in regard to OTM put options. A higher volatility implies a higher premium, and placing a put spread would be a less expensive choice.

Example:

The spread premium at the opening of the contract was net positive: $2,605 − $2,220 = $385 (see Figures 24.7 and 24.8).

This time both options contracts were left to expiry and ended with a loss. I bought a long put and sold a short put on the AUD/USD on May 16, 2011, at 5:23 p.m., and should have selected an OTM option for the long option, which would have been cheaper. Instead, the strike price was set at 1.0800 (the AUD/USD rate at the moment was 1.0591) and at 1.0850 for the short put option. I made a $642 profit on the short put, but this was offset and outweighed by the $757 loss on the long put.

Figure 24.7   Put bull spread trade example

Figure 24.8   Put bull spread chart

Long put AUD/USD (rate 1.0591) with the strike price at 1.0800
Short put AUD/USD (rate 1.0591) with the strike price at 1.0850

The contracts were left to expire (expiry date May 19, 2011).

Long put AUD/USD (rate 1.0642) expired with a $757 loss
Short put AUD/USD (rate 1.0642) expired with $642 profits
Net loss on the strategy = $642 − $757 = − $115

BEARISH STRATEGIES

Short Synthetic
This is the inverse procedure of a long synthetic, to be used when we are bearish on the market direction of the underlying currency pair. To implement this strategy, you will need to open one short call option and one long put option, both with the same strike price. The risks and potential profits are similar as well: unlimited loss if the market rallies in the opposite direction and unlimited gains if the rates fall.

A short synthetic is the equivalent to being short the currency pair.

Example:
On May 19, 2011, I decided to open a short synthetic contract on the AUD/NZD, as I was expecting the pair to fall and break below its recent lows on the 30-minute chart (see Figures 24.9 and 24.10). I sold a call and bought a put with the strike price at 1.3500.

On May 19, 2011, at 4:00 p.m., I placed a short call and a long put on the AUD/NZD (rate 1.3466), both with the strike price at 1.3500.

The next day (May 20), the rate of the currency pair had effectively fallen about 80 points and exhibited a possible bottoming pattern. The price went back to retest that support at 1.3480–1.3485, and I decided to close the options, obtaining a profit of $252.54 on the long put and $202.10 on the short call.

Closed long put at 5:03 p.m. with $251.54 profits
Closed short call at 5:04 p.m. with $202.10 profits
Net profits made = $251.54 + $202.10 = $453.64

Put Backspread
For this bearish strategy, two long put options OTM and one short put option ITM are needed.

Order		Order Date (GMT)	Product	Exp. Date	Buy/Sell	Pos.Type	Order Type	Qty	Strike	Filled	Filled Amt	Fees	Total Cost	Net P/S
38384	1.3466	5/19/11 4:00 PM	AUD/NZD	Jun'11	OPEN SELL	CALL	MARKET	1	1.35000	.01082	851.18	0.00	851.18	851.18 USD
38563	1.3383	5/20/11 5:04 PM	AUD/NZD	Jun'11	CLOSE BUY	CALL	MARKET	1	1.35000	.0814	-649.08	0.00	-649.08	-649.08 USD
Net Result														202.10 USD
														=========
38385	1.3466	5/19/11 4:00 PM	AUD/NZD	Jun'11	OPEN BUY	PUT	MARKET	1	1.35000	.01714	-1,349.64	0.00	-1,349.64	-1,349.64 USD
38561	1.3384	5/20/11 5:03 PM	AUD/NZD	Jun'11	CLOSE SELL	PUT	MARKET	1	1.35000	.02008	1,601.18	0.00	1,601.18	1,601.18 USD
Net Result														251.54 USD
														=========

Net profit = 202.10 + 251.54 = 453.64

Figure 24.9   Short synthetic trade example

285

Figure 24.10   Short synthetic trade chart

The risk is limited to the difference between both strike prices minus the premium received on the short put option. This is what you will lose if the market rates for the underlying currency pair rally against your directional bias, while on the other side you can expect two profit alternatives. On rising prices, the gains will be limited to the net premium received, but if the currency pair falls further, your profits can be unlimited. You will choose this method when the directional bias is turned to the downside but a higher volatility is expected.

The net premium at the moment of buying all three options should be a positive amount, being that you are short more than you are long. You can still profit from a wrong direction although with limited gains. This strategy bears some similarity to the long straddle; however, the cost of a put backspread will be cheaper, and profits are limited on one of the sides.

Example:

On May 16, 2011, I was expecting the AUD/USD to keep falling below its recent lows and decided to use a put backspread strategy (see Figures 24.11 and 24.12).

Order		Order Date (GMT)	Product	Exp. Date	Buy/Sell	Pos.Type	Order Type	Qty	Strike	Filled	Filled Amt	Fees	Total Cost	Net P/S
37768	1.0558	5/16/11 12:22 PM	AUD/USD	May'11	OPEN BUY	PUT	MARKET	1	1.05000	.00470	-470.00	0.00	-470.00	-470.00 USD
37817	1.0604	5/16/11 6:23 PM	AUD/USD	May'11	CLOSE SELL	PUT	MARKET	1	1.05000	.00246	246.00	0.00	246.00	246.00 USD
Net Result														-224.00 USD
														═══════
37769	1.0558	5/16/11 12:22 PM	AUD/USD	May'11	OPEN BUY	PUT	MARKET	1	1.04500	.00334	-334.00	0.00	-334.00	-334.00 USD
37819	1.0604	5/16/11 6:23 PM	AUD/USD	May'11	CLOSE SELL	PUT	MARKET	1	1.04500	.00148	148.00	0.00	148.00	148.00 USD
Net Result														-186.00 USD
														═══════
37773	1.0554	5/16/11 12:24 PM	AUD/USD	May'11	OPEN SELL	PUT	MARKET	1	1.06000	.00858	858.00	0.00	858.00	858.00 USD
37821	1.0601	5/16/11 6:24 PM	AUD/USD	May'11	CLOSE BUY	PUT	MARKET	1	1.06000	.00696	-696.00	0.00	-696.00	-696.00 USD
Net Result														162.00 USD
														═══════

Net loss = 162 – 186 – 224 = –248

Figure 24.11   Put backspread trade example

Figure 24.12   Put backspread chart

The option premiums paid were −$470 and −$334 on the long puts for a total negative of −$804; and the amount received on the short put was $858, giving a net positive of $54 credit.

Long put AUD/USD (rate 1.0558) at 12:22 p.m. with strike price at 1.0500

Long put AUD/USD (rate 1.0558) with strike price at 1.0450

Short put AUD/USD (rate 1.0554) at 12:24 p.m. with strike price at 1.0600

About 6 hours later, I saw a chart pattern that made me change my views on the currency pair, and I decided to exit at a loss after the price bounced back up from the support formed at around 1.0590–1.0600.

I closed both long puts at 6:23 p.m. with losses of $224 and $186, respectively. And I closed the short put at 6:24 p.m. with $162 profits.

Net loss on the transaction = $162 − $224 − $186 = − $248

I should have waited a little more, as the price thereafter went back down and I could have avoided some of the loss. But I chose not to take the risk of losing the maximum amount.

Call Bear Spread

The elements for this method are one short call option at a lower strike price and one long call option at a higher strike price.

The maximum loss potential is the difference between both strikes less the net premium received. The maximum profits to be made with this strategy are also limited to the net premium received (the short call premium received less the long call premium paid).

You will want to employ this strategy when you believe the rates of the underlying currency pair will be going lower.

Example:

On May 16, 2011, the EUR/USD was in a strong bearish trend on the 30-minute charts, and I decided to place a call bear spread set of options, profiting from the recent 61.8 percent pullback on the previous swing low (see Figures 24.13 and 24.14).

At 3:27 p.m. on May 16, 2011, I opened with a short call EUR/USD (rate 1.4224) at a strike price of 1.4000, and at 3.28 p.m. I placed a long call at a strike price of 1.4300.

A few hours later and fearing that the euro-dollar price might bounce back up off the support zone around 1.4150, I decided to close the setup with the rate at 1.4168: I closed the short call at 7:47 p.m. (rate 1.4168) with $364 profits and the long call with a loss of $300.

Net profits made = $364 − $300 = $64

Put Bear Spread

The benefits of this setup are similar to those of the call bear spread, and both strategies aim for a fall of the underlying currency pair rates.

The spread is composed of one short put option at a lower strike price and one long put option at a higher strike price.

The maximum profits to be made are limited to the difference between both strike prices less the net premium paid for the whole position. On the other side, the maximum losses incurred are limited to the net premium paid (the long put premium paid less the short put premium received).

The decision between choosing the call bear spread versus the put bear spread will be taken by comparing the market prices on both to see which of them is going to yield a higher payoff.

Order		Order Date (GMT)	Product	Exp. Date	Buy/Sell	Pos.Type	Order Type	Qty	Strike	Filled	Filled Amt.	Fees	Total Cost	Net P/S
37793	1.4224	5/16/11 3:27 PM	EUR/USD	May'11	OPEN SELL	CALL	MARKET	1	1.40000	.02342	2,342.00	0.00	2,342.00	2,342.00 USD
37833	1.4168	5/16/11 7:47 PM	EUR/USD	May'11	CLOSE BUY	CALL	MARKET	1	1.40000	.01978	-1,978.00	0.00	-1,978.00	-1,978.00 USD

Net Result   **364.00 USD**

=============

Order		Order Date (GMT)	Product	Exp. Date	Buy/Sell	Pos.Type	Order Type	Qty	Strike	Filled	Filled Amt.	Fees	Total Cost	Net P/S
37794	1.4224	5/16/11 3:28 PM	EUR/USD	May'11	OPEN BUY	CALL	MARKET	1	1.43000	.00500	-500.00	0.00	-500.00	-500.00 USD
37835	1.4168	5/16/11 7:47 PM	EUR/USD	May'11	CLOSE SELL	CALL	MARKET	1	1.43000	.00200	200.00	0.00	200.00	200.00 USD

Net Result   **-300.00 USD**

=============

Net profits = 364-300 = 64

Figure 24.13   Call bear spread trade example

Figure 24.14   Call bear spread chart

Example:

The contract is still open with an expiration date of June 16, 2011 (see Figures 24.15 and 24.16).

On May 19, 2011, at 4:14 p.m., I opened a long put on the GBP/USD (rate 1.6178) with a strike price at 1.6250 and a short put with a strike price at 1.6050. My expectations are for a projection for the GBP/USD rates to reach March lows in the first instance and January lows as a second possibility, before the date of expiry.

At that moment, the net premium for this position was $2,052 paid less $1,062 received, a $990 net potential loss if the market doesn't fall. The breakeven rate for this strategy is 99 points lower than the opening rate (1.6079), and the expected first target payoff was around 1.5979, thus 100 points for a $1,000 potential payoff. The risk-to-reward ratio here is slightly better than 1:1.

Order Date (GMT)	Product	Buy/Sell	Expiry	Strike	Type	Order Type	Qty	Filled
5/19/2011 4:14 PM	GBP/USD	BUY	Jun 2011	1.62500	PUT	MARKET	1	.02052
5/19/2011 4:14 PM	GBP/USD	SELL	Jun 2011	1.60500	PUT	MARKET	1	.01062

GBP/USD RATE = 1.6178

Figure 24.15   Put bear spread trade example

Figure 24.16   Put bear spread trade chart

NEUTRAL STRATEGIES

Neutral strategies are useful whenever we do not have a clear direction for the underlying currency pair. Straddles, strangles, guts, calendar spreads, vertical spreads, butterflies, and condors will offer us an opportunity to obtain profits under stable conditions or in front of volatile fundamental events with no specific trend in sight.

Long Straddle

This setup will be composed of one long call option and one long put option, both with the same strike price. Profit potential is unlimited in either direction the market moves, and the risks you will incur are limited to the total premium paid on both long options.

The straddle can be employed when you are expecting the market to break out of a given range with much volatility, for example, under impending news releases. You will make money if the scenario is bullish or if the prices of the underlying currency pair fall, provided the breakeven point is reached, covering the cost of both premiums paid.

Example:

The transaction is still open and has an expiration date set at June 16, 2011 (see Figures 24.17 and 24.18).

On May 19, 2011, I placed a long straddle on the AUD/USD, expecting this pair to break above the 1.0680–1.0700 resistance level and reach last April's all-time highs at 1.1010 as the first target and further highs at 1.1200–1.1250 in extension from the previous daily swing high.

On May 19, 2011, at 3:43 p.m., I opened with a long put AUD/USD (rate 1.0615) and a long call, both with a strike price at 1.06500. If this setup fails, I will lose a maximum of $3,053 (total cost of both premiums paid). The potential gains, should the rate of the

Order Date (GMT)	Product	Buy/Sell	Expiry	Strike	Type	Order Type	Qty	Filled
5/19/2011 3:43 PM	AUD/USD	BUY	Jun 2011	1.06500	PUT	MARKET	1	.01883
5/19/2011 3:43 PM	AUD/USD	BUY	Jun 2011	1.06500	CALL	MARKET	1	.01170

AUD/USD RATE = 1.0615

Figure 24.17   Long straddle trade example

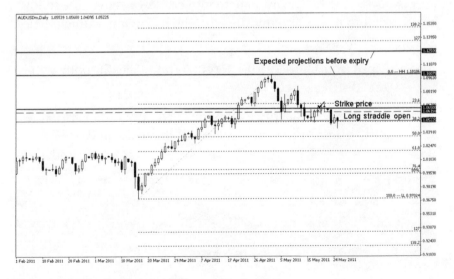

Figure 24.18   Long straddle trade chart

AUD/USD reach the first target before or at expiry, would be $3,600 for a net profit of $547 and on the second target $6,000 for a net profit of $2,947.

Short Straddle

This setup is similar to the long straddle, except that we would be expecting stable prices and a low volatility. An example would be prices of the underlying currency pair evolving inside a given range. Here we will be selling a short call option and a short put option, both with the same strike price.

Short straddles are much riskier than other straddle trades or other trades in general, as the losses can be unlimited in either direction the market moves, while the profits will be limited to the net premium amount received when selling the options. The idea behind this method is to profit from the effects of time upon the options premium value, while prices must exhibit very little change for it to be really profitable.

Example:

The transaction is still open and expires on June 16, 2011 (see Figures 24.19 and 24.20).

I expected the EUR/GBP rate to move sideways over the following weeks; I took a short straddle with the following characteristics:

May 26, 2011, at 12:22–12:23 a.m.
Short put and short call EUR/GBP (rate 0.8647), both with a 0.8600 strike price

I chose a lower strike price than the current rate, as I am expecting a slightly bearish projection to around that price and 0.8570 near

Order Date (GMT) ▼	Product	Buy/Sell	Expiry	Strike	Type	Order Type	Qty	Filled
5/26/2011 12:23 AM	EUR/GBP	SELL	Jun 2011	.86000	PUT	MARKET	1	.00606
5/26/2011 12:22 AM	EUR/GBP	SELL	Jun 2011	.86000	CALL	MARKET	1	.01056

EUR/GBP rate = 0.8647

Figure 24.19   Short straddle trade example

Figure 24.20   Short straddle trade chart

the expiration date. If the price remains on that range, I will keep both premiums minus the remaining value of the options if I decide to close them before the expiry or to close them completely should both options expire worthless.

Long Strangle

This strategy, like the long straddle, is best employed when volatility is high and is expected to increase while the market direction is not clear or when a large move is forecast. The difference is that the strike prices will be at a greater distance from each other.

With this strategy, we buy one long call option and one long put option, both OTM; that is, the strike price of the call has to be at a higher strike price in regard to the current underlying rate, and the strike price of the put needs to have a lower strike price.

Being OTM lowers the cost of the premium, but in return we also have a higher amount of points that the market will have to rise or fall to be profitable.

The potential profits on this strategy are unlimited in whichever direction the market moves. The maximum loss will be limited to the total premium paid for both call and put long options.

Example:

This long strangle is still open and expires on June 16, 2011 (see Figures 24.21 and 24.22).

On May 26, 2011, at 12:31 a.m., I decided to open a long strangle option setup on the USD/CHF, after a 61.8 percent retracement on the previous daily swing low, and expecting the currency pair to move further but still not being sure if the downtrend is coming to its end or not. I believe the pair might reach 0.9000 before the expiration date, which was set at June 16, 2011.

Long call USD/CHF (rate 0.8726) with strike price at 0.8750
Long put USD/CHF (rate 0.8726) with strike price at 0.8650

Order Date (GMT)	Product	Buy/Sell	Expiry	Strike	Type	Order Type	Qty	Filled
5/26/2011 12:31 AM	USD/CHF	BUY	Jun 2011	.87500	CALL	MARKET	1	.00942
5/26/2011 12:31 AM	USD/CHF	BUY	Jun 2011	.86500	PUT	MARKET	1	.00714

USD/CHF rate = 0.8726

Figure 24.21   Long strangle trade example

Figure 24.22   Long strangle trade chart

Whichever direction the market chooses to take, I will need the rates to move about 148 points for the options contracts to be at a breakeven level:

$942 + $714 (premiums paid) = $1,656/$11.20 pip
   value = $147.85

The projected target to the upside at 0.9000 will, if reached, yield net profits around $1,400 (points above the breakeven level multiplied by the pip value).

Short Strangle

This has a similar profile to the short straddle and the same differences that we find between long strangles and long straddles. This option setup is to be used when we expect the volatility to be low and the prices of the underlying currency pair to remain stable or inside a tight range. As we did for the long strangle, we will use OTM options.

The elements of this strategy are one short call with a higher strike price (above the current rate) and one short put with a lower strike price (below the current rate). The potential profits are limited to the net premium amount received in writing the options, while the maximum losses are unlimited whichever direction the market moves.

Here the strike prices are at a greater distance from each other than on the short straddle, which will reduce the premium received but in return will increase the opportunities for ending with a profitable result.

Example:

The short strangle is still open and expires on June 16, 2011 (see Figures 24.23 and 24.24).

Order Date (GMT)	Product	Buy/Sell	Expiry	Strike	Type	Order Type	Qty	Filled
5/26/2011 12:44 AM	EUR/GBP	SELL	Jun 2011	.86000	PUT	MARKET	1	.00571
5/26/2011 12:43 AM	EUR/GBP	SELL	Jun 2011	.87000	CALL	MARKET	1	.00625

EUR/GBP rate = 0.8658

Figure 24.23   Short strangle trade example

Figure 24.24   Short strangle trade chart

At 12:44 a.m. on May 26, 2011, I decided to write the put and call contracts for the EUR/GBP, as I expect the rates of the currency pair to remain inside a 100–130-pip range until expiration.

Short put EUR/GBP (rate 0.8658) with strike price at 0.8600
Short call EUR/GBP (rate 0.8658) with strike price at 0.8700

I will have to watch the evolution of this setup closely, because if the price crosses further on either side, I might have to close them earlier to limit the potential losses.

Long Guts

Elements of the strategy setup include one long call option at a lower strike price (ITM) and one long put option at a higher strike price (also ITM).

The profits for this method are unlimited in either direction the market evolves, while the maximum loss will be limited to the total premium paid plus the difference between both strike prices.

This setup is similar to the long strangle; the difference is that in a long guts you will only be buying ITM options, while for a long strangle you need to buy OTM options. The functionality of the long guts is to be used when you are bullish on volatility. Figure 24.25 presents an example of a long guts chart.

Figure 24.25   Long guts chart

Short Guts

Similar to the short strangle, this strategy differs in that it will use ITM options, whereas the short strangle employs only OTM contracts.

The elements that confirm the setup are one short call option at a lower strike price (ITM) and one short put at a higher strike price (also ITM).

Risk and reward profiles are inverse to that of the long guts; the maximum profit potential is limited to the net premium received on writing both short options, while the maximum loss is unlimited whichever direction the market moves. A short guts chart is shown in Figure 24.26.

Calendar Spreads

This type of spread option intends to take advantage of time decay. Both call and put time spreads are employed when the trader believes the prices will remain relatively stable (low volatility) and there is a neutral to slightly bearish market bias. Also, both profits and losses are limited in either direction to the underlying rate moves.

The strategy involves selling the option that will expire first and buying the option that will expire later. Usually there is about a month distance between the dates on both contracts. In writing

Figure 24.26   Short guts chart

the options, you will receive the premium up front and benefit from the devaluation of the contract over time; the risks inherent in selling naked short positions are then protected by the subsequent buying of the long position with a farther date of expiration, should the underlying currency pair move against the first expiring position.

The best time distance for the first option is less than 30 days to expiration, and OTM contracts will yield better results.

Call Time Spread

The elements of the setup are to write a short call option with a closer expiry date and buy a long call option to expire later.

Put Time Spread

If you want to place a put time spread, you will have to short a put option that will expire sooner and then buy a long put option with an expiration date at a greater distance.

The only difference between the call and put time spreads is that with the calls you expect the market rates to increase, while with the puts you expect the underlying currency pair prices to fall.

Call Ratio Vertical Spread

This neutral strategy is to be employed when the outlook on volatility is bearish (see Figure 24.27).

- *Elements*. One long call option ITM and two short call options OTM.
- *Risk and reward*. The profits are limited to the difference between both strike prices minus the net premium paid. Losses will be unlimited if the underlying currency pair rallies, but will be limited on a bearish scenario.

Figure 24.27   Call ratio vertical spread

Put Ratio Vertical Spread

The same way as we would use the call ratio vertical setup, this strategy is to be employed when there is an expectation of a stable, low-volatility evolution of the underlying currency pair prices and an expectation of a neutral bias in market direction (see Figure 24.28).

- *Elements*. Two short put options OTM and one long put option ITM.
- *Risk and reward*. Here again, the profits will be limited to the difference between both strike prices minus the net premium paid. Losses will be unlimited if the underlying currency pair falls, but will be limited to the net premium paid on a bullish scenario.

Figure 24.28   Put ratio butterfly spread

Butterfly Strategies

Long Call Butterfly

The long call butterfly can be employed when we expect the underlying market to show low volatility (see Figure 24.29). The strategy resembles a short straddle, but here the losses are limited. In addition, the straddle is cheaper to acquire, since you get the premium amount at the moment of writing the options, while with the long butterfly you have to pay the premium up front. You will earn profits when the market remains stable for the duration of the options.

- *Elements.* Two short call options ATM, one long call option ITM, and one long call option OTM.
- *Risk and reward.* Losses and profits are limited in this strategy. The maximum gain to expect is limited to the net premium received from the spread, while the maximum loss will be limited to the net amount that results from deducting the ITM strike price from the ATM strike price, minus the net premium paid.

Figure 24.29 Long call butterfly

Short Call Butterfly

The short call butterfly can be employed when we expect the underlying market to be volatile and break out of a given range in either direction (see Figure 24.30). The payout for this strategy is similar to that of the long straddle, as both have limited downside risks.

- *Elements.* Two long call options ATM, one short call option ITM, and one short call option OTM.

- *Risk and reward.* As is the case with the long call butterfly, losses and profits are also limited in this strategy. The maximum gain will be limited to the net premium received from the whole spread, while the maximum loss will be limited to the net amount that results from deducting the ITM strike price from the ATM strike price, minus the net premium received. It will be limited to the premium paid for the three options.

Figure 24.30   Short call butterfly

Long Put Butterfly

Options trading strategy is taken when the options trader thinks that the underlying security will not rise or fall much by expiration.

- *Elements.* Two short put options ATM, one long put option ITM, and one long put option OTM.
- *Risk and reward.* As with the long call butterfly, the long put butterfly is similar to a short straddle in that you need to expect a low volatility market, but here your losses are limited if the market goes against your direction, while in a short straddle you would risk unlimited losses. The maximum amount to profit from this strategy is limited to the net premium that you have received from the whole setup. Losses are also limited to the difference between the ATM strike price and the ITM strike price, minus the net premium paid.

Figure 24.31 shows an example of a long put butterfly.

Short Put Butterfly

The short put butterfly (see Figure 24.32) can be employed when we expect the volatility to be high and the market to move heavily in

Figure 24.31   Long put butterfly

Figure 24.32   Short put butterfly

either direction—for example, before an important news release. The payout for this strategy is similar to that of the long straddle, as both have limited downside risks. Although profits are limited, the strategy itself can give you greater returns on your investment, since the cost to implement is close to nothing.

- *Elements.* Two long put options ATM, one short put option ITM, and one short put option OTM.
- *Risk and reward.* Losses and profits are also limited in this strategy, just as they are for the short call butterfly. The maximum gain to expect is limited to the net premium received from the whole spread, while the maximum loss will be limited to the net amount that results from deducting the ITM strike price from the ATM strike price, minus the net premium received.

Condor Strategies

Condor setups are quite similar to butterfly strategies. The difference between them is that the double strike price "ATM" is split in two strike prices, one ITM and the other OTM.

In order to calculate the risk and reward potential for a condor, it is easier to break down the setup into two spreads: long call or put spread and short call or put spread. Maximum losses as well as maximum profits are limited for either long or short condor contracts.

Long Condor

Elements (call or put options)

- One long option, ITM (below the current underlying rate for a call and above for a put)
- One short option, ITM
- One short option, OTM (above the actual price of the currency pair for a call and below for a put)
- One long option, OTM

Equivalence of the two spreads

- One long call or put spread at a lower strike price
- One short call or put spread at a higher strike price

A long condor (see Figures 24.33 and 24.34) will be used when the trader is expecting the market prices to remain inside a stable range until the expiration date.

- *Profitability.* The maximum profits of a long condor are made when the rate of the underlying currency pair is trading between the two middle strike prices. To calculate this with the two-spread equivalence, you need to take the spread with the greater distance between strike prices and subtract the net premium paid for the spread; that would be the maximum profit.
- *Risks.* The maximum loss of a long condor will occur when the rate of the underlying currency pair is trading at the "wings" of the total spread (near or at the rate of either the option with the lowest strike price or the option with the highest strike price). In regard to the two-spread equivalence, the amount of the loss is the lesser of the difference between the lower strike spread minus the higher strike spread, minus the total premium paid for the whole set of contracts.

Figure 24.33 Long condor calls

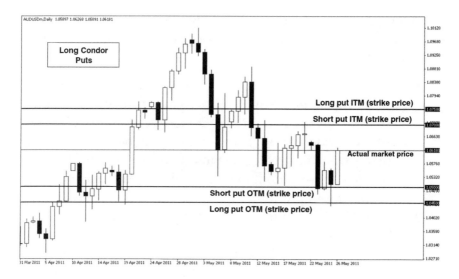

Figure 24.34   Long condor puts

Short Condor

Elements (call or put options)

- One short option, ITM (below the current underlying rate for a call and above for a put)
- One long option, ITM
- One long option, OTM (above the actual price of the currency pair for a call and below for a put)
- One short option, OTM

Equivalence of the two spreads

- One short call or put spread at a lower strike price
- One long call or put spread at a higher strike price

A short condor (see Figures 24.35 and 24.36) will be used when the trader is expecting that the market prices will break out of a range but does not have a clear bias concerning the direction of the move.

- *Profitability.* The maximum profits of a short condor are made when the rate of the underlying currency pair is trading beyond the wings (the highest and lowest "external"

Figure 24.35   Short condor calls

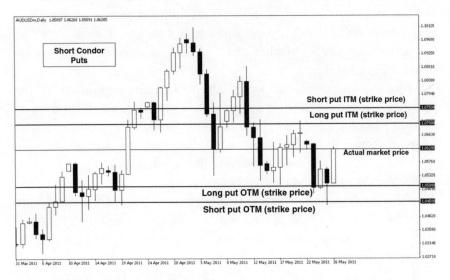

Figure 24.36   Short condor puts

strike prices). To calculate this with the two-spread equivalence, the maximum profit will be the greater in regard to the difference between the lower strike price spread minus the higher strike price spread, plus the total premium received for the whole setup of options contracts.

- *Risks*. The maximum loss of a short condor will occur when the rate of the underlying currency pair is trading in the center of the total option spread. In fact, in the two-spread equivalence, the maximum loss will be the result of selecting the spread that has the greater distance between strike prices and adding to this the net premium received.

EXOTIC OPTIONS STRATEGIES

Binary Options

To begin trading binary options, you need to search for a binary options broker and open an account; binary options are a specialized type of option, and only a few select brokers will offer this. You can go to www.jdfn.com to find a list of some brokers that offer binary options. These types of options are usually not offered on a centralized exchange but are usually OTC financial instruments.

The first step is to choose the underlying currency pair, preferably one you are familiar with and usually follow or trade. You can specialize in a single market or trade several options at a time on different markets.

You will then have to decide about the expiration date for the binary option, whether you intend to obtain results in the short term or plan for a longer time frame. The analysis to perform thereafter must take this time element into account.

Most binary options brokers offer contracts with expiration times and dates that can range between 1 hour to 1 month or more. A few of them also offer extra short-term options availability where you can choose an option that will expire in 15 minutes or even 5 minutes. This is important to know in order to determine a prediction with the best possible accuracy.

Finally, you will need to select the direction in which you think the rate of the currency pair will evolve at the expiration. If you are bullish and think the rate will be higher, you'll have to buy a call option; if you are bearish and think the rate will decrease by the expiry, you will need to place a put option.

If your forecast is correct, you will earn a high return on your original investment, as binary options usually offer payout percentages that range between 70 and 85 percent. You can also choose to trade multiple options as an additional advanced strategy, which will allow you to always be ITM.

Money Management

The same basic money management rules of forex trading will apply to options as well. No strategy will perform all the time, and there will be losses along the way that you have to be prepared to assume as part of the whole trading picture. You should also try to minimize the risks in regard to your total trading amount.

- *Risk amount.* Never risk more than 8.5 percent of your total account on a single options contract. This way you could be wrong 11 times in a row and still have enough money to keep trading.
- *Confidence.* Do not trade when you are unsure or have not performed enough research or analysis in selecting the options. Options were designed for insurance purposes on open positions. So options can be a great way to generate some cash. However, options can be very risky; so make sure you have paper-traded and have built up your confidence.
- *Diversification.* Reduce the overall risks by trading different types of options on different currency pairs and also combining them with regular forex trades; also use different expiration times.
- *Fundamentals.* Keep an eye on economic releases and either wait for the announcements to predict the market direction or use them to anticipate the market's volatility and to trade specific range-breaking strategies.
- *Trend.* As you would for a regular forex trade, identify the main trend and follow its direction.

Some Basic Binary Strategies

Bullish Binary Strategy

I will employ a bullish strategy when I believe the rate of the underlying currency pair is going to appreciate in the following period up to the expiration time or date.

For example, after an important sell-off on the AUD/USD, the price is now sitting above a strong support at 1.0500, and I think that in the next few hours there will be a significant pullback, resuming the upward trend.

I examine the options available and decide to buy a call that expires in 2 hours, with a premium of $1,000 and a 75 percent pay-out. This means that if my analysis was correct and the AUD/USD rate climbs above its current price, the option will be ITM, and I will then receive the initial investment back plus the 75 percent profits = $750 net profit on the transaction.

Bearish Binary Strategy

A bearish strategy is appropriate whenever I expect that the rate of a particular currency pair will decrease in value and there is a downward trend.

Let's say the market just made an important correction on the USD/CHF bearish trend. My analysis tells me that the price of the currency pair will now turn back and resume its move to the down-side, and so I decide to buy a put option with a premium of $1,200 and an 80 percent payout. If the USD/CHF rate is lower at the time of the option expiration, I will receive the $1,200 back plus the 80 percent, for a net profit of $960.

Range/Volatility Strategies

"In-the-Range" Options

When prices of the underlying currency pair have evolved inside a steady and stable range, the best strategy is to buy an option where the price at the expiration will be inside that range for the option to be ITM. See Figure 24.37.

"Out-of-the-Range" Options

When the market appears to be highly volatile or if we expect a fundamental release to cause a break of a particular range for a currency pair, we will select an out-of-the-range binary option. See Figure 24.38.

Binary Fence Strategy

Fence trading offers the trader a greater potential to win, whichever direction the underlying currency pair moves. For this strategy, I would use two distinct binary options: one put and one call.

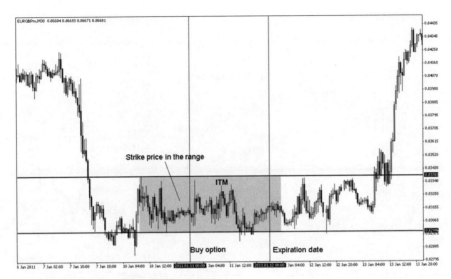

Figure 24.37   In-the-range options

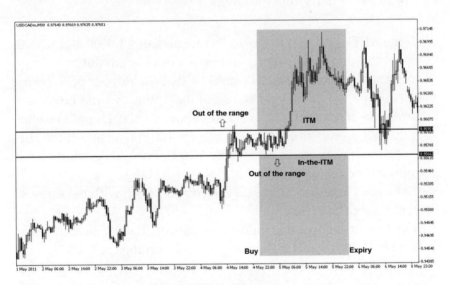

Figure 24.38   Out-of-the-range options

In the example shown in Figure 24.39, I decided to buy a put option after the AUD/USD broke below the support and was trading at 1.0800. A few hours later, the price seemed to be holding above another support zone at 1.0600, and I bought a second option, this time a call with the same expiration date and aiming to end above 1.0600.

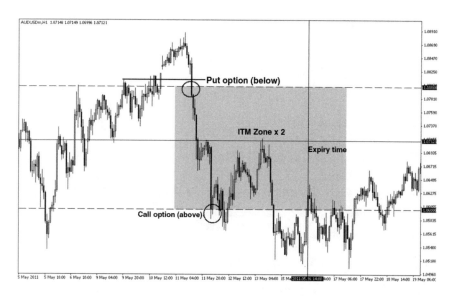

Figure 24.39   Binary fence strategy

If the AUD/USD expires with its rate between 1.0600 and 1.0800, I will be winning both options and earn a double payout.

Another possible scenario would be that the price expires above 1.0800 (or below 1.0600), and so one of the options would be a loser. For example, if the AUD/USD expires above 1.0800, I would be winning the call option and losing the put option; conversely, if the currency pair expires with its rate below 1.0600, I would be winning the put option and losing on the call.

Let's say I invested $1,000 on each option, both with the same 80 percent payout at expiry.

On the first absolute winning scenario, the net profits made would be $1,600 ($800 on the put plus $800 on the call).

On the second alternative, I will have invested $2,000 (for both options) and get back $1,800 (my investment plus 80 percent profits); thus my loss would only be $200, equivalent to 10 percent of the total initial investment.

With this strategy, I could trade up to eight times and lose seven times; still making a net profit on the whole series if the eighth option trade is a total win:

7 losses of $200 = $1,400 plus 1 win of $1,600 = $200 net profit

FOREX AUTOMATED TRADING

25

FOREX AUTOMATION

Forex automated trading is certainly the wave of the future. It wasn't too many years ago when there was really nothing out there on a retail basis when it came to trading automation in the retail forex. Typically there has always been automation in the financial markets. As computing power got stronger and more robust, computer manufacturers were able to make smaller, less expensive machines that individual traders could afford. Today our systems are very affordable, and most traders have all the technology and speed they need and an easy-to-obtain computer trading system.

When I first started using basic forex automation, there was only a handful of programmers making their systems available for traders to use. After a few months, though, programmers started coming from everywhere, offering the next great thing. Some of the systems are okay, while others are a flat-out scam, just trying to get your money. I have tried hundreds of automated systems, and I have created just as many proprietary systems of my own. In the end, it does not matter what the system is if it works. The proof is in the pudding, so to speak.

As noted above, automation is not something new. It has been prevalent among both stock and forex brokers, and they have been using computing power increasingly over the last several years to automate price feeds and to route orders. Black Friday was a product of automated trading. In fact, it was necessary to upgrade automated stock systems after the October 1987 market crash to ensure they could deal with unexpected spikes in trading volume for the foreseeable future.

During major news announcements, retail forex traders and institutional traders cause large volume spikes in anticipation of the news to be released. If a forex broker's automated systems or dealing desks cannot keep up with the trading volumes, then price requotes, slippage, and other undesirable trade errors will inevitably occur while trying to either fill or liquidate positions. Several forex brokers are implementing systems to automatically widen the spread before, during, and after news events, to discourage traders from overloading their systems. Most of the more sophisticated forex robots contain code that allows the trader to minimize possible slippage. The robot will actually bypass the trade if there is slippage or the spread is too wide.

FOREX ROBOTS

Over the last 10 years, the use of these forex robots has risen drastically. Starting out as "black-box" systems with the institutional traders, automated systems are now a staple of just about every kind of trader. Retail forex traders are increasingly turning not only to partial automation but also to forex robots for complete automation. Forex automated, or algorithmic, trading has many advantages. Some qualities cannot be duplicated by a human trader. One of the main advantages of forex automation is that many complex calculations can be performed across several currency pairs in just milliseconds as the price or currency changes in real time. Decision-based rules that stem from these calculations allow the automated forex robot to automatically enter or exit a trade at the best price, and almost instantaneously.

Because of market volatility, when a human trader finally decides on a manual entry point or exit point, the price may have moved by several points or possibly more. This can be partially mitigated by entering stop-loss and take-profit orders. However, those options have been eliminated in the United States by their own regulatory bodies. With partial automation come some benefits as well, since an automated forex script can close trades 100 times as fast as their human counterparts; requotes are dealt with much more efficiently.

EXPERT ADVISORS

The forex expert advisor, known as an EA, is a mechanical trading system used for forex trading. EAs are designed to allow automatic trading to take place. This frees the trader from continuously having to watch the market. In addition, there are some major mistakes that investors make; EAs can eliminate some of these mistakes altogether, allowing traders to concentrate their focus on making a profit.

An EA can inform clients about the possibility of arbitrage situations, checking multiple price feeds and letting the trader profit from the disparity between the spreads. EAs are used by beginners and experienced traders alike. Regardless of the level of experience, EAs can be used to assist traders by allowing them to work in different markets and under different conditions.

EAs are designed in MetaQuotes Language 4, which is a built-in language for programming trading strategies. This language allows EAs to be programmed to trade accounts automatically by managing trading operations that range from directly sending orders to the broker's server, to placing and adjusting pending orders, to placing trailing stops.

There are hundreds of different and unique EAs in the market, all functioning in accordance with different rules. The common factor they share is the adherence to a strict trading strategy and the consistent way of evaluating all parameters at the same time—often more successfully than any human could. Nonetheless, it is important to remember that an EA is a trading robot and should be used with caution. It is essential to understand how it operates and how it can affect your trading and strategy, and it is equally important to have a trustworthy source and point of contact for the EA.

I have been in the software business for many years, and so I have access to many programmers. I have spent years working with the EAs developing my trading strategies into an automated system using MetaTrader. The problem is that MetaTrader has its own inherent problems. The biggest is the MetaTrader plug-ins. So regardless of how good your system is, the output or results will be skewed. A perfect example is an EA I am testing right now.

The EA is trading on the EUR/USD and is placing about 30 trades a day. The EA is doing very well; it is about 95 percent accurate. But as with most EAs, the losses are big enough to keep the balance about even. What I have seen lately is that the broker is slipping the trades a few pips each time. My results are skewed: many of the smaller losses should be gains, and many of the smaller gains should be larger gains. Since this is a scalping EA, I am trading larger lots. The difference in profitability is huge. Great EA, but the MetaTrader provider or broker is killing the real results. Not much you can do . . . or so you may think; more to come.

TYPES OF EAS

Many different types of EAs are out there. Each one has its unique differences and has its own trading conditions in which you would deploy the EA. Below is a list of some of the different types of EAs that you may have tried or come across:

- *News EA.* A news EA is designed to take advantage of news events that lead to a big movement in price at the time the news is being released. These types of EAs were great a few years back, but many of the brokers are now using deceitful tactics such as slow servers, plug-ins, and wide spreads to eliminate the news experts. I can remember the good old days when you could get in just before news announcements using straddle-type orders and really make some big returns, but it's pretty hard to do now.
- *Breakout EA.* The breakout EA is designed to open a trade when the price breaks through predefined support and resistance levels. Breakout EAs can be very effective in consolidating markets when the price is static or moving around in a tight range.

- *Hedge EA.* A hedge EA is any EA that places two separate and opposing positions and minimizes the loss on one while capturing maximum profit on the other. I have tested many of these types of EAs, but none of them have been that great. With the rules that have changed in the United States, you cannot hedge in the same currency pair. However, you can still trade offshore and hedge.

Many of these EAs will open up lots of trades on either side of the bid/ask and then manage their way out of the trade for a profit. The problem here is the transaction cost. If your EA is placing lots of trades, you could end up down just because of the pip spread you are paying per each trade.

- *Scalper EA.* A scalper EA is the most active type of EA, placing and monitoring trades very frequently. It aims to secure small profits as soon as they are available. I have built and tested as many of these types as I could. I have always liked the scalping model. It dates back to my times of being a day trader. I like to be in and out of the market, know what my risk is, and be out of that trade quickly. The scalper EAs can get you in and out of a lot of trades pretty quickly.

There are numerous brokers out there that allow forex automation, and there are more every day; MetaTrader is not the only one. You can go to www.jdfn.com to see a current list of forex brokers and software that have the capability of placing trades automatically.

FOREX ROBOT REVIEWS

Automated trading has been around for many years. The big banks
and institutions have been doing this sort of trading far longer than
retail customers have had access to or the ability to do such trading.

We have previously discussed automated trading, and let me
just say I have personally tested many of the most highly touted
EA "robots" out there today. In addition, I have created many proprietary automated trading algorithms of my own. Some of the
EAs that I have used trade on the ever-popular MetaTrader systems, while others trade on my internal proprietary software. The
two robots that I want to discuss here are Fap Turbo and
Megadroid.

FAP TURBO REVIEW

Many years ago, after receiving all the various marketing e-mails
and reading all the hype on the Internet concerning Fap Turbo, I
decided to test it.

Overall, I found Fap Turbo to be a good trading robot; I was
very successful using the program and felt that it was written well.

I have spent hundreds of hours going through and back-testing the various settings. I always used demo accounts and back-testing processes that allowed me to manage the results. There are inherent problems with back-testing, which will be discussed in the next chapter.

One of the things I liked about Fap Turbo was the ability to change the offsets and time frames for the various strategies I used. My demo trading results were, oftentimes, much better than live trades; however, my live accounts made very good returns as well. In fact, I went many months without a month-over-month loss on a live account using Fap Turbo. Keep in mind that I used Fap Turbo with many other trading strategies that I would use when manually trading.

So here was the problem I had with Fap Turbo and, of course, with many of the other robots out there. If you are using Fap Turbo on your account and you are successful and making lots of money, you are going to fail in the end unless you work diligently to keep your profits. The brokers will work just as hard to know exactly what you are using, and they will be using the latest robots as well in an effort to help them determine how to beat you out of your hard-earned money.

This is why it was important to find settings that were not known to the brokers; that way, even if the brokers were able to determine what robot I was using, they would not be able to easily determine my settings, since I was not using the preset settings. Having a personal custom setting will at least provide some help with better executions.

Fap Turbo has offered many different versions and add-ons, and I have tried them all. In my opinion, Fap Turbo works best if you trade small amounts and keep taking your profits out as they increase; that way you can stay under the radar of the broker.

FAP TURBO SHORT-TERM SCALPING STRATEGY

One of the main reasons that Fap Turbo has become one of the top-selling forex trading robots is because of its short-term scalping strategy, which is the one I have used most. FapTurbo is considered a high-frequency trading robot because it uses scalping to get in and out of the market for quick pips. When employed with tight stops, an account can quickly grow. You do have to take into account transactional costs at some brokers.

SCALPING MULTIPLE CURRENCIES

Fap Turbo monitors many currency pairs depending on the version you have. It can use the scalping method to trade all of them simultaneously if you want to use that method. Keep in mind, though, that you do not want to use too many robots at one time unless you have a big account. You can quickly overleverage, and that would be bad news.

SAFE FILTERS TO RESTRICT BIG LOSSES

Ever wonder why so many EAs and other robots have great-looking equity curves or track records? Well, most often you can simply look at the trading results and look for the stop loss used in the test. You will find that many of these touted robots use big stop losses, sometimes 300 to 500 pips. This allows for the markets to cycle from the highs to the lows without the trader being taken out of the trade on a stop.

The problem with that is even if you use good money management, your drawdown will be too large to absorb and thus will create an account liquidation situation. So make sure that if you are trading a robot that uses big stop losses, you trade very small amounts and factor a 300–500-pip drawdown into your money management.

Fap Turbo has a built-in stop-loss feature that can be manually set to the number of pips or the percentage you are willing to lose on any given trade. This feature will allow you to use the robots within their money management systems. Unlike some of the other robots out there that have built-in stops, Fap Turbo can create an extremely user-defined risk tolerance.

A STEALTH MODE OPERATION

Some unscrupulous brokers like to increase spreads and hunt stops on accounts using forex trading robots. But Fap Turbo uses a stealth mode operation that can hide the profit and stop-loss values from the brokers. The robot will store the stop loss on the user's computer, and when the price reaches the stop, the robot will send the order as a market order.

This keeps the broker in the dark about where the stop is. The problem with this is that when the robot sends the order automatically to the broker as a market order, the broker could kick it back with a multitude of errors, resulting in a bigger loss.

The same thing can hold true on the other side for profitability using a limit. I have witnessed this far too many times. The trade goes your way, hits your limit, and then sends the order in. The broker slow-fills the trade, and you come to find out that your profitable trade just became a losing trade.

SOFTWARE LICENSING

I am not a big fan of how Fap Turbo sells its software. You pay a onetime fee, which is nice, but you have to go to the Fap Turbo Web site periodically and obtain new codes to enter for the authentication. If you forget to do this, your Fap Turbo will quit working, and you will discover that you haven't had any trades, which is very frustrating, especially if you have been experiencing profitable trades. Then your robot goes offline, and you may have missed a few more profitable trades. When you get your robot back up running again, you catch the first losing trade. All in all, it will affect the results of your trading. So you don't want your system to go down.

One of the things I have found with Fap Turbo, and with other robots, is that if you are using a setting that is producing good results on a live account, don't be surprised if that changes down the road. Many times the robots, and the many unique settings, only work in certain market conditions. But that is okay; just save all your settings, which is easily done by using the save feature for the settings menus included with the robots. You can then go back to the settings when you find yourself in that same market condition again.

Overall I like the robot, and I currently use it a little differently by running through some proprietary software programs that we have written, which allows the trades to execute and then sends them through a portal to other brokers.

MEGADROID REVIEW

This is one of the first robots I ever tested. I spent a lot of time both back-testing and forward-testing this robot. I have had great success with my results on a live account. Remember to always start using your robots on a demo account; that way you can see the idiosyncrasies of a particular robot. Each robot will have little quirks that you will need to understand before going live. When you do decide to go live, I would suggest that you start with your robot "dialed down," so to speak, meaning use small lot sizes. This will allow you to compare the demo trading versus the live trading executions of your robot.

The Megadroid robot only trades on the EUR/USD pair, and there are some settings you can use to manipulate the trading frequency. It does not trade as much as one would like. However, it is designed to be very specific and target its entry times, thus making it one of the most successful robots on the market today.

When you first set up the robot, it may take some time before it places the first trade. Have patience; it will place trades, and you will see why it is one of the best robots on the market.

I use multiple robots when trading, and I do this because it allows for a more diversified approach to my trading. The automation is a way to diversify, and so is using multiple robots. By adding this strategy to my manual trading, I am able to put down a well-diversified trading system.

One of the key features you will want a good robot to have is a stop-loss component that will keep your account from blowing up. You cannot afford to lose your previous winning trades to one big single loss. I have seen this happen too many times. The robot will make 20 successful trades in a row, and then one big loser wipes all the profits away. Forex Megadroid, on default, will try to use a 3:1 risk-to-reward ratio.

REVERSE CORRELATED TIME AND PRICE ANALYSIS

Most robots can make money in the right market conditions. It's when the market conditions or the trend changes that causes the robots to start losing. That is one of the reasons why I save all my settings and maintain a significant archived log of them. That way I know which robot was used, what setting was maximized, and what the market conditions were. I can take the same robot and change the settings to maximize my profit potential during different trending markets. By doing this, I can eliminate one of the biggest drawbacks of robots, the inability to determine market conditions and adjust trading strategy to maximize current market trends.

Megadroid has a reverse correlated time and price analysis feature that helps the robot to adapt to different changing market conditions. Megadroid then continues to profit in the new trend. I don't necessarily use this feature as set in stone; I still like to maximize the settings for different market conditions.

BUILT-IN CLOAKING

As I have discussed in this book, some brokers are only in it for themselves at the expense of their customers. My robot trading is what first tipped me off that something was really wrong with some of these brokers. Some brokers will not even allow you to use robots, and others are known to specifically reject any orders that come from robots, especially if the broker finds out which one you are using—and especially if you are profitable.

As I mentioned before, one of the things I have done to combat this is to run the robots on a demo account (or a small live account), use a middleware program we developed that will see the trade, and make the trades with numerous brokers simultaneously. You cannot do this with proprietary robots, as that would be against their user agreements. We use this strategy on our internal proprietary robots that we have developed.

To help combat the problem with brokers detecting which robots you might be using, Megadroid uses two unique ID settings. Megadroid recommends that you change these two settings weekly to keep the brokers from detecting your robot.

I have installed and tested hundreds of EAs; Megadroid is one of the easiest ones to install. It should only take you about five minutes to get this robot up and running. Remember, it could take a week or more before the first trades pop on.

Overall, of all the EAs I have tested, Fap Turbo and Megadroid are the best. There are lots of robots out there, and as the forex market grows, there will be many more. I have a team and a testing lab set aside specifically to test robots and develop new ones. I believe in this technology. It has been around for a long time and will only get better. The brokers are not stupid, and so they will be working just as hard to stop you from making money. That is why you really need a true ECN-type broker, one who is going to put your trades through to the bank.

27

BACK-TESTING

Most know that it is important, but few know how to use it. A fundamental tool for your success in forex trading, back-testing is nothing more than gathering a series of data or events and applying to them the strategy or trading system we want to test so we can measure its efficiency. The key question is, if the great majority of forex traders "in the know" know that back-testing is essential, why is it that new traders and even experienced ones do not employ this feature at its full potential?

There are two distinct answers to this. One is that many can find it boring or tiresome. They don't understand or simply don't care and prefer to jump into the market with their strategy in a demo account or even in a real account. This is a huge mistake; in the end, those people will always be consistent losers. Always. And why? Because greed, impatience, and even the love for easy shortcuts that many people possess and their attitude toward life make them adventurous, and they enter the market "blinded." Then, after blowing up their first account, comes frustration.

There is another group that uses back-testing, but the people in this group do not know how to implement its features. These people are good-willed, but good intentions by themselves do not generate pips; these individuals can also end up as losers.

Both groups of traders also lose because this business is highly individualistic; you have nobody by your side to tell you what to do and especially what *not to do*. And so mistakes pile up that are not analyzed or understood. I am certain that, given enough and appropriate guidance when using demo accounts and later in real accounts, thousands of dollars could be saved. Just keep in mind that the demo account will be skewed somewhat from live trading. We dedicated an entire chapter to that topic in this book.

That's why even getting good results after a lot of practice in demo accounts does not automatically guarantee you won't make mistakes on a real account because of your lack of experience and lack of guidance to understand fully a particular strategy and do a follow-up of the errors encountered.

If you do not perform back-testing accurately, you will have a fair chance of becoming a permanent losing trader. If you try to implement a method on the real markets without a previous statistical verification of its performance, you will only be destroying your own money.

Why is back-testing so important?

1. Because it gives you a statistical certainty about the tool you are using and about its efficiency, with the probability of success when opening and closing a position.
2. Because it will reduce your fears on entering the market.
3. Because when you trade forex, you need a high amount of confidence and trust in your strategy, knowing that anything can happen in the markets—and quite often, when you least expect it.
4. Because it will allow you to identify and correct possible flaws within your system before going live and will also allow you to identify the best market conditions to employ.
5. Because forex traders are not fortune-tellers. Don't try to play casino with your account and trade on instinct or because of a hunch. Employing a thoroughly proven method is being responsible, and this precisely is a fundamental quality that a trader must possess.

In short, back-testing is the action of applying a trading strategy toward historical data. You will be verifying all the parameters and rules that characterize your particular trading method by testing them against the past behavior of the markets; and depending on the results, you will modify or refine the conditions to add strength to your system.

Parameters will have to include the time frame, expected profit and maximum allowed loss, profit goals, and entry and exit conditions based on technical or fundamental indicators. Results will be analyzed in regard to overall profitability, percentage of winning and losing trades, and risk-to-reward ratio.

BACK-TESTING METHODS

Manual Back-Testing

This is the slowest of all three methods and consists of advancing through historical data one candle or bar at a time, writing down the trading signals, and recording projected entry and exit prices. This method is limited by the amount of data that can be held in one chart. Manual back-testing will require that you keep accurate records, which will help you build a sound experience in treating forex trading as a business.

Let's face it; this is not the reality of today's marketplace. Most back-testing methods are going to need to run on tick data to be efficient or accurate. That means every time the market is changing, your computer system is storing that information. Can you imagine trying to store that much information manually? I don't see that happening. Even computers have a difficult time running back-testing. In fact, back-testing is so intensive, it will oftentimes kill a computer. Lots of data and time points to crunch.

Software Back-Testing

This is, in my opinion, the best way to back-test a strategy, as it will allow you to work faster and over longer periods of time, being that the software automatically processes the data. You will be experiencing the same conditions as if you were trading live, with the added feature of being able to go backward and forward at a higher speed and set the preferred pace for the data output.

This is essentially one of the things that I built when I was on my mission to build a proprietary software user interface for traders to use in retail forex trading. As I was building the software, I had to create the back end of the software, the storage, the 7-days-a-week–24-hours-a-day data center. Because I had access to all this technology, I was able to create my own data storage. I can utilize the data in our testing labs, and that gives me a clear advantage over smaller retail customers. I have in the past shared what I learned; this book is no different.

Programmed Back-Testing

Setting up a programmed interface with all the rules and parameters of your strategy is the most complicated of all three methods, but it could be useful if you intend in the end to trade by means of a robot or automated system. The computer goes back in time and takes the trades according to your system rules.

This kind of back-testing is the fastest, as you do not need to see the chart unfolding. The calculations and trades are made automatically based on the parameters you have set, and you only see the end results.

The limitations it has are, first, that it is difficult to program the system with precision and, second, that at the moment the robot "decides" to take the trade, it takes into account only the real-time data. You will also still need to manually check some of the trades taken to make sure that the program is really trading in agreement with your rules, and you probably will have to make many adjustments until the robot interprets the conditions with total accuracy.

Forward-Testing

Clearly this is not back-testing, but it is testing, and so I wanted to cover it in this chapter. One of the absolute best things you can do for your trading is to forward-test your strategy. You can do this with an EA, other robot, manual system, whatever.

Essentially what you do is take your robot or your trading plan and follow it to the letter. But instead of taking old information and back-testing your strategy, you are taking real-time data and making trades in real time based on that real-time information. You can forward-test with a live account or a demo account. But when doing this sort of trading, you want to be watching your screen; that way you can see what is really happening and how your trades are opening and closing. You will be able to see some of the games the brokers are playing. I like to forward-test my roots and systems for months on end, maybe even years. That way when I do my research, I can see what the actual system was doing with the bids and asks of the market, the real data flow versus closed time frames that are somewhat static.

HOW TO BACK-TEST

At first this can take some effort, but as soon as you develop a complete template, it will be useful to evaluate any strategy thereafter.

Your trading method must be clearly defined and have specific and nonsubjective entries and exits, based on signals given by indicators or price action patterns. You should not use too many indicators, as those could be conflicting and interfere with decision making. Then you need to choose the currency pair to evaluate as well as the particular time frame, according to your personal trading style. For example, if you only trade a specific market session, those should be the hours upon which to implement the back-test.

With these data, you can set up a template in Excel to show the currency pair you are using along with its entry and exit price. Between both prices you will also show the maximum profits made and maximum losses. This information will be vital for your analysis. You can group all maximum profits as a series of events from which to obtain the average and its standard deviation. This will offer some statistical certainty about the area of greater concentration of those maximum values so that later on you can define your take-profit level. For example, if 65 percent of the concentration of the maximum values of your method is between 70 and 90, you could choose any value of that zone for your future take-profit.

You can also increase or decrease the scope of your concentration of pips and make the corresponding adjustments. The same occurs in regard to the maximum losses, and it would have to be reasoned as follows: How many pips can my method withstand against my original direction before closing or not closing a position and come back to be a winner (that is, discovering which is the more accurate stop loss).

The key question is, how many data points should I evaluate? I personally think that a range between 200 and 400 trades (which would represent 3 to 5 months approximately, depending on your trading style) is the minimum needed for a back-test in order to obtain efficient results. This requires a lot of effort, of course, but will empower you with a strategy testing machine that will help you find the best system for consistent winnings and not just for a few weeks or a few months.

Always remember that your take-profit level has to be greater than your stop loss. If your method or type of trading gets 35 pips on winners and loses 40 pips, you are risking your capital considerably. Other cases are worse; winning 5 pips and then losing up to 20 pips is something absolutely illogical, and these kinds of systems must be discarded.

I have tested all sorts of strategies, even the ones that claim to be accurate 99.9 percent of the time, and I have found some where that was actually the case. The problem with these sorts of systems is that when you actually go live in a real account, you don't get the same results. The first thing you will notice is that some of the brokers have begun to play the games that I have talked about in this book. And so your automated strategy can't make all the trades it is supposed to.

Guess what? That changes the tested results; now you have new variables. You also have some strategies touted out there that have huge stop losses, and so if you are willing to take a 300- to 400-pip stop loss, then you may find some success. You better have a big account, though, so that you can absorb the intertrade drawdowns.

Other strategies take the negative risk-to-reward approach; this kind of strategy will risk 100 pips to get 10 pips, and it will make eight good trades in a row and then lose two trades in a row. Now you are upside down. You can't beat good money management. That is paramount. So make sure you are testing that in your system as you back-test.

Summarizing, we would have four basic steps to construct a sound back-testing strategy:

1. Obtain the appropriate and most complete historical market data for the currency pair under test.
2. Decide upon the indicator or set of indicators you will be using as entry and exit signals.
3. Build your trading rules.
4. Optimize your strategy by modifying the appropriate parameters against the trading rules, such as total balance, margin level, maximum drawdown, maximum profit, and consecutive losing or winning trades, as well as different leverages and spreads.

FOREX SIMULATORS

Learning, developing, and refining your own trading strategy requires a great amount of practice, repetition, and optimization. A forex simulator is specialized software that has been designed to reproduce the conditions of the markets in real time, allowing you to simulate forex trading. It is a very useful tool for training and improving your trading skills, and so you can build up confidence in a particular method and compare several different strategies without having to risk any real money.

With such a tool, you are able to upload and review historical data at any given time, going backward and forward as many times as you need. This will allow you to perform a continuous training on your understanding of the behavior of a particular currency pair, with its chart patterns, price action, and signals, over and over until you can feel confident about your comprehension and of the probable results of your methods.

Some traders seem to think that it is better to jump directly into the markets with a demo account to perform a live forward-test. However, the use of a forex simulator allows you to cover months of data in just a few days, limiting your work to a specific market session and test in several different time frames. Besides, if you want to test a trading strategy on a demo, you first need to know exactly what you are doing, and the training confidence and market knowledge that you will acquire through the use of the simulations is priceless.

Several independent and specific tester software programs are available, as well as trading platforms that include strategy testing options, and you can also find testing plug-ins that will allow you to implement the testing on your platform of choice. Some of them are free of charge; others have to be purchased once or require a subscription. If your own trading platform allows you to go back in time and move the chart forward one candle at a time, you can also perform manual back-testing, although this alternative will be slower. Forex simulators allow you to set up a much faster pace to the sequence of market tick data and to fast-forward to precise points in time, and so you can just employ the time you really need and can work on wider ranges, even over many years.

Simulators can also be used to back-test automated strategies. You will need to build your rules completely in the automated module, and the results will be determined based on the historical data and your parameters over the time range selected, with no further intervention on your part during the test. This is the fastest way to obtain an accurate evaluation if your own trading method is suitable to be automated.

Benefits of Back-Testing versus Forward-Testing

- *Time-saving.* You can evaluate years of data in just a few days, which allows you to correct any parameters and retest over the same data.
- *Statistically more accurate.* On a demo account, any mistake you make will stay recorded and will mess up the statistics of your strategy, while the simulator allows you to go back and start over, correcting the mistake. Also, let's say that your method requires you to open a trade every day at market close and you happen to miss one or more days on the demo account; your statistical results will be flawed.
- *No time limitation.* You can perform the testing even when the markets are closed or on weekends, and you can pause whenever you need to and continue later. With a forex simulator, you control the time.

AVOIDING BACK-TESTING MISTAKES

One of the most common errors of back-testing a strategy is to use approximated information in place of information not yet available at the moment of the decision-making process. For example, some software programs will give you closing data in anticipation. If your own method includes closing prices, you cannot open the trade until the candle or bar of the time frame you are using has effectively closed.

To avoid this, you need to make sure that you are only using the exact information available at a given point, especially if you are employing an automated alternative. This is usually done by chosing a tick-by-tick option for the chart price evolution. On manual back-testing it is easier to check.

Another mistake that often comes up is the use of too many variables for the test, for example, too many indicators. This can work well for a while on past time periods, but it can become a problem when the strategy is applied to future events. Keep your strategy simple.

Finally, your trading strategy should be able to stand powerfully against any unforeseen events, when the markets react to particular fundamentals and behave erratically. How can you protect yourself and still get positive results out of the back-testing? By anticipating the eventuality of those events and the subsequent drastic market reactions:

- Increase the loss expectations in regard to the results given by the back-test, and check whether the strategy will still be profitable under those new conditions.
- Increase the expected risk level per trade based on your maximum risk level allowed. At a certain point, you might face an unforeseen event and the losses could be greater.
- Set an appropriate maximum risk level and maximum drawdown that you are able to tolerate. Make sure you plan for drawdowns according to the maximum historical drawdowns that your method can experience over an extensive period of time. Increase the expected percentage for eventual worse drawdowns in the future.

The stronger trading strategies will be profitable under various market conditions. There are also strategies that are difficult to back-test, especially those that rely on trendlines and some technical patterns that cannot be adequately quantified. Finally, you have to accept that there will be times in real market conditions where your strategy will not function as well as expected because of the irrationality of the markets or unpredictability of certain fundamental events.

METATRADER BACK-TESTING

As discussed in the previous chapter, I have used MetaTrader extensively while testing EAs and automated strategies. Here I want to discuss a few key things that I have witnessed in my back-testing using this software platform.

I have noticed that if you do an extensive amount of back-testing using MetaTrader, your computer will eventually get slower. What you need to do is periodically close MetaTrader and then just reopen it. I am no computer guy, but I have witnessed that the back-testing will give you different results on the same parameter scans the more you run the back-test. One of my IT guys told me that the MetaTrader platform has some sort of memory leak. Closing and restarting the program will solve the problem, so just keep that in mind when you are back-testing a lot of strategies.

I have read a lot of chat room posts and message boards debating the MetaTrader strategy tester. There are lots of pros and cons about how it works, and as I mentioned, there are some inherent problems. But if you want to run through some different parameters of an EA, it is a pretty good way to isolate what is going on.

One thing to be aware of is that the system is faulty in that it sometimes doesn't place trades. The strategy tester will test your EA, but some of your trades in a live account won't be taken because of the error message you get from the broker, such as invalid price and trade content busy. So that skews your results a bit.

MetaTrader History Center
Make sure that when you are using MetaTrader's strategy tester, you are using the best data possible; to do this, you will need to

maximize the efficiency to get the best result. If you are going to use every tick, then you will want to do the following to make sure that you are getting the most complete and accurate data available. When you run your test and you see mismatched data errors of less than 89 percent modeling- quality data, then you need to adjust your historical data.

To adjust your historical data, go to the tools menu, open the history center, and double-click the chart pair in the left column that you plan to back-test. The next thing you will see is a list of different time frames. The time frame that you should start with is the M1, or one-minute time frame. The M1 is the tick data, and so this will give you the most complete data to use during your back-test. If you download the latest data when you first turn on your computer, you will have better modeling-quality data.

The best way to get the most accurate and complete data to back-test is to turn on your MetaTrader software and leave it running as long as you can. This brings in real data in real time. If you can find a broker that will give you a nonexpiring demo, then you are in the money, so to speak. You can then leave the demo account open in real time for as long as you want. What happens is that your demo ends up collecting months of real-time data, allowing you to have a much better back-test result.

BACK-TESTING LOG

When back-testing, I have always kept a log. On the other hand, rather than keeping a log, if you are using MetaTrader or some of the other software platforms out there, they have an optimizer that can help you find the best configuration of your strategy. For me, I like to keep a log.

I take whatever strategy I am working on and start back-testing each variable. It is important to be specific and make sure you write the results in your log. Start with the currency pair and then work down from there. Try all the different time frames and then all the different market conditions. If you are using an EA, try the different offsets available. I like using offsets because they will help you throw the broker off your trail.

The money management parameters are big parameters that you need to test. Test each one separately: stop loss, take profits, etc.

Back-testing is an important part of the trading process; spend the appropriate time on this stage of your trading process to help you maximize your trading profit potential.

28

EA DEMO VERSUS LIVE

For someone who has tested EAs, I can tell you there is a lot to know, and it requires lots of patience. We have discussed EAs in previous chapters. Here I just want to cover some of the thought processes behind using the EAs in a demo situation versus a live situation.

EAs will trade very differently on a live account versus a demo account, and these differences are what I want to talk about. Brokers are not all created equal. The first thing you are going to want to do before you start using your EA on a demo or live account is to ask your broker who provides the MetaTrader software it uses.

Some companies are not as honest as others. I will leave that up to your Google searches if you want to know more specifics about which brokers to avoid. However, most of the brokers today are going to say they use some sort of STP model or processing model.

The brokers will say that they send the order directly to their liquidity provider. This may be the case, but the brokers are going to play with the trade before sending it through. The MetaTrader plug-ins allow the brokers to quickly skim a few pips off the order execution and manipulate the trade to put more money in their pockets.

It seems even the good brokers play with the orders some. For example, I was trading on MetaTrader with my broker, which I feel is one of the better ones. I just had four short trades on the EUR/USD, and they were all up with a gain. I wanted to close them out, and so I manually closed out each of the four orders. And every one of the orders I closed had a 1-pip slippage on it. The orders were initially placed by an EA, and I manually closed the orders in a slow-moving market. I guess the market wasn't slow enough.

The point is, pay attention to your orders and you will see what the brokers are doing; even the best brokers are still playing games. So when you are using an EA on a demo account, you will notice that the results you get from forward-testing don't exactly match the results you get from trading live.

A forward-test is simply running the EA in the marketplace in real time. If you are using a demo account and you turn your EA on, it will take into account slippage and spreads while making its trading determinations. If you are back-testing with past data, the EA will not be able to take into account accurately the slippage on each trade and the spreads being manipulated by the broker.

One of the things you will see when trading an EA live is that sometimes it won't place any trades. If you go in and look at the journal, you will see all the error messages that come up when the EA is trying to place a trade. The errors are the off-price quotes, server buys, spread too wide, etc.

When you are testing your EA in a demo account, your EA will more than likely place a lot more trades and will not have all the errors that it gets when running on a live account. The demo account most likely won't have the middleware running the plug-ins. Without the plug-ins turned on, the games aren't being played.

OPEN A DEMO ACCOUNT

It is best to open up a new demo and start with a good round number—say, $10,000–$100,000 if you have the ability to choose—that way you can try and use a number that will be a little closer to what you are going to actually trade. When you are using your demo account with your EA, you can work on your money management; you can set your appropriate drawdowns. This is one of the most critical things that you will need to watch. How much will your EA trade at one time? You don't want your EA to place a trade and then, on some aggressive setting, place another trade, doubling your position and doubling your exposure. If you haven't taken into consideration what the double exposure will do to your account and you take a loss, it could get pretty bad very quickly.

OPEN A LIVE ACCOUNT

Whenever I move from a demo investment into a live environment, I like to dial my EA down and place some small lot sizes to begin. That way I can basically start my testing over again with limited drawdown and exposure. Over the next few days I will be looking to see what my EA is doing, and I will want to compare my trade logs with those of the same EA trading on a demo account. If I don't see many differences and I have a handful of trades to compare, I will turn up the volume on my EA and let it go.

If I start seeing some pretty big inconsistencies, I will stop trading live and go back to the demo account to do some more forward-testing. A perfect example is an EA I have been testing for about three months on a demo account. I was forward-testing the results, and so I was letting the EA trade in real time on a demo account. That way I could see exactly how the EA was placing its trades and managing risk.

Let's take the next step; just the other day I placed the EA on a live account, and the first thing I noticed was that the EA was placing more trades, almost double that of when I had it on a demo account. The second thing I noticed was that I was having swap rates charged to my account for holding the positions past rollover. This was different from what I had been seeing when my EA was trading on a demo account.

This caused me to start looking into all the trades that had been placed using the same software system. As I mentioned earlier, when I move an EA from the demo side to the live trading account side, I dial the EA down so that I have limited risk. In this case I did just that, and so my risk was limited, and that allowed me to see what my EA was doing in a live account with real money.

I still liked the results I was getting; in fact, I was pretty happy. However, I had to make some adjustments to my money management plan that I had worked on while my EA was in demo mode, since I was getting almost twice as many trades now. I didn't want to have twice as many trades open and then go against me and basically double the drawdown I was expecting.

I was also able to talk to the broker and solve the overnight swap issue. There was actually an error in how the MetaTrader provider was passing on the swaps to my broker. Regardless, I was being charged incorrectly. Can you imagine how many other people trading are being charged incorrectly? *Yikes!* is all I can say.

Be diligent in your trading. Make sure that you are watching all your trades or at least reviewing them all. It never hurts to sit and watch your EA when it is opening and closing its trades. If you really want to make sure that your broker doesn't have you on the plug-ins, the next time your EA places a few trades, manually close the trades. Make sure to pay close attention to the price when closing; and if possible, close the trade during some slow market conditions so that the broker cannot say that the market was moving fast and that slippage is expected during fast-moving markets. As you are closing your trades, look at the price and then see what the price is after the trade has closed.

You will also want to watch to see how long it takes the trade to close once you click on the CLOSE TRADE button. If the trade takes more than a few seconds (less than 5), then there is a problem, and you will want to investigate more. One of the settings within the MetaTrader plug-ins is server delay, or trade execution delay. You can set it for 5 seconds, 10 seconds, etc. So if you are closing your trades and they seem to be lagging about the same amount of time, you have a problem and need to discuss it with your broker.

Don't expect the people at your broker's to be very up front when you confront them about the games going on. You may have to just plan on changing brokers. I keep an updated list of brokers that I use on www.jdfn.com. And a survey is always running on the site so that you can see what other traders are recommending and where they are trading.

I am always testing brokers with real money and have moved many times, and I know I will probably move again at some point, at least until I set up my own system that I know doesn't play games. But for now, I will just pay close attention to my trades.

CONCLUSION

Now you have just about finished the book. It has taken me more than 10 years to gain the knowledge that I have written about in this book related to what I have found going on in the retail forex industry behind the scenes. When I first began, I had no idea what the retail forex brokers were doing to their customers. I, like many of you, have been taken advantage of by some of the unscrupulous brokers out there. I have lost large amounts of money in single trades specifically because of the tactics we are talking about here. But that didn't stop me from trading, and each time I learned a little more and learned how to better protect myself. Unfortunately I am sure this won't be the last time I lose money on a trade because of a broker. Until I start a firm myself, I will always have broker issues. Quite frankly, even if I had my own firm, I would have problems with my liquidity brokers. But that is trading, and I choose to trade.

In the beginning when something looked strange in my account—say, a slow execution or the price slipping—I just didn't know any better. It took the 10-plus years to piece it all together. Over the last 12 months is when the light bulb started to go off. That led me to my own personal investigations and opened my eyes to what was really going on. I have tried to share many of my discoveries with you, as well as some of the strategies that I use to trade this market today.

I love the forex market; it is the only market that I really trade actively. It is the largest financial market in the world and will only grow. We have seen tremendous growth over the last few years; I remember when I first started in early 2000 when daily turnover was reported at $1.9 trillion a day. Today the daily turnover is reported to be about $3.9 trillion. The growth has been staggering and what is more amazing is the U.S. growth in retail forex trading. When I first started, not a hand in the room would go up when I would ask who was trading the forex. Now you can hear mention of the forex just about anywhere you go; the topic certainly controls the TV financial news shows today. And why not? Currency is the driving force behind the world's economies, which are now more interconnected than ever before.

There are some 25 million equities traders in the United States today and only about 2 million forex traders. This will change as time goes on. A shift will begin to happen, as equities brokers begin to offer retail forex to their customers and as retail forex brokers begin to offer equities to their customers. In the end, there is a lot more upside to customer acquisition and account growth in the forex than in the equities markets. Brokers know this and will be looking to cash in on the growth. The growth will be good for all of us, as it will bring more regulations and oversight. I'm not sure if all those changes will be good or not, but it will make a much fairer marketplace for us all.

Don't let what you have read close the door on your ideas of being a foreign currency trader. You are better off now that you know what is going on than you were before you started reading this book. Just keep in mind that there are brokers trying to take your money, so trade accordingly. This market will still give up huge profits to the traders who are using the right tools and have the right training—the traders who have the right mindset and great money management will prevail.

Make sure that you trade smart, and if you find yourself the victim of broker foul play, pick up the phone and confront that broker.

Put the broker on the spot and don't give up until you get your money back. If you see a pattern in the way your trades are executed and you are losing money, then change brokers.

As you finish this book, keep it handy so that when you recognize some of the games happening in your own trading, you can refer back to the book. Also remember to check www.jdfn.com on a regular basis for up-to-date information on various topics that I have written about in the book and will be updating on my Website. Also, if you find new insider tactics that are not addressed in this book, please go to the Web site and post your findings for all to read.

GLOSSARY

Appreciation The increase in the value of an asset.

Arbitrage A technique that lets traders profit from differences in the price of a single currency pair that is traded on more than one market.

Ask The price at which a currency pair or security is offered for sale. The quoted price at which an investor can buy a currency pair. Also known as the *offer, ask price,* and *ask rate.*

Asset An item having commercial or exchange value.

Back-testing The process of testing a trading strategy on prior time periods. Instead of applying a strategy for the time period forward, which could take years, a trader can do a simulation of his or her trading strategy on relevant past data in order to gauge the strategy's effectiveness. Most technical analysis strategies are tested with this approach. When you back-test a theory, the results achieved are highly dependent on the movements of the tested period. Back-testing a theory assumes that what happens in the past will happen in the future, and this assumption can cause potential risks for the strategy.

Bank rate The percentage rate at which the central bank of a country lends money to the country's commercial banks.

Base currency The first currency in a currency pair. The base currency is the currency against which exchange rates are generally quoted in a given country. *Examples:* USD/JPY—the U.S. dollar is the base currency; EUR/USD—the euro is the base currency. See also *quote currency*.

Bear market An extended period of general price decline in an individual security, an asset, or a market.

Bid The price at which an investor can place an order to buy a currency pair. The quoted price at which an investor can sell a currency pair. Also known as the *bid price* and *bid rate*.

Bid/ask spread The point difference between the bid and offer (ask) price.

Binary option A type of option in which the payoff is structured to be either a fixed amount of compensation if the option expires in-the-money or nothing at all if the option expires out-of-the-money. These types of options are different from plain vanilla options. Also known as *all-or-nothing options* or *digital options*.

Book of business (BB) Common parlance in the U.S. financial services sector. It refers to the collection of clients that a broker has assembled. It is often used to refer to the valuation of such client following.

Bretton Woods The site of the conference that in 1944 led to the establishment of the postwar foreign exchange system that remained intact until the early 1970s. The conference resulted in the formation of the IMF. The system fixed currencies in a fixed exchange rate system with 1 percent fluctuations of the currency to gold or the dollar.

Broker An agent that executes orders to buy and sell currencies and related instruments either for a commission or on a spread. Brokers are agents working on commission and not principals or agents acting on their own account. In the forex market, brokers tend to act as intermediaries between banks, bringing buyers and sellers together for a commission paid by the initiator or by both parties. There are four or five major global brokers operating through subsidiaries, affiliates, and partners in many countries.

Bull market A market that is on a consistent upward trend.

Buy limit order An order to execute a transaction at a specified price (the limit) or lower.

Buy on margin The process of buying a currency pair where a client pays cash for part of the overall value of the position. The word *margin* refers to the portion the investor puts up rather than the portion that is borrowed.

Cable Forex trader's slang word that designates the British pound–U.S. dollar exchange rate, GBP/USD.

Candlestick chart A chart that displays the daily trading price range (open, high, low, and close). A form of Japanese charting that has become popular in the West. A narrow line (shadow) shows the day's price range. A wider body marks the area between the open and the close. If the close is above the open, the body is white (not filled); if the close is below the open, the body is black (filled).

Carry The income or cost associated with keeping a forex position overnight. This is derived when the currency pairs in the position have different interest rates for the same period of time. Also known as *interest rate carry*.

Carry trade In forex, the practice of holding a position with a positive overnight interest return in the hope of gaining profits, without closing the position, just for the central bank's interest rates difference.

Central bank A bank, administered by a national government, which regulates the behavior of financial institutions within its borders and carries out monetary policy.

Chartist A person who attempts to predict prices by analyzing past price movements as recorded on a chart.

Closing a position Selling or buying a forex position resulting in the liquidation (squaring up) of the position.

Closing market rate The rate at which a position can be closed based on the market price at the end of the day.

Commission The fee that a broker may charge clients for dealing on their behalf.

Confirmation Written acknowledgment of a trade, listing important details such as the date, the size of the transaction, the price, the commission, and the amount of money involved.

Consumer Price Index (CPI). The statistical measure of inflation based upon changes in the prices of a specified set of goods.

Contract for difference (CFD). Special trading instrument that allows financial speculation on stocks, commodities, and other instruments without actually buying. An arrangement made in a futures contract whereby differences in settlement are made through cash payments, rather than the delivery of physical goods or securities.

Correspondent bank A foreign bank's representative that regularly performs services for a bank that has no branch in the relevant center, e.g., to facilitate the transfer of funds. In the United States this often occurs domestically due to interstate banking restrictions.

Counterpart A participant in a financial transaction.

Cover (1) To take out a forward forex contract. (2) To close out a short position by buying currency or securities that have been sold.

Cross rate The exchange rate between two currencies where neither of the currencies is the USD.

Currency Money issued by a government—this includes coins and paper money. It is a form of money used as a unit of exchange within a country.

Currency pair The two currencies in a forex transaction. The EUR/USD is an example of a currency pair.

Day order A buy or sell order that will expire automatically at the end of the trading day on which it is entered.

Day trade A trade opened and closed on the same trading day.

Day trader A trader who buys and sells on the basis of small short-term price movements.

Day trading A style or type of trading where trade positions are opened and closed during the same day.

Dealer An individual or firm that buys and sells assets from its portfolio, acting as a principal or counterpart to a transaction.

Dealer plug-ins Devices used to intentionally delay traders' orders, in order to induce slippage. If the slippage is in the customer's favor, the customer's order is executed at the requested price instead of the better price, allowing the broker to keep the savings. If the slippage is not in the customer's favor, the difference is passed on to the customer and the customer loses.

Dealing desk A desk where transactions for buying and selling securities occur. Since the forex market is open around the clock, many institutions have dealing desks around the world. Dealing desks can also be found outside the forex markets, such as in banks and finance companies, to execute trades in securities. The term *desk* may be a bit of a misnomer, given its connotation of a table shared by a couple of traders. Large financial institutions often have dealing facilities that are staffed by hundreds of dealers. In a large institution, major currencies, such as the euro and yen, may have several dealing desks staffed by dozens of traders who specialize in these currencies.

Demo account A trading account that allows investors to practice their trading with imaginary money. A demo account trades similarly to a live account by allowing execution of orders, money management, and strategy testing in a safer atmosphere than a live account can offer since any losses sustained are not "real" in the demo account environment.

Depreciation A fall in the value of a currency due to market forces.

Desk Term referring to a group dealing with a specific currency or currencies.

Devaluation The act by a government to reduce the external value of its currency.

Digital option An option whose payout is fixed after the underlying stock exceeds the predetermined threshold or strike price. The value of the payout is determined at the onset of the contract and doesn't depend on the magnitude by which the price of the underlying moves. So whether you are in-the-money by $1 or $5, the amount that you receive will be the same. Also referred to as a *binary* or *all-or-nothing option*.

Discretionary account An account in which the customer permits a trading institution to act on the customer's behalf in buying and selling currency pairs. The institution has discretion about the choice of currency pairs, prices, and timing, subject to any limitations specified in the agreement.

ECB See *European Central Bank.*

ECN broker A type of forex brokerage firm that provides its clients direct access to other forex market participants. ECN brokers don't discourage scalping, don't trade against the client, don't charge spread (low spread is defined by current market prices), but do charge commissions for every order.

Economic release A scheduled announcement related to a particular fundamental indicator, which includes the data of the previous release and the forecast value. At the moment of the release, revisions can be made to the previous release values, and these will become the actual release. Also called an *economic news release.*

Euro The single currency of the European Economic and Monetary Union introduced in January 1999. This is the amalgamation of the following currencies; after January 1, 2002, these currencies have been considered legacy currencies: German deutsche mark, Italian lira, Austrian schilling, French franc, Belgian franc, Dutch guilder, Finnish markka, Portuguese escudo, Greek drachma, Irish punt, Luxembourg franc, and Spanish peseta.

European Central Bank (ECB) The central bank for the new European Monetary Union. It is the main regulatory body of the European Union financial system.

Execution The process of completing an order or deal.

Exotic options An option that differs from common American or European options in terms of the underlying asset or the calculation of how or when the investor receives a certain payoff. These options are more complex than options that trade on an exchange, and they generally trade OTC. For example, one type of exotic option is known as a *chooser* option. This instrument allows an investor to choose whether the option is a put or call at a certain point during the option's life. Because this type of option can change over the holding period, it is not be found on a regular exchange, which is why it is classified as an exotic option. Other types of exotic options include barrier options, Asian options, digital options, and compound options, among others.

Expert advisor (EA) A plug-in tool used with trading platforms like MetaTrader 4 that allows for automated trades based on parameters set by the developer of the EA program. These programs integrate into the trading platform, allowing automation of order entry and execution.

Fap Turbo An automated forex trading robot. It offers short-term scalping strategies that monitor five currency pairs: EUR/CHF, GBP/CHF, EUR/GBP, USD/CAD, and EUR/USD. The software automatically enters and exits trades based on predetermined parameters.

Fast market Rapid movement in a market caused by strong interest by buyers and sellers. In such circumstances, price levels may be omitted and bid and offer quotations may occur too rapidly to be fully reported.

Federal Deposit Insurance Corporation (FDIC) The regulatory agency responsible for administering bank depository insurance in the United States.

Federal Open Market Committee (FOMC) The committee that sets money supply targets in the United States which tend to be implemented through Fed Fund interest rates, etc.

Federal Reserve System The central banking system in the United States. This is the main regulatory body of the U.S. financial system; its division, the FOMC, regulates, among other things, federal interest rates. Also known as the *Federal Reserve* and the *Fed*.

Fibonacci retracements The levels with a high probability of trend break or bounce, calculated at the 23.6 percent, 32.8 percent, 50 percent, and 61.8 percent levels of the trend range.

Fill The process of completing a customer's order to buy or sell a currency pair.

Fill price The price at which a buy or sell order is executed.

Financial risk The risk that a firm will be unable to meet its financial obligations.

Flat (square) Term describing a trading book with no market exposure. A neutral state that occurs when all your positions are closed.

Foreign exchange The purchase or sale of a currency against the sale or purchase of another. Also known as *forex* and *FX*.

Forex Term commonly used when referring to the forex market.

Forex clubs Groups formed in the major financial centers to encourage educational and social contacts between forex dealers.

Forex simulator Unlike a live forex demo account that functions in real time, a forex simulator enables users to upload, view, and review historical data at any given time. A forex simulator is used to confirm a trader's understanding of trading pattern recognition and trading signals. It allows traders to practice strategies through repetition without the need to be in the market at the time the movements take place.

Forward A transaction that settles at a future date.

Forward-testing The process in which you take a small set of data, analyze all the attributes, and generate the optimized set of attributes. This optimized set of values is applied to a set of unanalyzed data. Every new result generated plays its part in generating the next result and participates until the final result is generated. Forward-testing is a calculator for forecasting future performance.

Fundamental analysis Analysis of economic and political information with the objective of determining future movements in a financial market.

FX See *foreign exchange.*

Good-till-canceled order (GTC) A buy or sell order that remains open until it is filled or canceled.

Hedging A type of transaction that limits investment risk with the use of derivatives, such as options and futures contracts. Hedging transactions purchase opposite positions in the market in order to ensure a certain amount of gain or loss on a trade. They are employed by portfolio managers to reduce portfolio risk and volatility or lock in profits. Hedge funds use this sort of transaction extensively.

Initial margin The deposit a customer needs to make before being allocated a trading limit.

Initial margin requirement The minimum portion of a new security purchase that an investor must pay for in cash.

Instant execution The process of passing market orders directly to the liquidity providers and executing the orders instantly at the current market price. *Instant execution* is a term most commonly used when discussing the forex market and STP.

Invalid quote An error message used by MetaTrader 4 and most often associated with a fast-moving market using expert advisors and manual trading.

Kiwi A forex slang name for the New Zealand currency, the New Zealand dollar.

Leverage The use of various financial instruments or borrowed capital, such as margin, to increase the potential return of an investment or the amount of debt used to finance a firm's assets. A firm with significantly more debt than equity is considered to be highly leveraged.

Limit order An order to execute a transaction at a specified price (the limit) or better. A limit order to buy would be at the limit or lower, and a limit order to sell would be at the limit or higher.

Liquidity A term that refers to the relationship between transaction size and price movements. For example, a market is liquid if large transactions can occur with only minimal price changes.

Live account A trading account that allows investors to trade "live" in the market with real money through a forex brokerage firm.

Long position In forex, when a currency pair is bought, it is understood that the primary currency in the pair is long and that the secondary currency is short.

Lot The standard size of an order or trading position. One lot is equal to US$100,000 on currency pairs where the U.S. dollar is the base currency and is equal to its equivalent in dollars where the base currency is from another country. The amount is usually expressed in multiples of 100.

Maintenance A set minimum margin that a customer must maintain in his or her margin account.

Margin The amount of money needed to maintain a position.

Margin account An account that allows leverage buying on credit and borrowing on currencies already in the account. Buying on credit and borrowing are subject to standards established by the firm carrying the account. Interest is charged on any borrowed funds and only for the period of time that the loan is outstanding.

Margin call A call for additional funds in a margin account either because the value of the equity in the account has fallen below a required minimum (also termed a *maintenance call*) or because additional currencies have been purchased (or sold short).

Market close The time of day that a market closes. In the 24-hour-a-day forex market, there is no official market close. Often, 5:00 p.m. EST is considered the market close because value dates for spot transactions change to the next new value date at that time.

Market maker (MM) A person or firm that provides liquidity, making two-sided prices (bids and offers) in the market.

Market order A customer order for immediate execution at the best price available when the order reaches the marketplace.

Market rate The current quote of a currency pair.

Maturity The date on which payment of a financial obligation is due.

Megadroid A forex robot that attempts to mimic how successful traders trade. Megadroid uses a 1-hour time frame to trigger its entry.

MetaTrader A type of trading software used to help currency traders with forex trading analysis and trade execution. Metatrader provides charts and order-taking methods.

Momentum The tendency of a currency pair to continue movement in a single direction.

Offer The price at which a currency pair or security is for sale; the quoted price at which an investor can buy a currency pair. Also known as the *ask, ask price*, and *ask rate*.

Off-price quotes Quotes that occur when order limits are set to a certain price and the price has already moved to some other value. For example, you want to buy at 1.3050, but by the time the order arrives on the market, the price is at 1.3060. The order is then rejected because there is too much difference in the price.

One-cancels-the-other order (OCO) A combination of two orders in which the execution of either one automatically cancels the other.

Open order A buy or sell order that remains in force until executed or canceled by the customer.

Open position Any position (long or short) that is subject to market fluctuations and has not been closed out by a corresponding opposite transaction.

Option Greeks The mathematical characteristics of the Black-Scholes model, named, for the most part, after the Greek letters used to represent them in equations. The five option Greeks measure the sensitivity of the price of stock options in relation to four different factors: changes in the underlying stock price, interest rate, volatility, and time decay.

Order A customer's instructions to buy or sell currencies with a certain rate.

Overbought See *overbought/oversold indicator*.

Overbought/oversold indicator A technical analysis tool that attempts to define when prices have moved too far and fast in either direction. This is usually calculated based on a moving average of the difference between the number of advancing and declining issues over a certain period of time. If the market is considered overbought, the technical analyst will sell; and if the market is considered oversold, he or she will buy.

Overnight position A trader's long or short position in a currency at the end of a trading day.

Oversold See *overbought/oversold indicator*.

Pip The smallest increment of change in a foreign currency price, either up or down. The last digit in the rate; for example, for EUR/USD, 1 point = 0.0001.

Pipette Fractional pip, 1/10 of a point. Additional decimal point quoted by some forex brokers. It provides a greater accuracy of price movements. *Examples:* 1.27503 for EUR/USD or 110.052 for USD/JPY.

Pivot point The primary support or resistance point that is calculated based on the previous period's high, low, and close prices. It is usually calculated on daily rates, but other time frames can also be used.

Point See *pip*.

Price The price at which the underlying currency can be bought or sold.

Price transparency The ability of all market participants to "see" or deal at the same price.

Principal value The original amount invested by the client.

Profit A positive amount of money gained for closing the position. Also known as a *gain*.

Quote A simultaneous bid and offer in a currency pair.

Quote currency The second currency mentioned in a currency pair. The quote currency is the one that determines the exchange rates. *Examples:* in the pair USD/JPY, the Japanese yen is the quote currency; in the pair EUR/USD, the U.S. dollar is the quote currency. See also *base currency*.

Rate The price at which a currency can be purchased or sold against another currency.

Realized profit or loss The gain or loss for already closed positions.

Resistance The price level at which technical analysts note persistent selling of a currency. The price level for which the intensive selling can lead to an increase in price (uptrend).

Revaluation The daily calculation of potential profits or losses on open positions based on the difference between the settlement price of the previous trading day and that of the current trading day.

Risk In regard to the forex, the risk that the exchange rate on a foreign currency will move against the position held by an investor such that the value of the investment is reduced.

Risk management The employment of financial analysis and use of trading techniques to reduce or control exposure to financial risk.

Rollover The process of extending the settlement value date on an open position forward to the next valid value date.

Scalper A trader who trades for small, short-term profits during the course of a trading session, rarely carrying a position overnight.

Scalping A trading strategy that attempts to make many profits on small price changes. Traders who implement this strategy will place anywhere from 10 to several hundred trades in a single day in the belief that small moves in prices are easier to catch than large ones.

Sell limit order An order to execute a transaction only at a specified price (the limit) or higher.

Selling short A situation where a currency has been sold with the intent of buying back the position at a lower price to make a profit.

Server busy A message related to trading forex using the MetaTrader 4 platform. This is limited to the market demand. As more trades are entered, the server will be overloaded and cause a "server busy" message to appear when a trader wants to buy or sell a currency. As a result, the trader will have to enter the trade again.

Settled position A closed position for which all needed transactions have been made.

Settlement The actual delivery of currencies made on the maturity date of a trade.

Short position In forex, when a currency pair is sold, the position is said to be short. It is understood that the primary currency in the pair is short and that the secondary currency is long.

Short squeeze The pressure on short sellers to cover their positions as a result of sharp price increases.

Slippage The difference between the expected price of a trade and the price at which the trade actually executes. Slippage often occurs during periods of higher volatility, when market orders are used and also when large orders are executed when there may not be enough interest at the desired price level to maintain the expected price of the trade. *Slippage* is a term often used in both forex and stock trading, and although the definition is the same for both, slippage occurs in different situations for each of these types of trading. In forex, slippage occurs when a limit order or stop loss occurs at a worse rate than originally set in the order. Slippage often occurs when volatility, perhaps due to news events, makes an order at a specific price impossible to execute. In this situation, most forex dealers will execute the trade at the next best price. Traders can help to protect themselves from slippage by avoiding market orders when not necessary.

Spot market The market where people buy and sell actual financial instruments (currencies) for two-day delivery.

Spot price The current market price of a currency that normally settles in two business days (one day for dollar/Canada).

Spread The point or pip difference between the bid and ask price of a currency pair.

Spread betting A type of speculation that involves taking a bet on the price movement of a security. A spread betting company quotes two prices, the bid and offer price (also called the spread), and investors bet whether the price of the underlying stock will be lower than the bid or higher than the offer. The investor does not own the underlying stock in spread betting; he or she simply speculates on the price movement of the stock.

Stealth mode A feature in some forex expert advisor programs that is designed to hide a trader's take profit and stop loss from the broker. By hiding the take profit/stop loss, a broker is unable to see where the traders have placed their take-profit and stop-loss orders, and therefore the broker cannot move the bid/ask in an attempt to execute orders for their own benefit instead of for the benefit of the trader.

Sterling Another term for the British currency, the pound.

Stop hunting A strategy that attempts to force some market participants out of their positions by driving the price of an asset to a level where many individuals have chosen to set their stop-loss orders. The triggering of many stop losses generally leads to high volatility and can present a unique opportunity for investors who seek to trade in this environment. Understanding that the price of an asset can experience sharp moves when many stop losses are triggered can be useful when seeking potential trading opportunities.

Stop order An order to buy or sell when a given price is reached or passed to liquidate part or all of an existing position. Also known as a *stop-loss order*.

Stop order An order to buy or to sell a currency when the currency's price reaches or passes a specified level. Also known as a *stop*.

Straight-through pricing (STP) An initiative used by companies in the financial world to optimize the speed at which transactions are processed. This is performed by allowing information that has been electronically entered to be transferred from one party to another in the settlement process without manually reentering the same pieces of information repeatedly over the entire sequence of events.

Support The price level for which intensive buying can lead to a decrease in price (downtrend).

Support levels A price at which a currency or the currency market will receive considerable buying pressure.

Swap A transaction that moves the maturity date of an open position to a future date.

Take-profit order A customer's instructions to buy or sell a currency pair which, when executed, will result in the reduction in the size of the existing position and show a profit on said position.

Technical analysis An analysis based only on technical market data (quotes) with the help of various technical indicators.

Tick The smallest possible change in a price, either up or down.

Trade context busy A message related to trading the forex using the MetaTrader 4 platform. Brokers claim that all market execution orders on MetaTrader 4 will be filled at the best price available in the market, although there can be a delay in getting a confirmation from their banks. This message appears if the CANCEL button is pressed while an order is in the process of execution.

Trade desk A desk where transactions for buying and selling securities occur. Trading desks can be found in most organizations (banks, finance companies, etc.) involved in trading investment instruments such as equities, fixed-income securities, futures, commodities, and forex. A trading desk provides traders with access to instantaneous trade executions. Also known as a *dealing desk*.

Transaction date The date on which a trade occurs.

Trend The direction of a market which has been established with the influence of different factors.

Turnover The total volume of all executed transactions in a given time period.

Two-way price A quote in the forex market that indicates a bid and an offer.

Unrealized profit or loss An usually fluctuating profit or loss that derives from nonclosed (active) positions. Also known as a *floating profit* or *loss*.

Usable margin Amount of money in the account that can be used for trading.

Used margin Amount of money in the account already used to hold open positions open.

U.S. Dollar Index (USDX) An index that measures the performance of the U.S. dollar against a basket of currencies: EUR, JPY, GBP, CAD, CHF, and SEK.

Value date The maturity date of the currency for settlement, usually two business days (one day for Canada) after the trade has occurred.

Vanilla options A normal option with no special or unusual features. A plain vanilla option is your plain run-of-the-mill option, with your standard expiry and strike price.

Variation margin Funds required to bring the equity in an account back up to the initial margin level. They are calculated on a day-to-day basis.

Volatility (VOL) The statistical measure of the change in price of a financial currency pair over a given time period.

BIBLIOGRAPHY

BROKERS

Silvani, Agustin, *Beat the Forex Dealer: An Insider's Look into Trading Today's Foreign Exchange Market*, Wiley, 2008.

Solin, Daniel R., *Does Your Broker Owe You Money? If You've Lost Money in the Market and It's Your Broker's Fault—You Can Get It Back*, Penguin Group (USA), 2006.

FINANCIAL REGULATIONS

Acharya, Viral V., Thomas F. Cooley, Matthew P. Richardson, Ingo Walter, and NYU Stern School of Business, *Regulating Wall Street: The Dodd-Frank Act and the New Architecture of Global Finance*, Wiley, 2010.

Bonello, Frank, and Isobel Lobo, *Taking Sides: Clashing Views on Economic Issues*, McGraw-Hill, 2011.

Buckley, Ross, *International Financial System: Policy and Regulation (International Banking and Finance Law)*, Kluwer Law International, 2008.

Davies, Howard, and David Green, *Global Financial Regulation: The Essential Guide*, Wiley, 2008.

Dewatripont, Mathias, Xavier Freixas, and Richard Portes (eds.), *Macroeconomic Stability and Financial Regulation: Key Issues for the G20*, London Publishing Partnership, 2011.

Elliott, David, and Carlos A. Pelaez, *Financial Regulation after the Global Recession*, Palgrave Macmillan, 2009.

Goodhart, Charles, David Llewellyn, and Philipp Hartmann, *Financial Regulation: Why, How, and Where Now?* Taylor & Francis, 1998.

Kawai, Masahiro, and Eswar Prasad, *Financial Market Regulation and Reforms in Emerging Markets*, Brookings Institution Press, 2011.

MacNeil, Iain, and Justin O'Brien. *The Future of Financial Regulation*, Hart Pub, 2010.

Skeel, David, and William D. Cohan, *The New Financial Deal: Understanding the Dodd-Frank Act and Its (Unintended) Consequences*, Wiley, 2010.

Spencer, Peter D., *The Structure and Regulation of Financial Markets*, Oxford University Press (USA), 2000.

Tarullo, Daniel K., *Banking on Basel: The Future of International Financial Regulation*, Peterson Institute, 2008.

Tatom, John A., *Financial Market Regulation: Legislation and Implications*, Springer-Verlag, 2011.

U.S. Congress Senate Committee, *Turmoil in U.S. Credit Markets: Examining the Recent Actions of Federal Financial Regulators*, Bibliogov, 2010.

Vittas, Dimitri (ed.), *Financial Regulation: Changing the Rules of the Game*, World Bank Publications, 1993.

FOREX SCAMS

Miller, Frederic P., Agnes F. Vandome, and John McBrewster (eds.), *Forex Scam*, VDM Publishing House Ltd., 2010.

OPTIONS

Chicago Board of Trade, *CBOT Handbook of Futures and Options*, McGraw-Hill, 2006.

Chorafas, Dimitris, *Introduction to Derivative Financial Instruments: Bonds, Swaps, Options, and Hedging*, McGraw-Hill, 2008.

Garner, Carley, and Paul Brittain, *Commodity Options: Trading and Hedging Volatility in the World's Most Lucrative Market*, FT Press, 2009.

Hull, John, *Fundamentals of Futures and Options Markets*, 5th ed., Prentice Hall, 2004.

Hull, John, *Options, Futures and Other Derivatives*, 6th ed., Prentice Hall, 2005.

Izraylevich, Sergey, and Vadim Tsudikman, *Systematic Options Trading: Evaluating, Analyzing, and Profiting from Mispriced Option Opportunities*, FT Press, 2010.

McCafferty, Thomas, *Options Demystified*, McGraw-Hill, 2005.

Natenberg, Sheldon, *Option Volatility & Pricing: Advanced Trading Strategies and Techniques*, updated ed., McGraw-Hill, 1994.

Reehl, C. B., *The Mathematics of Options Trading*, McGraw-Hill, 2005.

Shover, Larry, *Trading Options in Turbulent Markets: Master Uncertainty through Active Volatility*, Bloomberg Press, 2010.

Sinclair, Euan, *Option Trading: Pricing and Volatility Strategies and Techniques*, Wiley, 2010.

Whistler, Mark, *Volatility Illuminated: Empowering Forex, Stocks, Options & Futures Traders*, CreateSpace, 2009.

TRADING PSYCHOLOGY

Elder, Alexander, *Trading for a Living: Psychology, Trading Tactics, Money Management*, Wiley, 1993.

Steenbarger, Brett N., *The Daily Trading Coach: 101 Lessons for Becoming Your Own Trading Psychologist*, Wiley, 2009.

TRADING STRATEGIES

Capre, Chris, *Price Action Pivot Points*, Harriman House, 2011.

Carter, John F., *Mastering the Trade: Proven Techniques for Profiting from Intraday and Swing Trading Setups*, McGraw-Hill, 2005.

Cohen, Guy, *The Bible of Options Strategies: The Definitive Guide for Practical Trading Strategies*, FT Press, 2005.

Kaufman, Perry J., *Alpha Trading: Profitable Strategies That Remove Directional Risk*, Wiley, 2011.

Kaufman, Perry J., *New Trading Systems and Methods*, 4th ed., Wiley, 2005.

Knuth, Elaine, *Trading between the Lines: Pattern Recognition and Visualization of Markets*, Bloomberg Press, 2011.

Norris, Jay, and Al Gaskill, *Mastering Trade Selection and Management: Advanced Strategies for Long-Term Profitability*, McGraw-Hill, 2011.

Pesavento, Larry, and Leslie Jouflas, *Trade What You See: How to Profit from Pattern Recognition*, Wiley, 2007.

Ponsi, Ed, *Forex Patterns and Probabilities: Trading Strategies for Trending and Range-Bound Markets*, Wiley, 2007.

Stridsman, Thomas, *Trading Systems That Work: Building and Evaluating Effective Trading Systems*, McGraw-Hill, 2000.

Velez, Oliver, and Greg Capra, *Tools and Tactics for the Master DayTrader: Battle-Tested Techniques for Day, Swing, and Position Traders*, McGraw-Hill, 2000.

INDEX

Note: *f* and *t* following page numbers refer to figures and tables, respectively.

ABOUT THE AUTHOR

James Dicks is president and CEO of a group of financial companies, including a forex hedge fund. He founded Forex Made Easy, one of the largest introducers of spot retail forex customers in the United States. He has been investing in various aspects of the financial markets for more than 25 years, including the areas of portfolio diversification that include asset classes such as real estate, equities, and foreign currency. For more information, visit www.JamesDicks.com.